SHOULDER TO SHOULDER?

SHOULDER TO SHOULDER?

THE AMERICAN FEDERATION OF LABOR, THE UNITED STATES, AND THE MEXICAN REVOLUTION

1910–1924

GREGG ANDREWS

University of California Press
Berkeley · Los Angeles · Oxford

University of California Press
Berkeley and Los Angeles, California

University of California Press
Oxford, England

Copyright © 1991 by
The Regents of the University of California

Library of Congress Cataloging-in-Publication Data

Andrews, Gregg.
  Shoulder to shoulder?: the American Federation of
Labor, the United States, and the Mexican Revolution,
1910–1924 / Gregg Andrews.
      p.   cm.
  Based on the author's thesis—Northern Illinois University. Includes bibliographical references and index.
  ISBN 0–520–07230–8 (cloth: alk. paper)
    1. Trade-unions and foreign policy—United States.
2. American Federation of Labor.   3. United States—
Foreign relations—Mexico.   4. Mexico—Foreign relations—United States.   5. Mexico—History—Revolution,
1910–1920.   6. Mexico—History—Revolution, 1923–
1924.   7. Pan-Americanism.   I. Title.
HD6490.F582U613   1991
322'.2'0973—dc20   91–11343
                                                         CIP

Printed in the United States of America

1   2   3   4   5   6   7   8   9

The paper used in this publication meets the minimum
requirements of American National Standard for Information Sciences—Permanence of Paper for Printed Library
Materials, ANSI Z39.48–1984 ⊗

Contents

Acknowledgments

I would like to thank Colin M. MacLachlan, James Wilkie, and Benjamin Keen for reading and critiquing the entire manuscript. They raised challenging questions about my arguments and offered valuable editorial suggestions. I am especially indebted to Keen, whose scholarship and teaching have significantly shaped my conceptual approach to Latin America. More importantly, he has been a good friend.

J. Carroll Moody, Carl Parrini, and Michael Gonzales provided important help when the manuscript was in the dissertation stage at Northern Illinois University. I would especially like to thank my wife, Vikki Bynum, who took time away from working on her own book to read major parts of the manuscript and offer constructive criticism. I also wish to thank Scott Mahler for his role in soliciting my manuscript and facilitating its publication.

Gregory McNamee edited the manuscript with a critical eye, and I am indebted to the entire editorial staff at the University of California Press. Part of Chapter Six appeared earlier as "Robert Haberman, Socialist Ideology, and the Politics of National Reconstruction in Mexico, 1920–25," *Mexican Studies/Estudios Mexicanos* 6 (Summer 1990): 189–211. I want to thank John M. Hart for his comments and suggestions on an earlier draft of that article.

Unfortunately, Colin MacLachlan's *Anarchism and the Mexican Revolution: The Political Trials of Ricardo Flores Magón in the United States* was unavailable to me before I wrote this book. His study should significantly enhance our understanding of the impact of anarchism on the Mexican Revolution, left-wing politics, and political repression in the United States.

The publication of this book will please Travis and Shane, my children. Finally, I dedicate this book to my mother, Virginia Sudholt, who raised Kevin, Cheryl, and me on a minimum-wage income and sacrificed enormously so that we could have a better life through education.

Introduction

The activities of the American labor movement in Latin America have generated considerable controversy. Especially since World War II, American labor leaders have often acted as instruments of United States foreign policy. Time and time again they have collaborated with government officials and corporate representatives to prevent or subvert radical change in Latin America. Countries in which radical and even middle-class nationalist movements have posed what the United States regards as a threat to its economic and strategic interests in the region have suffered intense economic and diplomatic pressure and sometimes military intervention. Although American labor leaders and U.S. officials have at times disagreed over tactics, they have shared a fundamental philosophical objective: to contain revolutionary nationalist movements that threaten to remove Latin America from the geopolitical orbit of the United States.

American labor's conception of Pan-Americanism developed to a large extent during the national debate over how the United States should respond to the Mexican Revolution—the first major social upheaval in twentieth-century Latin America.[1] As they maneuvered to contain the Revolution, which broke out in 1910, within ideological boundaries defined by their perceptions of U.S. strategic interests, government officials sometimes used the American Federation of Labor (AFL) as a formal or informal policy instrument. On other occasions, AFL leaders publicly condemned interventionist forces and thereby irritated U.S. policymakers.

To a certain extent, these differences over foreign policy were rooted in conflicts over domestic political economy. AFL president Samuel Gompers often reserved his sharpest criticism for American investors in Mexico who were vigorous opponents of organized labor at home. An English immigrant who began to work in cigar shops at the age of ten, Gompers believed that the Amer-

1

ican trade-union movement should focus on practical economic objectives and stress craft orientation. After working in a local union of cigarmakers in New York City, he headed a movement that broke away from the Knights of Labor and founded the AFL in 1886 as an organization representative of American skilled workers. He dominated the AFL until his death in December, 1924.[2]

As a young man, Gompers had studied the writings of Karl Marx and associated with a group of socialists in New York's cigar shops. By the 1880s, however, he had moved sharply away from the more radical ideas that informed the union activities of his earlier years. He defeated a socialist proposal at the 1894 AFL convention for the collective ownership of the means of production and distribution, and the tone of his antiradical rhetoric became increasingly strident as he responded to growing internal challenges from the left.[3]

Despite Gompers's denunciation of radicals, his calls for strong trade union organizations clashed with employers who wanted a union-free America. The National Association of Manufacturers, for example, campaigned for open-shop legislation and court injunctions to halt strikes and labor boycotts. Such employers declared an all-out war on organized labor at home and abroad.

Under Gompers's leadership, the AFL established contacts with Mexico's first large-scale labor movement—a movement which grew out of and played a significant role in the Revolution. When Gompers died, his popularity among Mexican labor leaders and the politicians who occupied the National Palace was at an all-time high. His activities in Mexico earned him the honor of a special seat at the presidential inauguration of Plutarco Elías Calles in December 1924. Gompers became ill and died shortly after attending the inaugural ceremonies.

To a large extent, the AFL's response to the Mexican Revolution reflected the dynamic interplay of domestic forces that shaped Progressive Era efforts to come to grips with the social and political realities of a corporate capitalist order. A strong reformist impulse underpinned the many-sided efforts of Progressivism to confront the problems of an industrial society. Reformers from different social backgrounds, with divergent aims, attacked political corruption, abuse of corporate power, urban problems, and the instability of widespread labor-capital conflict. To many American reformers the dictatorial regime of Porfirio Díaz (1876–1910) in Mexico represented a counterpart of the evil, corrupt institutions which they deplored at home. The fact that many powerful U.S. trusts had acquired extensive interests in Mexico underscored the connections between the two evils. Thus attacks on monopoly and corruption at home shaped the Progressive critique of conditions in prerevolutionary Mexico.[4]

Criticisms by American reformers of the links between American trusts and the repressive institutions of Porfirian Mexico sharpened during the decade before the Mexican Revolution. These increasing attacks paralleled the rise of an organized political movement by Mexican opponents of Díaz, and they reflected the diverse ideological influences within the American progressive community. Engaged in a difficult struggle against corporations at home, the AFL criticized the lack of democracy under Díaz and denounced the activities of trusts in Mexico. Gompers publicly condemned U.S. collaboration with Díaz to imprison Mexican political exiles.

The most vocal American advocates of deeper change at home and in Mexico, however, were the socialists and members of the Industrial Workers of the World (IWW), or "Wobblies," as they were called. The early ideological tendencies of revolutionary syndicalism in the Mexican labor movement attracted the IWW, the AFL's chief rival. Gompers feared the possible influence of dynamic IWW internationalism in radicalizing the Revolution. During the early 1900s, the AFL also faced a stiff challenge from socialists who worked to increase their strength inside the AFL. Gompers could not ignore the socialists' efforts to shape the AFL's domestic policies or their possible influence on American labor's activities in Mexico.[5]

Several socialists played important roles in the extension of AFL influence south of the border. Although they represented the major progressive force within the AFL, they generally belonged to the right-wing faction within the prewar Socialist Party of America (SPA). Advocates of close cooperation with the AFL, gradualism, and political democracy to achieve socialism, these social democrats did not believe that advancing socialism within the AFL required them to attack Gompers. They endorsed his policies in Latin America, subordinated themselves to his leadership, and supported the AFL's patriotic endorsement of U.S. involvement in the First World War. They promoted inter-American labor solidarity while simultaneously combating revolutionary syndicalist and, later, bolshevik influences in the region.

Although Gompers granted this small group of right wing socialists a role in the AFL's response to the Mexican Revolution, he opposed the Second International's efforts to expand its postwar influence in Mexico. Under his leadership, the AFL pursued "Pan American" policies that required Latin American labor movements to accept its tutelage. The AFL, however, reserved its sharpest criticism for the Third International. At its convention in 1925, the AFL's Committee on Resolutions added a "labor" corollary to the Monroe Doctrine that declared Latin America off limits to communism:

> What the United States Government, through President Monroe, expressed to Europe as a warning against armed territorial aggression, we convey in equally emphatic terms regarding aggression by propaganda. . . . Neither the Red Internationale of autocratic Moscow nor any other internationale may in complacency ignore this definition of American labor policy. It will contest to the last every inch of ground whenever and wherever autocracy seeks to invade the hallowed soil of this hemisphere. And we shall accept no pretense of "world labor unity" as a mask for invading disrupters and destroyers.[6]

To understand the AFL's reaction to the Mexican Revolution we must examine the foreign program of domestic working-class Progressivism. We must also consider the ways in which the tendencies toward corporatism that appeared during the Progressive Era influenced the AFL's activities in Mexico. From the corporate boardrooms of progressive businessmen and the offices of sympathetic politicians flowed a stream of reform that emphasized the need to harmonize labor-capital relationships in order to conjure away the threat posed by radical elements to the corporate order. Through the National Civic Federation (NCF), founded by Ralph Easley in 1900, many representatives of major corporations met with AFL leaders and middle-class intellectuals and professionals to discuss ways to improve industrial relations and avoid the violent conflicts that had rocked American society during the 1890s. These businessmen often attacked the shortsighted policies of other businessmen who refused to recognize the AFL, despite its conservative ideology. Although many NCF leaders found the abstract principle of cooperation with conservative union leaders more appealing than the unpleasant reality of having to bargain with AFL unions in their business establishments, Gompers continued to collaborate with them. This collaboration invited sharp attacks from socialists and others who complained that participation in the NCF robbed the AFL of its vitality.[7]

It was during Woodrow Wilson's presidency that the political economy of "corporate liberalism"[8] reached its fullest expression in the Progressive Era, especially during the First World War. Much more effective than the voluntary cooperation between labor and capital that the NCF espoused, the Wilson administration's efforts to regulate class conflict through the political apparatus of the state provided important legislative concessions and patronage to labor. The wartime emergency encouraged tripartite cooperation to ensure uninterrupted industrial production for the Allied effort. The federal government used its resources and power to promote more conciliatory relationships between employers and prowar unions and smash antiwar opposition.[9]

To a limited extent, the Wilson administration also encouraged tripartite initiatives in foreign policy. It is therefore helpful to use the conceptual tool of "corporatism" to examine the U.S. response to the Mexican Revolution. Thomas J. McCormick underscores the need to systematize a conceptual framework within which American foreign policy can be examined. He calls for a corporatist synthesis to address what he regards as the "lack of analytical sophistication" that plagues the field of diplomatic history. The basis of such a synthesis is the premise that large, powerful functional groups such as organized labor, corporate capital, and agriculture forge collaborative relationships with one another and the State to shape domestic and foreign policy arrangements. The State is more willing to formalize its power sharing with private-sector agents during times of crisis. At other times, the relationship between nongovernmental actors and the State is more informal. Whatever the formal or informal arrangements that enmesh these groups in a national policymaking web, the object of such collaboration is to promote public policies designed to rationalize American industrial capitalism and avoid deep social conflicts.[10]

"The key to using corporatism in foreign policy studies," McCormick writes, "is the simple proposition that people do not think one way about their national society and a different way about the world society. Instead, they tend to project and internationalize conceptual frameworks first articulated at home."[11] The incorporation of organized labor into the foreign-policy apparatus of the United States rests on the willingness of labor leaders, public officials, and representatives of corporate capital to reach a consensus that American economic expansion abroad is vital to domestic prosperity. Although conflicts often occur between and within the functional groups over how best to ensure that expansion, an underlying embrace of what Charles Maier has called "productionism" brings these groups into tripartite partnerships to carry out American foreign policy. Productionism diverts labor's attention from trying to increase its slice of the nation's economic pie at capital's expense and instead focuses on creating a larger pie through greater cooperative efforts to increase productivity at home and promote marketplace expansion abroad. Crucial to labor's endorsement of the "politics of productivity" is the ability of the State and the private sector to provide material rewards for class collaboration within corporatism.[12]

By exploring the dynamics of this tripartite cooperation, which was promoted on a voluntary basis but under the auspices of the State, we can perhaps better understand how corporate liberalism influenced the AFL's response to the Mexican Revolution. Gompers's enthusiasm for corporatist structures during the war did not diminish after the war. He continued to seek government and private-sector endorsements for an expanded AFL role in a reconstructed world order along the lines set forth by President Wilson. Although the AFL's political influence declined precipitously as a result of a Republican presidential victory in 1920, Gompers continued to lobby for the AFL's inclusion in an integrated economic and strategic approach to Mexico and all of Latin America.

Scholars who have investigated the AFL's activities in Mexico during this period generally belong to two camps. Earlier studies like Philip Taft's *The A.F. of L. in the Time of Gompers* emphasize the anti-interventionist nature of the AFL's Mexican policies and view the growing interest of AFL leaders in Mexico as an expression of genuine labor internationalism. Divorcing AFL leaders from the policies of the U.S. government, these studies praise the idealistic objectives of Gompers's Pan American activities.[13]

A more recent representative of this historiographic tendency is William G. Whittaker, who describes Gompers as an anti-imperialist and stresses the AFL's consistent defense of Mexico's right to have a revolution free of U.S. interference. According to Whittaker, the AFL's Pan-American activities enabled Latin American workers to "discover a new American face, apart from that of the Department of State and the American corporation."[14]

These uncritical studies emphasize the policy conflicts between the U.S. government and AFL leaders over the Mexican Revolution. Sinclair Snow claims that secret government funding of the Pan American Federation of Labor (PAFL) to try to undermine Mexico's neutrality during the First World War marked only a temporary deviation from the sturdy independence of the AFL's role in Mexico. "The end of the war," he writes, "destroyed the secret aim of the organization, that is, the winning of Mexico for the Allies, but it made possible a return to the original goal of a federation of Pan-American labor organizations which would counteract organized capital in the Western Hemisphere."[15]

Recent studies have challenged this interpretation of the AFL's activities in Mexico and elsewhere. Numerous critical analyses of the AFL's international activities depict its leaders as agents of U.S. foreign policy and thus participants in the construction of an American empire in Latin America. Perhaps the most stinging attack on American unions in Latin America comes from Jack Scott, who minimizes the conflicts between union leaders and U.S. officials over foreign policy. He argues that a basic consensus has united them, along with business representatives, in defense of imperialism. He stresses that Gompers and other labor leaders have promoted the organization of Latin American workers only to protect their members from the competition of cheap labor and to prevent the growth of radical unionism. According to Scott, although capitalist manipulation of the international labor market may compel American unionists to oppose U.S. foreign policy on occasions, a firm commitment to imperialism limits labor's criticisms of U.S. interference in the internal affairs of Latin American nations.[16]

Scott largely follows the tradition established by Ronald Radosh, whose important revisionist work, *American Labor and United States Foreign Policy*, links labor's "backward and reactionary" foreign policy to its embrace of "corporate unionism." Radosh points out that although the AFL's endorsement of economic expansion abroad dates back to the Spanish-American War era, material benefits from this commitment to trade expansion did not really reach labor until World War I, when President Wilson offered concessions to the AFL in exchange for wartime loyalty. Radosh argues that the AFL's objectives in Mexico were in fundamental harmony with those of the corporate community.[17]

Scott, Radosh, and others who have written critical studies of the AFL's actions in Latin America provide an important corrective to the idealistic version found in the writings of Whittaker and Snow. By stressing labor's integration into the foreign policy apparatus of the United States, they call attention to the underlying consensus which has facilitated labor, capital, and government cooperation to fashion public policy. Although they show that this tripartite alliance became institutionalized after World War II, they are less successful in explaining how the twists and turns of the Mexican Revolution either encouraged or impeded the evolution of a policymaking consensus. They also ignore or minimize significant conflicts and thus oversimplify the dynamics of American labor's international activities. Their failure to consider the dialectic of conflict and consensus distorts the full significance of the AFL's response to the Mexican Revolution and obscures the interplay of forces which shaped evolving corporatist strategies to confront revolutionary nationalism in Latin America.

The most balanced treatment of the AFL's involvement in Mexico is Harvey Levenstein's excellent *Labor Organizations in the United States and Mexico*, which contains important chapters on the AFL's response to the Mexican Revolution. Critical yet mindful of the complexities of the AFL's motivations in Mexico, Levenstein recognizes the limitations of Gompers's "internationalism" but is somewhat fuzzy on the issue of labor's relationship to imperialism. He fails to explore the AFL's reaction to the U.S. occupation of Veracruz in 1914 but acknowledges that Gompers never opposed the dispatch of troops to chase Pancho Villa in 1916. Equally important, Levenstein does not examine Gompers's involvement in financial diplomacy to undermine Mexico's economic nationalism during the war. Neither does he adequately explore the AFL's theoretical position on the prerogatives of foreign capital in Mexico.[18]

A major part of Philip S. Foner's study of the American labor movement in Latin America also explores the AFL's response to the Mexican Revolution. Foner emphasizes that although many labor and socialist elements opposed U.S. intervention in Latin America, Gompers was committed to keeping the region within the economic and geopolitical orbit of the United States.[19]

A comprehensive study of the AFL's response to the unfolding drama on the southern border of the United States between 1910 and 1924 enables us to probe the areas of conflict and consensus among labor, capital, and government with regard to intervention and the rights of foreign capital in underdeveloped (or misdeveloped) areas. American capitalists had investments in Mexico that totaled more than $1 billion when the Revolution began in 1910.[20] Under the dictatorship of Díaz, foreign capital poured into Mexico to underwrite the so-called economic miracle, which included the development of a modern banking system, increased foreign trade, impressive railroad construction, and the modernization of infrastructural facilities in the export sector.

This economic growth nurtured the rise of a Mexican middle class that became unhappy over the privileged position enjoyed by foreigners and the monopolization of political power by Díaz and his cronies. During the twilight of the *porfiriato,* as Díaz's tenure (1876-1910) is commonly known, native entrepreneurs and middle-class professionals voiced increasing opposition to the concessionary policies that enabled foreign interests to dominate the strategic sectors of the economy. Lavish subsidies especially attracted foreign investors to railroad construction, mining, real estate, oil production, and the metallurgical industry. American capital dominated many of these economic activities, and trading patterns heavily linked Mexico to the United States. Nationalist resentments gave birth to the popular maxim, "Mexico, mother of foreigners and stepmother of Mexicans."[21]

Labor and agrarian unrest during the last years of the *porfiriato* exposed the rickety social foundations of Díaz's dictatorship. Seizures of Indian village lands by speculators, large landowners (*hacendados*), and the government had accelerated to produce a large-scale expansion of the hacienda system and harsh living conditions for the dispossessed peasantry. The plight of agricultural workers was especially dismal in the south, where debt peonage and even outright slavery were prevalent in states such as Yucatán. Industrial workers who protested or tried to organize trade unions to improve their conditions found an increasingly repressive government ready to use troops in support of management.[22]

As Eric R. Wolf notes, the Mexican Revolution "moved by fits and starts, and in numerous directions at once; it carried with it the bastions of power and the straw-covered huts of the peasantry alike."[23] What began in 1910 as a struggle within the Mexican elite exploded into a bloody social conflict that mobilized the masses. Two wings of the movement emerged to contend for power. An alliance with organized labor enabled urban middle-class forces under the leadership of Venustiano Carranza to defeat the peasant armies of Emiliano Zapata and Pancho Villa. The integration of workers and peasants into the armed struggle meant that it would be difficult for any postrevolutionary plan of reconstruction to ignore the social and political demands of these forces.[24]

By the time the dust had settled and the fighting had taken a devastating toll on the population and national resources, the Revolution had produced an impressive new constitution with provisions for land and anticlerical reform, an advanced labor code, greater state control over Mexico's natural resources, and regulation of the activities of foreign capital. It had also withstood two direct military interventions by the United States, which applied considerable financial and diplomatic pressure in an effort to extract guarantees of protection for American investments and safeguard its geopolitical interests.[25]

The consolidation of Mexico's postrevolutionary state in the 1920s depended to a large extent on how the architects of national reconstruction responded to the economic, social, and political demands of peasants and workers whose expectations had been raised as a result of their participation in the military campaigns. It also depended on the outcome of efforts to placate the United States without completely renouncing Mexico's political sovereignty. Mexico's economic dependence on the United States and the persistent problem of militarism encouraged President Álvaro Obregón (1920-1924) to reach an agreement with the United States in late 1923 in order to secure badly needed financial support and consolidate his regime. Included in his blueprint for national reconstruction were corporatist formulas to regulate social conflict. The Confederación Regional Obrera Mexicana (CROM), the dominant labor organization which was created in 1918, endorsed this blueprint and became a part of the official ruling coalition in the 1920s. It also established a close relationship with the AFL. Robert Haberman, an American Socialist who became an important liaison between the CROM and the AFL, found a career in Mexican politics as a result of his links to labor, socialist, and progressive forces in the United States.[26]

In order to understand more clearly how and why the AFL responded to the revolutionary awakening of social forces in Mexico, it is important to examine briefly the wider context in which this response occurred. As the United States emerged as a world industrial and military power around the turn of the twentieth century, seeking expanded markets, outlets for the investment of surplus capital, and access to strategic raw materials, the young AFL entered the national debate over imperialism following the war with Spain in 1898. As a member of the Anti-Imperialist League, Gompers represented the dominant tendency in the AFL which opposed the annexation of territories "liberated" from Spanish rule. He feared that the annexation of Cuba, Puerto Rico, Hawaii, Guam, and the Philippine Islands would undermine wage standards in the United States by increasing the competitive threat posed by contract immigrant labor and the possible production of cheaper goods in those areas. He often used racist arguments to oppose the incorporation of "semi-savage" peoples into the United States.[27]

Condemning those who favored imperialism as a way to divert attention away from important domestic problems, Gompers emphasized that American workers would bear the greatest burden of increased armaments necessary to support imperialism. However, he endorsed American economic expansion abroad and accepted the challenge of international industrial competition. In his view, territorial annexation was unnecessary to ensure the triumph of the United States in the world's commercial contest. At a national conference held in Saratoga Springs, New York, in August 1898 and organized by Ralph Easley, founder of the Chicago Civic

Federation, Gompers expressed his faith that American industrial supremacy could be achieved without colonialism:

> The nation which dominates the markets of the world will surely control its destinies. To make of the United States a vast workshop is our manifest destiny, and our duty, and thus side by side with other nations, in industrial and commercial rivalry, we basing [sic] the conditions of the workers upon the highest intelligence and the most exalted standard of life, no obstacle can be placed in our way to the attainment of the highest pinnacle of glory and human progress. But to attain this end is the acquirement of the Philippine Islands, with their semi-savage population, necessary? Surely not. Neither its gates nor those of any other country of the globe can be closed against our constantly growing industrial supremacy.[28]

Henry W. Berger emphasizes that Gompers, despite his opposition to colonialism, did not oppose the growth of an informal economic empire or the extension of non-colonial American influence abroad. Indeed, Gompers embraced the concept of manifest destiny and argued that acceptance of the AFL as a partner in the industrial system would promote rather than hinder national greatness. According to Berger, the AFL's endorsement of an American economic empire facilitated the growth of a rudimentary consensus between "imperialists" and "anti-imperialists" after 1900 and weakened American labor's opposition to corporate capitalism at home. He argues that "this meant more sophisticated efforts by the unions to obtain employer recognition of their organizations, larger material benefits for workers, and increased political power for themselves in the system at home and abroad rather than seeking any fundamental alteration of the political economy."[29]

Gompers tried to promote the integration of AFL concerns into a national foreign policy agenda which would nurture a more progressive United States-led economic expansion into Latin America. Accompanying this expansion would be a less militaristic policy and a more sensitive approach to the material needs of the working class. In his view, the extension of AFL-style unions into the region posed no threat to U.S. hegemony; on the contrary, business unionism could insulate Latin America from revolutionary theories. It could also promote friendly attitudes toward the United States in an area where the interventionist activities of American commercial interests had generated anti-American feelings.

The employment of an interpretive framework that recognizes

the interplay between progressive forces in the AFL and the tendencies toward corporatism enables us to evaluate more effectively the AFL's response to the Mexican Revolution. Since Gompers and the AFL executive council generally handled the disposition of issues related to foreign affairs, this study focuses considerably on the attitudes of AFL leaders toward the Mexican Revolution. In his study of AFL foreign policy during the First World War, Simeon Larson points out that the control of convention machinery enabled Gompers to appoint as members of committees men whose reports on major issues would conform to his policies. Larson finds no instance in which a committee report or resolution on international affairs conflicted with Gompers's views.[30]

This study examines the ideological forces that influenced Gompers and other AFL leaders as they reacted to the political ferment of Mexican workers between 1910 and 1924. Clearly important to AFL leaders were "bread and butter" issues, such as limiting Mexican immigration, blocking the importation of Mexican strikebreakers, and increasing labor's bargaining strength in the face of capital's growing penetration of Latin America. These concerns must be viewed, however, in the context of labor's reaction to the broader political, economic, and strategic issues raised by the Mexican Revolution. This study investigates several important questions that extend beyond the narrow interests of labor. What was the AFL's position on American intervention and the prerogatives of foreign capital in Mexico? How did AFL leaders view the economic nationalism embodied in Article 27 of Mexico's Constitution of 1917? To what extent were AFL representatives acting independently of capital and the state? How did the AFL define Mexico's status as an underdeveloped nation in the international economic and political community? What were the implications of the AFL's activities for future revolutionary nationalist movements in Latin America? Finally, what was the AFL's overall effect on the Mexican Revolution? These questions provide a yardstick with which to measure the AFL's commitment to change in Mexico— change that was taking place in the wider context of world war and social revolution in Russia.

1

In Search of Reform and Stability

The strong impulse of Progressivism to reform and democratize American society in the early 1900s had an internationalist dynamic that influenced the AFL's critique of prerevolutionary conditions in Mexico. Before the outbreak of the Mexican Revolution in 1910, the AFL's growing interest in Mexican affairs indicated genuine opposition to the dictatorship of Porfirio Díaz and the degraded conditions of Mexican workers. Locked in a fierce struggle with corporate interests at home, the AFL criticized the links of foreign trusts with an oppressive government in Mexico and the impoverished conditions of the Mexican masses. In the eyes of the AFL and other reformers, Díaz symbolized the corruption and political repression spawned by the activities of powerful trusts in underdeveloped countries.

Although he had long abandoned his early flirtation with socialism, AFL president Samuel Gompers retained a general commitment to the socialist ideals of international labor solidarity, peace, and democracy, but he adjusted his internationalist views to accommodate his collaborationist policies and perception of the strategic interests of the United States. He shared with American skilled workers a deep attachment to the nation's democratic political traditions. His contacts in the 1880s with Mexican cigarmakers who opposed the dictatorship of Díaz nurtured an interest in Latin American affairs. Western mineworkers and trade-union socialists who had a special interest in Latin America persuaded Gompers to go beyond the narrower concerns of the AFL's eastern craft unions and endorse an activist approach to Mexican politics in the early 1900s.[1]

During the decade preceding the Revolution, Gompers joined the chorus of radical and progressive voices that denounced the jailing of Mexican political opponents of Díaz in the United States.

Organized opposition to Díaz crystallized in the Mexican Liberal Party (*Partido Liberal Mexicano*, PLM), whose leaders found that conducting political activities from exile in the United States did not immunize them against repression. Having fled Mexico in 1904 after being arrested several times by Díaz, the Flores Magón brothers—Ricardo, Jesús, and Enrique—moved to St. Louis, Missouri, after a brief stay in San Antonio, Texas, where an attempt upon their lives by a Díaz-appointed assassin convinced them to move farther from the border. In St. Louis they published a newspaper, *Regeneración*, to mobilize opposition to Díaz. Harassment by local authorities and private detectives in the service of Col. William Greene, a copper baron who blamed the PLM for labor unrest at his mine in Cananea, Sonora, forced the Flores Magón brothers to leave St. Louis, however, and shift the PLM's headquarters to Los Angeles.[2]

The PLM published a platform in 1906 that called for the abolition of child labor, debt peonage, company stores, and discriminatory wage payments that favored North Americans over Mexicans who performed equivalent tasks. It also advocated the eight-hour day, a six-day work week, payment of wages in cash, a minimum wage law for Mexican workers, and employer liability for on-the-job injuries. Also included in the platform were provisions for land reform, secularization of the educational system, nationalization of church property, and basic individual and political freedoms.[3]

The PLM's reformist blueprint found a receptive audience among radicals and liberals in the United States,[4] but the collusion between Díaz and U.S. officials to harass the exiled political activists meant imprisonment for many PLM members in the United States. The arrests of Ricardo Flores Magón, Antonio I. Villarreal, and Librado Rivera in 1907 for having allegedly broken U.S. neutrality laws disturbed the American progressive community, which rallied to the defense of the PLM leaders. The outpouring of support for the jailed political refugees was especially strong in Los Angeles, the scene of the arrests. Socialists, anarchists, trade unionists, and other progressive elements protested the arrests and launched a campaign to block the imprisoned refugees' extradition to Mexico. Gompers's public defense of Flores Magón, Villarreal, and Rivera added greater visibility to the AFL's opposition to Díaz. Acting upon Gompers's suggestion, the 1908 AFL convention passed a resolution condemning the arrests and urging financial contributions to defend the jailed PLM leaders.[5]

A key figure in the fundraising drive was the legendary Mary Harris Jones, known as Mother Jones, socialist and official organizer for the United Mine Workers (UMW), who enlisted the financial backing of AFL unions in Los Angeles, the UMW, and the Western Federation of Miners (WFM). Writing from their cell in the Arizona Territorial Prison, Flores Magón, Villarreal, and Rivera appealed to her for help on November 31, 1909, but she had already swung into action on their behalf, having urged their release during an interview with President William Howard Taft on June 16 of that year. In a speech to the 1909 UMW convention, she attacked the economic interests that propped up Díaz, and she appealed for donations to defend the imprisoned PLM members. The UMW convention responded by appropriating $1,000. According to Mother Jones, the AFL donated a total of $4,000 to the defense fund.[6]

The plight of PLM activists in the United States also attracted the attention of John Murray, a trade-union activist who had met many PLM members in Los Angeles through Job Harriman, his friend, fellow socialist, and lawyer who represented the incarcerated PLM leaders. Murray, who had helped to establish the Political Refugee Defense League to protect Russian refugees, now widened the scope of the organization's activities to defend Mexican political refugees. Ricardo Flores Magón provided him with credentials to travel to Mexico in May 1908 to investigate conditions and relay information to PLM sympathizers in Mexico City. A skilled journalist and editor, Murray wrote articles on the repressive political climate and backward social conditions that he observed during his trip. The Mexican government hired American detectives to keep him under surveillance. These detectives, working in cooperation with U.S. postal authorities, opened his mail and sent copies of pertinent letters to the Mexican minister of foreign relations. U.S. authorities arrested him and PLM leader Lázaro Gutiérrez de Lara in October 1909, when President Taft and Díaz held a conference in El Paso.[7]

A member of the International Typographical Union and an

advocate of "boring from within" the AFL to advance socialism, Murray emerged from his brief imprisonment on false charges more determined to publicize the persecution of Díaz's political opponents in the United States. Although he later became one of Gompers's faithful lieutenants in Mexico, he did not trust the AFL president at this time because of his opposition to socialism. He bypassed Gompers in his effort to rivet congressional attention on U.S. policy in Mexico. Instead he approached Democratic congressman William B. Wilson, a former UMW official from Pennsylvania, with the suggestion that Congress investigate the persecution of Mexican exiles in the United States. Wilson chaired the House Rules Committee, which held hearings into the matter in June 1910. Testifying were Lázaro Gutiérrez de Lara, John Kenneth Turner (the socialist author of *Barbarous Mexico*, the classic exposé of Díaz's oppressive regime), Murray, and Mother Jones, who had developed a friendship with Wilson during her organizing efforts in the Pennsylvania coal fields. Although not consulted by Murray, Gompers submitted to the committee a letter that condemned Díaz and U.S. officials for conspiring to persecute Mexican political refugees in the United States.[8]

The hearings did not spark a thorough investigation, but the jailed PLM leaders received favorable publicity and an early release later that year. At a time when Socialists were exerting considerable pressure within the AFL to challenge Gompers's leadership, his nonpartisan approach to politics, and policies of class collaboration, the decision to cooperate with socialists in the campaign to defend the jailed PLM leaders had important consequences. When the Mexican Revolution broke out shortly thereafter, leaders of the movement sought AFL support. For the rest of his life, Gompers reminded Mexican labor leaders and politicians that he had championed the cause of PLM exiles in the United States. His cooperation with socialists undoubtedly began to weaken Murray's previous reservations about his conservative philosophy. As he later reminded Murray, Gompers did not find it easy to cooperate with socialists on behalf of Mexican political refugees, given the intensity of socialist attacks on his labor policies:

> I want to tell you, too, it was not an easy matter for me to cooperate with the Socialists at that time. I had been so thoroughly abused and

misrepresented that if they were to be believed I was not even a man
that any self-respecting man or woman would shake hands with or
talk to. I was the lieutenant of capitalism.[9]

Besides expressing American labor's support for civil liberties and
democracy, Gompers's growing involvement in Mexican politics on
the eve of the Revolution reflected concern over an issue that had
a more direct impact on the American labor movement: the influx
of Mexican workers into the United States. The special interest that
American miners had in Mexico indicated, in part, that they felt
the pinch of competition from the cheap labor often provided by
Mexican immigrant workers, especially in the West. Although concerned on the one hand that this stream of workers would depress
the wages of Americans, Gompers feared on the other that Mexican immigrant workers would join the IWW. Such fears were not
groundless, for by 1906, the AFL faced a major challenge from the
WFM, one of the chief forces in the IWW at the time, in its attempts
to organize Mexican workers in the mining industry in Arizona.
The WFM's militant philosophy and recruitment strategy, which
stressed the AFL's exclusionary, racist practices, attracted Mexican
workers and invited greater cooperation between the WFM and the
PLM in the area.[10]

Labor unrest during the twilight of the *porfiriato* contributed to
the growth of an anti-Díaz movement. During the early years of
his rule, Díaz's policy toward organized labor had encouraged
labor groups that would operate within acceptable guidelines. As
David Walker has noted, Díaz utilized "a flexible and sophisticated
array of labor policy instruments that was based upon cooperation
with and subsidies to pro-government labor organizations as well
as political rewards and the other fruits of cooptation for labor leaders loyal to the regime."[11] By 1906, however, a resurgence of labor
militancy, including the famous strike at the American-owned
copper company in Cananea, Sonora, close to the Arizona border,
elicited a less sophisticated response from Díaz, who used increasingly repressive methods to crush strikes. The government's use
of troops in 1907 against striking textile workers in Río Blanco
further fueled the mounting political discontent and demands for
improved social conditions among Mexican workers.[12]

Northern miners and railway workers displayed an especially
combative spirit. In Cananea, miners resented the preferential

treatment of American employees. These nationalist resentments fused with the influence of IWW ideas to produce the bloody 1906 strike, which brought Arizona Rangers and armed Arizona miners across the border at the request of the governor of Sonora amid reports that Mexicans were killing Americans. Contacts with IWW organizers on the Arizona side of the border encouraged the growth of radicalism among Cananea miners. This strike exposed the potential danger to the Díaz regime if the organized political opposition could capitalize on labor unrest.[13]

Nationalism was an important force in energizing Mexican railroad workers, who found that the extension of U.S. railroad unions into their country simply reinforced the privileged status of foreigners in an industry dominated by foreign capital. American railroad workers had established local chapters along craft lines in the 1880s. They monopolized the skilled jobs and often displayed contemptuous disregard for Mexican workers, who joined the brotherhoods but complained that fellow unionists from the United States ignored their grievances over discriminatory hiring practices, wage differentials, and lack of opportunities for advancement. As a result, Mexican railroad workers began to form their own unions to bargain with management and protest the privileged status of American workers in the industry. Their growing demands for "Mexicanization" of the railroads dovetailed with the Díaz government's attempt to establish majority stock ownership in the railway companies and contributed to the buildup of nationalist sentiment on the eve of the Revolution.[14]

While Gompers developed contacts with PLM leaders and criticized infringements on the civil liberties of Díaz's political opponents, American railroad workers in Mexico criticized Díaz for more chauvinistic reasons. Protesting the rising tide of Mexican nationalism, U.S. railroad unions tried to gain sympathy from the State Department, which conducted an investigation in 1903 and dismissed complaints that American workers in Mexico suffered discrimination. They complained again in July 1909, when the Díaz government announced its plans to "Mexicanize" the railroads. Despite government assurance that American workers would not be fired without just cause, American train dispatchers launched a general strike that month that resulted in their dismissal and replacement by Mexicans. The "Mexicanization" of the labor force on the National Railways had not become a reality by the time Díaz left office, but American railroad unions in Mexico were apprehensive about their future in the face of mounting demands by Mexicans to get the jobs held by foreigners. Although Mexican railroad workers benefitted from the precedents of trade-union organizing by the American brotherhoods, their complaints about union discrimination fused with the struggle against management to give a nationalistic cast to their organizing efforts.[15]

PLM representatives soon discovered that Gompers's opposition to Díaz did not translate into an endorsement of their revolutionary movement. By 1911 the PLM had split into two ideological camps, both of which sought AFL support. While Ricardo Flores Magón had converted to anarchism, Gutiérrez de Lara and Villarreal embraced the liberal, reformist campaign of Francisco Madero, the wealthy Coahuilan landowner who launched a revolution against Díaz in November 1910.[16] When told by Gutiérrez de Lara of the impending revolt against Díaz, Gompers refused to offer his support, replying evasively that "if the movement should permit a man of the type of Diaz to be placed in the presidency I would have nothing to do with it."[17]

If the liberal, reformist wing of the movement could not secure Gompers's endorsement, *magonista* radicalism could hardly be expected to attract his support. Denouncing Madero as well as Díaz, Ricardo Flores Magón launched a military invasion of Baja California, where he hoped to establish an anarchist society. Much of his support came from wobblies on the West Coast. His capture of the border cities of Tijuana and Mexicali, however, prompted President Taft to send twenty thousand troops to patrol the border in March 1911. Already engaged in bitter disputes with fellow revolutionaries and American socialists over his break with Madero, Flores Magón asked Gompers for a public statement of opposition to U.S. intervention. Gompers responded by asking for a clearer view of Flores Magón's aims: "If the present regime is to be supplanted by another, the present revolutionary party, without fundamentally changing conditions which shall make for the improvement of the workers' opportunities, and a greater regard for their rights and their interests, then the American labor movement can look upon such a change with entire indifference."[18]

Assurances from Flores Magón that his movement embraced

land reform, basic civil liberties, and higher wages and improved working conditions for Mexican laborers did not persuade Gompers to jump into the fray. In a letter to Gompers, Flores Magón urged AFL support to prevent capitalists from exploiting cheap Mexican labor to undermine the American labor movement. When Gompers raised the issue at an executive council meeting, only the UMW's John Mitchell favored issuing a protest against possible U.S. intervention. The executive council preferred to await further developments before taking any action.[19]

While the executive council decided against protesting Taft's mobilization of troops along the border, numerous union locals expressed militant opposition to the troop deployment. For example, a local of the International Association of Machinists in Newark, New Jersey, denounced the maneuver as an attempt "to further the interests of a handful of selfish capitalists in their efforts to throttle real democracy in Mexico." The Cigar Makers' Union in San Francisco urged a national demonstration to protest interference in Mexico. The Pennsylvania Federation of Labor passed a resolution introduced by a Philadelphia local of the Cigar Makers' Union that charged that Taft had deployed the troops "solely in the interest of those American capitalists whose surplus of wealth, wrung from American labor, is invested in Mexico, and whose opportunity to further mercilessly exploit the Mexican working class would be endangered by the success of the revolution."[20]

The Socialist Party of America (SPA) played a leading role in stimulating the outpouring of protests from unions, progressives, and socialists immediately after the troop deployment. In a statement prepared by Morris Hillquit, the SPA's executive committee publicly charged that the United States intended to shield Díaz and his Wall Street supporters from a popular revolution, and urged noninterference in Mexican affairs. The petitions of protest filed by numerous SPA locals generally echoed the position outlined in the SPA's national proclamation. When a female member of a teachers' union introduced at a Chicago Federation of Labor meeting an anti-interventionist resolution that conformed too closely to the SPA's national proclamation, a male member of the machinists' union tried unsuccessfully to block it by proposing instead that an all-male committee study the matter.[21]

The unity displayed by American radicals over the troop deployment could not conceal deeper differences created by the Flores Magón-Madero split. While IWW sympathizers supported the Baja activities of Flores Magón, many Socialists opposed his attempt to push the revolution to the left at this time.[22] On April 12, 1911, the socialist *New York Call* criticized Flores Magón for having provoked the split by attacking Madero's limited vision of a political revolution. Eugene V. Debs also began to distance himself from the Baja group, stressing that Madero would usher in an era of political democracy during which much could be accomplished toward socialism through union and party organizing. He and other socialists argued that the bourgeois-democratic stage of development was vital to the evolution of socialism in Mexico. Criticizing the *magonista* plea for "direct action" to seize lands from the rich, Debs argued that the Mexican masses suffered from a lack of consciousness and that the seizure of lands would only provoke savage retribution and senseless bloodshed. Besides stressing that the capitalists were too strong to engage militarily, he pointed out that an economic revolution could not be achieved overnight: "If the land can be taken from the rich in this insurrection so can also the mills, factories, mines, railroads, and the machinery of production, and the question is, what would the masses in their present ignorant and unorganized state do with them after having obtained them?"[23]

Following Díaz's resignation and departure for Europe in May 1911, the AFL executive council continued its cautious approach, voting on June 16 to defer action on a PLM request for support. However, trade-union socialists like Mother Jones and other representatives of American mineworkers accepted Madero's invitation to help organize Mexican miners. Madero, who assumed the presidency in November 1911, following the interim presidency of Díaz's secretary of foreign relations, Francisco León de la Barra, assured Mother Jones that he favored the organization of all Mexican workers in their respective crafts. Jones went to Mexico City, where she, UMW vice president Frank Hayes, and the WFM's Joe Cannon met with Madero. "Mr. President," she said, "if I come down and do what I can at Cananea, the big American interests in all those mines will arrest me and put me in jail." Madero responded, she later noted, by reassuring her: "If they do I will come down and make them take you out."[24]

While Madero expressed support for the organization of Mexican miners, Manuel Calero, the secretary of justice during De la Barra's interim presidency and Madero's future secretary of foreign relations, hoped to use Mother Jones, Hayes, and Cannon to accomplish more pressing political objectives. Fulfilling a promise made to Calero during their stay in Mexico City, Jones and Cannon visited Flores Magón in Los Angeles to prevail upon him and his supporters to lay down their arms and return to Mexico to participate in the political process. Praising the more open political climate created by the ouster of Díaz, Jones denounced the use of force as "the last resort of intelligent people" and urged the *magonistas* to promote their political agenda through the ballot box.[25]

Flores Magón and his colleagues scolded Jones for allowing herself to be manipulated and deceived by Mexican politicians, and they rejected the invitation to abandon their revolutionary tactics in favor of a more gradualist approach. They predicted that Madero's tenure in Mexico City would be short-lived. After failing to convince the *magonistas* to return to Mexico, Jones and Cannon concluded that further discussions with them would be useless. Nevertheless, Jones tried one more time with the help of Job Harriman, their attorney and Socialist mayoral candidate of Los Angeles. Neither Harriman nor Jones could sway them, however, and Jones issued a final warning to Flores Magón:

> Now I want to say to you you have one of two alternatives, and I want to be honest with you. You cannot go into Mexico by force and take the lands, for the United States is a friendly nation to Mexico. They will not uphold any violation of International laws. . . . You will either go into Mexico, accept the proposition of the Government that is given to you here today, or you will be arrested by the American Government and handed over to the Mexican Government. I am not prepared to say what will follow after that.[26]

After her last meeting with Flores Magón, Jones visited AFL offices around Los Angeles to ensure that the *magonistas* would receive no further money from the "qualified labor unions." Completely frustrated by Flores Magón's refusal to endorse Madero's presidency as an important stage in the peaceful transition to socialism, she told Calero that her efforts had been fruitless and that the *magonistas* were receiving money from Italian and Spanish anarchists. She assured him that AFL unions opposed Flores Magón and his allies, whom she denounced as "unreasonable fanatics."[27]

The *magonistas* quickly attacked Mother Jones and the AFL in their newspaper, *Regeneración*. These attacks prompted a letter from Jones, who denied that she was a tool of the Mexican government. Praising Madero as "a gentleman in every sense of the word, a man with the most remarkable grasp of the economic struggle and the underlying causes," she expressed a sense of betrayal over Flores Magón's lack of appreciation for her role in the AFL's defense of jailed PLM representatives. She rebuked Flores Magón for *Regeneración*'s attacks upon the AFL:

> You should have refused the $4,000 that they [AFL] donated if they are what you represent them to be. You should have notified me not to accept a dollar from them or their colleagues to defend you. . . . Neither my colleagues or myself shall ever again insult you by taking any money from the American Federation of Labor to defend you if you should again get into the clutches of the law.[28]

The more open political climate that followed the overthrow of Díaz encouraged the political ferment of Mexican workers. The rapid growth of unions, many of which were affiliated with or at least sympathetic to the IWW, during Madero's presidency suggested the possibility of a left-wing drift in the movement that Madero had unleashed but perhaps could no longer control. It was during his brief tenure that the Casa del Obrero Mundial,[29] an anarchosyndicalist labor center, opened its doors in Mexico City. Such developments had potential implications for Gompers, who, as Harvey Levenstein points out, "could certainly not look with equanimity upon the possibility of a strong ally of the IWW sitting just across the border."[30]

By the fall of 1912 the AFL executive council had overcome its earlier cautious reaction to the ouster of Díaz and endorsed Madero's government. Using his previous contacts with Gompers, Gutiérrez de Lara appeared before the executive council and won support for a protest against possible U.S. intervention. Andrew Furuseth and T. A. Hanson, delegates from the International Seamen's Union, introduced at the AFL convention in November a resolution that opposed American intervention in Mexico. The convention adopted the resolution, which defined the revolution in Mexico as an attempt to abolish debt peonage and promote land reform.[31]

Internal and external pressures soon undermined Madero, whose failure to remove the officer corps of the federal army and other allies of the old porfirian aristocracy within the federal bureaucracy proved fatal. Madero, no radical, selected a relatively conservative cabinet and shunned ambitious reform programs in his effort to demonstrate that granting the Mexican middle class a greater role in the political system would promote long-range stability and economic prosperity, attract foreign investment, and safeguard the hacienda as the productive unit of modernized agriculture. His refusal to press for a meaningful solution to the agrarian problem cost him the support of the peasant revolutionaries led by Emiliano Zapata, previously one of his chief allies, and exacerbated social and political unrest. Opposition also came from the old aristocracy, which found Madero's toleration of labor unions and embrace of civil liberties and political freedoms distasteful. Madero sent armies against the *zapatistas,* who had begun to seize lands from large landowners and restore them to Indian villages in southern and central Mexico; and he had to contend with numerous counterrevolutionary movements in various parts of the nation.[32]

A revolutionary peasantry and a reactionary porfirian aristocracy were not the only major threats to Madero, who could not please Mexico's cranky northern neighbor. Notwithstanding the predictions of American radicals that the Taft administration would intervene to save Díaz and protect U.S. investments in Mexico, Taft opted for a more moderate course. In fact, the initial U.S. response to Madero was quite favorable—a reflection of the view among government officials and some large American companies in Mexico that the new president would not tamper with the economic system and would favor American over European investors. Washington had taken a dim view of Díaz's attempts to neutralize the political clout of American capital in Mexico by courting European investors. Although Madero's financial and foreign policies were hardly anti-American, his honeymoon with the United States did not last long. He refused to grant special favors to American interests. The unhappiness of American offi-

cials and companies over this independent posture fused with concern over Madero's inability to maintain political stability and deal
with the peasant revolutionaries to produce an increasingly antagonistic policy toward him.[33]

In his campaign to step up pressure on Madero and paint a pic-
ture of growing instability, one of the issues emphasized by Henry
Lane Wilson, the U.S. ambassador in Mexico City, was Madero's
move to require that all employees of the National Railways be able
to speak Spanish. Led by engineers and conductors, American railroad workers in Mexico launched a general strike in April 1912 to
protest this attempt to "Mexicanize" the railways. When Madero
replaced the strikers with Mexicans, a mass exodus of American
railroad workers ensued, effectively closing the local chapters of
American brotherhoods.[34]

Madero's inability to straddle the fence between peasant revolutionaries and reactionaries led to his swift demise. Domestic
counterrevolutionary forces, led by General Victoriano Huerta and
encouraged by Ambassador Wilson, toppled his presidency on
February 13, 1913. Despite the AFL's 1912 statement of opposition
to U.S. intervention, Madero's failure to contain social and political
unrest had begun to undermine Gompers's hopes that a liberal
democracy could be immediately achieved in Mexico. Gompers
later described Madero as "theatrical" and "sentimental" and complained that Mexicans were simply not ready for democracy.[35]

The establishment of Huerta's dictatorship and the assassina-
tions of Madero and his vice president, José María Pino Suárez,
opened a more violent phase of the Revolution and posed problems for the incoming administration of Woodrow Wilson, who
withheld recognition of Huerta and recalled Ambassador Wilson.
A complex set of moral and material motives shaped President Wilson's response to the Mexican Revolution. Elected on a platform
of antimonopoly reform, he believed that government should not
be a captive of big business, and he criticized the attempts by large
corporations to interfere in Mexico. Often using anti-imperialist
rhetoric, he expressed sympathy for Mexico's struggle to achieve
democracy, eradicate semifeudal traditions, and resist the interventionist machinations of European and American corporations.
He opposed what he regarded as the crude economic exploitation

of Latin America by European powers that acted simply to protect the interests of their financiers and investors.

Underpinning this moral idealism and opposition to more traditional forms of imperialism, however, was the conviction that a stable Mexico should maintain a commitment to liberal capitalism, accept American tutelage, and refrain from placing any confiscatory restraints upon foreign companies. In short, Wilson believed that Mexico should do nothing to disturb its subordinate position in a world order dominated by the advanced industrial nations. By promoting democracy and combatting European influences in Mexico and Latin America, he hoped to stabilize the political situation and improve the opportunities for American trade and investment. He agreed with then-State Department counselor Robert Lansing's warning that European economic penetration of Latin America destabilized the region. Lansing stressed that the financial dependence of Latin American countries on Europe would lead to greater political domination. "With the present industrial activity, the scramble for markets, and the incessant search for new opportunities to produce wealth," he told the president, "commercial expansion and success are closely interwoven with political domination over the territory which is being exploited."[36]

It was within this ideological context that the Wilson administration confronted Huerta, who irritated U.S. officials when he cultivated British support by granting concessions to Lord Cowdray's Anglo-American Petroleum Company. Convinced that British oil interests were the sinister force responsible for Britain's Mexican policy, and frustrated over the recognition of Huerta by European nations, Wilson set out to isolate the man whose overthrow of Madero offended his view that democratic procedures were the most effective antidote to Mexican instability. He viewed Huerta as an instrument of British imperialism and believed that foreign powers were propping up his dictatorial regime. In Wilson's opinion, this justified U.S. efforts to topple Huerta, shape the character of the new government, and ensure a more favorable political climate for foreign investments. "If the influences at work in Mexico were entirely domestic," he argued, "this government would be willing to trust the people to protect themselves against any ambitious leader who might arise, but since such a leader relies for his strength, not upon the sympathy of his own people, but upon the influence of foreign people, this Government, whether that foreign capital is from the United States or from other countries, would be derelict in its duty if by silence or inaction it seemed to sympathize with such an interference in the rights and welfare of Mexico."[37] He assured British diplomat Sir William Tyrell in November 1913 that the United States aimed "not merely to force Huerta from power, but also to exert every influence it can to secure Mexico a better government under which all contracts and business concessions will be safer than they have ever been."[38]

Madero's ouster coincided with the arrival of an administration in Washington that supported important domestic labor reforms, including the Clayton Act in 1914, which exempted unions from prosecution under the Sherman Anti-Trust Act. Included in the package of reforms was the creation of the Department of Labor. President Wilson appointed William B. Wilson, the former UMW official and congressman who had chaired the House Rules Committee investigation of jailing of the PLM members in the United States, as the new department's first secretary. The close relationship with the Wilson administration affected the AFL's Mexican policies as Gompers carefully manipulated the expression of anti-interventionist tendencies within the AFL in a way that did not challenge the fundamental tenets of Wilsonian foreign policy. From this time forward, Gompers stepped up his efforts to shape the ideological orientation of the Mexican labor movement and determine Huerta's successor as President Wilson adopted an interventionist policy to mold the Revolution according to his specifications.

The challenge of steering the AFL away from a collision course with President Wilson over Mexico without completely alienating anti-interventionist elements quickly confronted Gompers. The specter of U.S. intervention sparked the introduction of a resolution at the AFL convention in November 1913 that would have committed the AFL to an unequivocal position against armed interference in Mexico. Introduced by George Berry of the Printing Pressman's Union, the resolution bothered Gompers, who persuaded Berry to withdraw the section that declared the AFL "in the most emphatic manner [to be] opposed to armed intervention by the United States." After discussions with members of the newly created Committee on International Relations, Berry agreed to a watered-down version of the resolution which condemned the campaign by American and other foreign corporations and jingoistic newspapers to promote armed intervention in Mexico.[39]

An analysis of the committee's discussions reveals that although Gompers denounced the "bloody record" of Huerta, much larger concerns underlay his defeat of the earlier draft of Berry's resolution. Fully aware of the broader economic and geopolitical interests at stake, Gompers, like President Wilson, saw the hidden hand of European powers behind Huerta's coup, and made clear he would not endorse an anti-interventionist policy for the AFL or the U.S. government. That Gompers's commitment to U.S. hegemony took precedence over the principles of anti-imperialism is evident in his comments justifying opposition to Berry's original resolution. Invoking the Monroe Doctrine, he began:

> Now, I am a peace-loving man and the American labor movement is a peace-loving movement; but I do not believe that we will continue forever and ever to fold our arms in humble submission to every indignity and outrage that may be committed against us. . . . If ever a man held a position of power in the land, Huerta holds it, by the blood upon his brow. And if the Huerta regime is permitted too long to gather [a] hold upon the Mexican people it means at least another quarter of a century before the people of that nation will assert their rights and inaugurate some sort of a protest for its undoing. . . . In the United States we have declared, or rather those who have gone before us have declared, that the Monroe Doctrine shall prevail. . . . Well, if we want to maintain that policy, if we want to make the great American continent secure for the purpose of working out our salvation, our theories, our ideas and our ideals of self-government, we must maintain the position that no foreign government may attempt by an armed demonstration or force to interfere in the internal affairs of an American government.[40]

The logic of Gompers's argument compelled him to support U.S. intervention in order to prevent what he regarded as European meddling in Latin America. As war loomed in Europe, he recognized the dangerous implications of foreign economic rivalries in Mexico and became convinced that European threats to U.S. hegemony also threatened to deprive Latin American nations of their national sovereignty. Accordingly, he refused to commit the AFL to an anti-imperialist policy, for he wanted the United States to retain the option of intervening to prevent European interference. "I will go as far as any man," he said, "in protesting against any armed intervention, against any disturbance of our international relations or to bring about any war; but there will be one of two alternatives for us, and that is to make the conditions habitable and tolerable or else, despite our protests, foreign governments will interfere and intervene and our Monroe Doctrine with all that it implies will be destroyed and thrown to the four winds of the heaven."[41]

As we shall see, Gompers often sharply criticized the interventionist machinations of American and other foreign investors in Mexico, but his willingness to endorse U.S. intervention against Huerta revealed the limits of his anti-imperialism. He understood the economic basis of imperialism and conceded the need under certain circumstances to intervene to create a more stable political climate that would safeguard the long-range interests of foreign capital and the United States. It would be unfair, however, to describe him as an advocate of knee-jerk intervention, ever ready to serve the narrow interests of capitalists. In effect, his position coincided with that of President Wilson, who condemned the selfish interventionist demands of corporate interests but sought to replace Huerta with a government more acceptable to the United States. In Wilson's view, an acceptable government would be one capable of ensuring a stable political environment in which capitalists from all nations could operate without special concessions or favors. Creating this kind of atmosphere would undercut possible intervention by European nations on behalf of the selfish interests of their capitalists. Gompers explained this position to members of the Committee on International Relations as he diluted Berry's anti-interventionist resolution:

> Here is the fact: Interests, honestly as well as dishonestly, have been invested in Mexico, and these interests . . . are protected or proposed to be protected by the governments of the countries in which the holders of these interests reside and of which they are subjects. If we say to England and Germany: "Keep your hands off Mexico, this is an American affair," then we have got to help in keeping our house in order.[42]

What is revealing about Gompers's comments is the absence of any explanation of how intervention would serve the interests of the labor movements in the United States and Mexico. His rationale for intervention spoke exclusively to American geopolitical interests. In many respects, Huerta's labor policies did not differ significantly from those of his predecessor. Huerta continued Madero's attempts to manipulate the fledgling Mexican labor movement and encourage non-radical organizations, and he expanded the size of the Department of Labor, which had been created under Madero. In an effort to consolidate his dictatorship, Huerta tolerated the modest labor reforms of Madero and even pushed a few of his own. The Casa del Obrero Mundial led the first May Day demonstration in Mexico's history, but Huerta soon thereafter cracked down by arresting many of its leaders and forcing it to close in early 1914.[43]

Given Gompers's defense of intervention against Huerta before the fact, it is not surprising that he did not criticize the U.S. occupation of Veracruz in April 1914, after diplomatic pressure by Wilson failed to oust Huerta. An incident in Tampico on April 9, 1914, provided Wilson with the pretext for intervention. In this incident, Huerta's troops arrested several sailors from the American cruiser *Dolphin* for landing in a restricted zone when they came ashore to buy fuel. Although Huerta's general apologized and quickly freed the American sailors, the White House insisted that Mexico honor the American flag by giving it a twenty-one gun salute—a demand Huerta refused to grant.

Learning on April 21 that the German merchant ship *Ypiranga* was steaming toward Veracruz with an arms shipment for Huerta, Wilson ordered American marines to seize the customs house in Veracruz. Huerta's troops withdrew from the city, but local volunteers and cadets of the naval academy fought bravely in an unsuccessful resistance against the American occupying forces. Wilson hoped that Huerta's domestic enemies would support the American action and grant the White House a role in shaping a provisional Mexican government once Huerta had been deposed.[44]

Wilson discovered, however, that his attempt to impose a solution to Mexico's political problems did not sit well with the Constitutionalist forces that were waging an armed struggle to oust Huerta. Zapata's peasant forces harassed Huerta's troops in Morelos and other southern states, while Pancho Villa led successful operations against Federal forces in the state of Chihuahua. Villa put himself under the command of Venustiano Carranza in Coahuila, and Álvaro Obregón led the campaign against the *huer-*

tistas in Sonora. As the "First Chief" of the coalition of Constitutionalist forces, Carranza demanded the removal of U.S. troops.
The nationalist response to American intervention included pledges
from Mexican workers to defend their country against aggression,
but Huerta chose to send new working-class enlistees to Morelos to
fight the *zapatistas* rather than the American occupiers of Veracruz.[45]

Unwilling to undertake a larger-scale military intervention in
Mexico, Wilson then tried a more flexible strategy designed to
remove Huerta and impose a provisional government that was
acceptable to the United States. The U.S. State Department persuaded Argentina, Brazil, and Chile to offer to mediate the conflict between Mexico and the United States. President Wilson's
unsuccessful effort to forestall a complete Constitutionalist military
victory through this mediation at the Niagara Falls conference in
May and June of 1914 reflected his fear that continuation of the
military struggle could only prolong political instability and jeopardize American interests. Secretary of State William Jennings
Bryan told American commissioners to the conference at the outset
to insist that the provisional government comprise members sympathetic to land reform. Whereas Bryan regarded land reform as
the key to stabilizing Mexico, other voices in the State Department
expressed pessimism that anything short of an American protectorate in Mexico could end the revolutionary turbulence. Leon J.
Canova, a special agent for the State Department in Mexico, argued that the United States should use financial leverage to win
Constitutionalist acceptance of direct American tutelage. "It seems
to me the only salvation for this country," he wrote from Saltillo,
"is a supervision over its affairs by the United States, which would
act as an advisor to the government, or under a plan similar to the
Platt Amendment."[46]

In the only reference to the American occupation in his autobiography, Gompers praised President Wilson's "extreme self-
control and wisdom" in preventing a full-scale war with Mexico.[47]
Having abandoned pacifism,[48] Gompers supported the move to
oust Huerta at a time when significant pockets of opposition to war
with Mexico existed within the American labor movement. The
IWW's William D. Haywood, who claimed to have been acting
upon the authority of the WFM and UMW, threatened in a speech
at Carnegie Hall to call a general strike if the United States declared

war on Mexico. Haywood, along with many other leftists, compared the invasion of Mexico to the killing of striking miners in Ludlow, Colorado, which occurred just before the occupation of Veracruz. "You may say that this action of the mine workers is traitorous to the country," he said, "but I tell you it is better to be a traitor to a country than to be a traitor to your class."[49]

Haywood's militant declaration prompted the *New York Times* to conduct surveys throughout the nation to determine how organized labor would react to war with Mexico. Publishing comments from many labor leaders, the newspaper concluded that while they opposed war, most flatly rejected the idea of calling a general strike and dismissed Haywood's threat as an empty one. However, labor leaders in Indianapolis expressed general opposition to war with Mexico and declared that they would do everything possible to discourage enlistments. The Chicago Federation of Labor (CFL) approved a resolution condemning what it regarded as efforts by commercial interests to provoke intervention. However, the CFL dismissed Haywood's assertion that the UMW would join the IWW in a strike, and UMW leaders in Pennsylvania's anthracite fields repudiated Haywood. AFL vice president James Duncan perhaps most accurately expressed the view of the executive council:

> Organized labor is opposed to strikes except as a last resort. A war is like a strike only to be resorted to when all other means of settlement have failed. Organized labor regards the situation as different from situations which often arise in Europe, where wars are generally gotten up for the benefit of the fellow who does not do much of the fighting. Labor in those countries is justified in its antagonism to such wars, but our wars are forced upon us by injustice or insult.[50]

Huerta finally resigned and left for Europe on July 15, 1914, but American troops did not evacuate Veracruz until November 23, 1914.[51] The AFL executive council adopted a suggestion by Gompers that he send a letter to Rafael Zubarán Capmany, a Constitutionalist representative in Washington, urging a lenient policy toward the *huertistas*. The executive council also endorsed Vice-President James Duncan's suggestion that the letter include a call for land reform.[52] Gompers contacted Zubarán Capmany to express AFL support for Carranza and suggest that no reprisals be taken against Huerta's followers. "What I have in mind," he wrote, "is that since the American Federation of Labor, as no other instrumentality outside the government of the United States, has aided for the success of the prospective government, we have the right to suggest to those who represent General Carranza and the victorious revolutionary army that the higher humanitarian consideration be given, aye, even to those who have been guilty."[53]

Following the fall of Huerta, the stability the Wilson administration and Gompers desired did not materialize. The Revolution entered a more bloody phase as fundamental differences over social issues quickly fractured the Constitutionalist coalition. Peasant revolutionaries Zapata and Villa demanded a thoroughgoing solution to the agrarian problem and other sweeping economic and social reforms. The unwillingness of Carranza, a fiercely conservative aristocratic landowner, to address the basic concerns of the peasant revolutionaries led to a more intense stage of fighting between the Constitutionalists and the armies of Zapata and Villa. The AFL convention endorsed Carranza in November 1914, just as the divisions in the Constitutionalist camp were widening into open conflict.[54]

The AFL's involvement in Mexican affairs grew when Carranza, forced out of Mexico City by Villa and Zapata, yielded to political and military pressures and heeded the advice of reform-minded members of his movement to reach out to urban labor. Although Carranza held a dim view of the Casa del Obrero Mundial and had little sympathy for labor reform, some of his supporters, particularly his capable general Álvaro Obregón, recognized the importance of incorporating the urban labor movement into the Constitutionalist struggle by offering reforms. Amid concern that the peasant revolutionaries might capitalize on the growing ferment of Mexican workers, Obregón, the famous painter Gerardo Murillo (popularly known as Dr. Atl), Zubarán Capmany, and other Constitutionalist reformers persuaded a reluctant Carranza to recruit workers for the military campaign against the peasant armies. In exchange for promised labor legislation, Casa leaders agreed to recruit workers' battalions for the Constitutionalist armies. The Constitutionalists successfully depicted their struggle as a movement against clerical, military, and bourgeois reaction, and six "Red Battalions" organized under the Casa-Carranza accord went into action against the peasant revolutionaries.[55]

Eight Casa leaders signed the pact with Zubarán Capmany, Carranza's secretary of *Gobernación* (the counterpart of the U.S. Department of the Interior), in February 1915, despite considerable opposition within the ranks of labor. The formation of the Red Battalions pitted workers against peasants and split the labor movement in some areas as many workers and a few leaders joined Zapata and Villa. The Casa's decision to abandon its earlier policy of nonalignment with any of the revolutionary factions represented a significant movement away from anarchosyndicalism. By participating in the armed struggle to capture the machinery of government, the Casa hoped to use its political connections to build a more solid organizational base from which it could better challenge Carranza and the capitalist order. In effect, however, it thereby recognized the legitimacy of the bourgeois state and helped to consolidate its power.[56]

Events soon demonstrated that the Casa-Carranza pact also opened the door for the AFL in Mexico. The Constitutionalists' overtures toward the urban labor movement took into consideration international as well as domestic forces. Besides mobilizing workers against the peasant armies, the pact required labor leaders to publicize the Constitutionalist cause inside and outside Mexico. The recent American occupation of Veracruz indicated that the Wilson administration would not play the role of a dispassionate spectator as the Revolution deepened. Zubarán Capmany, who already had contacts with Gompers, set up and financed a committee whose job it was to ensure that the Casa's publicity work was not at odds with his Ministerio de Gobernación.[57]

Shortly after the Casa-Carranza pact was signed, John Murray, who had by now overcome his reservations about Gompers, took off for Mexico to get more information on the agreement for the *New York Call* and lay the groundwork for establishing a relationship between the AFL and the Casa. It is not entirely clear whether Murray conferred with Gompers before embarking on his trip, but during his discussions with Casa leaders in Veracruz and Mexico City, he tried to make Gompers's philosophy more palatable to an audience that had sympathies for the IWW. Softpedaling Gompers's opposition to the IWW, he painted a favorable portrait of the AFL leader and stressed the importance of linking up with the AFL. Briefed by Casa leaders on the pact with Carranza, whom they described as prolabor, Murray returned to the United States convinced that the AFL should urge diplomatic recognition of Carranza.[58]

The AFL's evolving pro-Carranza position solidified during the spring and summer of 1915, thanks in part to Murray's efforts. On returning to the United States he discussed the Mexican situation with Santiago Iglesias, a trade-union Socialist, AFL organizer in Puerto Rico, and trusted adviser to Gompers on Latin American affairs. In an effort to inject a broader vision of internationalism into AFL policy, Murray and Iglesias agreed that it was time to foster a relationship with Mexican and other Latin American labor organizations. They discussed their views with James Lord, who headed the AFL's Mining Department, and other AFL officials. Gompers welcomed Murray into his inner circle of advisers as the AFL's point man in Mexico.[59]

In the view of Iglesias, the accelerated transnational movement of capital made a regional labor federation imperative as a mechanism to protect workers from greater exploitation in the Western Hemisphere. The Wilson administration was backing a drive to promote increased trade and investment in Latin America through a series of financial conferences held in conjunction with the Pan American Union. Having attended the first of such conferences in May 1915 as an observer, Iglesias regarded the concerted effort by governments and commercial interests to plan a more coordinated investment strategy as a possible threat to Latin American workers. He recommended that the AFL immediately move to convene a Pan-American Labor Conference. Although the executive council did not specifically urge the convening of a regional labor conference, it did endorse the groundwork which had been laid with the Mexican labor movement and sought AFL authorization to contact Latin American labor representatives with preliminary suggestions to hold a meeting of Pan-American labor organizations.[60]

Gompers tried unsuccessfully that summer to persuade Secretary of the Treasury William G. McAdoo to grant labor representation on the committees set up at the opening session of the Pan-American Financial and Trade Conference.[61] Encouraged by Iglesias and Murray to seek an expanded role for the AFL through regional labor discussions, Gompers increased the AFL's visibility in Mexico against a backdrop of concerns that extended beyond Iglesias's desire to strengthen the bargaining position of Pan-American workers. Opposition within the AFL to possible U.S. involvement in the European war concerned Gompers during the summer of 1915. The UMW held a conference attended by several AFL-affiliated unions on May 27 to announce opposition to the war. Gompers ignored the conference's request that he convene a special meeting of all labor organizations if U.S. entry into the war appeared imminent. He refused to endorse Secretary of State Bryan's call for peace, despite the fact that Bryan's position was popular with many trade unionists. Blaming strikes in the American munitions industry on German agents, Gompers lunched with important munitions manufacturers during the summer of 1915 and gained the confidence of the British Embassy. Arranged by Ralph Easley, executive secretary of the National Civic Federation (NCF), these contacts did much to ease concerns about possible labor support for an embargo on arms exports. "The NCF thus appears to be the catalyst," writes Simeon Larson, "that brought about a working relationship between the president of the AFL, the leading industrialists of the country, and the British Embassy."[62]

The NCF also expressed concern over the Mexican situation. Easley complained to Gompers that the socialists had been too successful in circulating their view of Carranza within the State Department. Bemoaning that the socialists were "taking Carranza under their wing," he pointed out that Carranza had sent to the United States many teachers "who are being more or less chaperoned by the socialists." Easley hinted at the need for a counterinfluence on Carranza's representatives and publicists in the United States.[63]

Fears of an expanded IWW influence in Mexico also encouraged Gompers to increase his contacts with Casa leaders during the summer of 1915. American press reports that described the Casa as a branch of the IWW alarmed Gompers, who feared the spread of Wobblie ideas among Mexican workers in the southwestern United States. American IWW publications hailed the rapid growth of the Casa. As Philip S. Foner points out, these reports, which stressed the dynamic growth of the Casa, "brought an end to the period when he [Gompers] was only partly interested in events South of the border."[64]

Opportunities appeared that summer for the AFL to increase its influence among Mexican workers and simultaneously encourage the stabilization of the Revolution by acting as peacemakers between Carranza and Wilson. The White House had become increasingly frustrated by Carranza's steadfast resistance to U.S. interference in Mexico's internal affairs. Carranza's refusal to yield to U.S. pressures that he reach a settlement with the various opposing Mexican factions irritated President Wilson. "I thing [sic] I have never known of a man more impossible to deal with on human principles," Wilson complained to his secretary of state, "that [sic] this man Carranza."[65]

Meanwhile, nationalist opposition to U.S. meddling intensified in the face of growing concern over the possible return of American troops. From Veracruz, the Revolutionary Committee of the World's Workers of Mexico called upon Gompers to protest the White House's hostile attitude toward the Constitutionalists and emphasized the determination of Mexican workers to resist U.S. intervention. Gompers relayed the communication to President Wilson and asked about reports that Duval West, one of the White House's special agents dispatched to Mexico, was hostile to the interests of Mexican workers. The White House assured Gompers that the impression about West was inaccurate, and Gompers informed the Mexican labor leaders of his action and the president's response.[66]

Later that summer Col. Edmundo E. Martínez, one of Carranza's representatives, contacted Gompers for help in securing U.S. recognition. Bearing credentials which confirmed that he belonged to the Federación de Sindicatos Obreros de la República Mexicana, Martínez claimed to be a special representative of Mexican labor. He praised Carranza's support for organized labor and explained the Constitutionalist movement to Gompers. Subsequent contacts with Gompers revealed that Martínez's chief mission was to promote Carranza, and that insofar as labor was concerned, his overriding preoccupation was the defeat of more radical tendencies within the Mexican labor movement. He asked Gompers to arrange a meeting for him with President Wilson. Following a conference with Martínez in AFL headquarters, Gompers tried unsuccessfully to convince the President to grant Martínez an interview. Wilson assured Gompers, however, that he would consider Martínez's views before making any major policy decisions on Mexico.[67]

The persistent Martínez then wrote directly to Wilson, identifying himself as a Mason and Protestant and describing the Constitutionalist movement as a struggle against the political tyranny of the Catholic church. Villa and Zapata, he said, were "vile murderers." Likening Carranza to Wilson, he praised the refusal of both leaders to be bought off by big corporations. Hailing Wilson as "the model for a Christian gentleman and citizen, the one who could unite all America for the Master," he also praised Gompers: "We think a good deal of him in Mexico, and trust that with his fatherly advice, we will settle many a rough path."[68]

Gompers assured Martínez of AFL support and apologized for Wilson's refusal to grant him an interview. He said that international events absorbed much of the president's time but promised that Wilson would deal with Mexico in an intelligent manner after studying the situation carefully. "I trust that the President will not feel obliged to in any way interfere with the internal affairs of Mexico," he noted to Martínez, "except in an advisory and friendly capacity."[69]

Like Martínez, Gompers had more on his mind than the well-being of the labor movement. His assurances about the president's "benevolent paternalism" stopped short of repudiating the right of the United States to intervene in Mexico. In Gompers's view, the possible deepening of the Revolution posed a threat to American geopolitical interests and warranted the kind of fatherly advice that Martínez told Wilson Mexicans welcomed. While reaffirming AFL support for Carranza and urging patience, a somewhat impatient Gompers lectured Martínez that it was "the bounden duty of the people of Mexico to bring their numberless revolutions to an end." He reminded Martínez that the United States was morally responsible for policing the Latin American beat: "Upon the United States rests a sort of responsibility to help maintain the integrity of the governments of the Pan-American countries independent from interferences, intrusion or invasion of other countries."[70]

Gompers's contacts with Martínez and the information that he received from Murray on the Casa-Carranza pact convinced him that Carranza deserved U.S. recognition. Shunning the role of a mere instrument of Wilsonian policy in Mexico, he now tried, in fact, to lead rather than follow the president. On September 22, 1915, he sent a letter to the White House urging recognition of Carranza and expressing sympathy with the Mexican people's struggle against tyranny. "Although that struggle may be associated with many things . . . not in accord with our ideals," he wrote, ". . . these things are the first crude efforts of a people long accustomed to despotism and denial of the rights of free citizens to realize ideals of freedom."[71]

Rumors that Gompers's influence was about to sway Wilson prompted Catholic interests to protest the AFL's endorsement of a movement which they regarded as violently anti-Catholic. Nevertheless, the AFL's efforts to expand its influence in Mexico received a boost when the United States granted de facto recognition to Carranza about three weeks after Gompers's letter to the president. Quick to exploit the timing of Wilson's action, Gompers requested a copy of the formal note recognizing Carranza and encouraged Mexicans to believe that the AFL had considerable clout in the White House.[72]

The degree to which the AFL had influenced the decision to extend recognition triggered an internal debate in Mexico. Critics who minimized the AFL's role also criticized Martínez, who resented these slights. Anguished by what he regarded as a lack of public appreciation for his efforts, he considered renouncing his Mexican citizenship. Gompers counseled against such action, stressing that the Mexican people needed Martínez. He instead recommended an extended vacation for Martínez in the United States. Gompers hinted that Wilson had recognized Carranza because of AFL advice, and he thanked Martínez for Mexican labor's decision to send him a medal as a token of appreciation for AFL support.[73]

By the end of 1915, Gompers had developed a considerable stake in Mexico in pursuit of the twin objectives of reform and stability. These seemingly contradictory objectives were consistent with his basic view that political repression and denial of workers' rights simply bred radicalism and instability. Encouraged especially by trade-union socialists, mineworkers, and other progressive elements within the AFL, he had protested the jailing of Díaz's political opponents in the United States, denounced the interventionist activities of powerful American interests, and supported Madero after refusing initially to endorse the military movement against Díaz. These efforts and his alignment with the Constitutionalists won many friends for the AFL in Mexico and undermined John Murray's skepticism about his conservatism. Murray made an important decision to work with Gompers in 1915, and this relationship would later have even more important implications for the labor movements in Mexico and the United States.

Although Gompers hoped that the Revolution would usher in a liberal, democratic order in which workers would be able to exercise their organizational rights and enjoy political freedoms, he did not want the pursuit of reform to threaten what he conceived to be the strategic interests of the United States. He viewed the overthrow of Madero as an act of European aggression and invoked the Monroe Doctrine to justify intervention against Huerta in 1914. He also reminded Edmundo Martínez in 1915 that the United States had the moral authority to police Latin America. Confident that a bourgeois democratic order would improve living standards for Mexican workers and stabilize the Revolution, he established contacts with Mexican labor representatives and politicians to support the Constitutionalists and promote friendly relations with the United States.

Encouraged by Murray and Iglesias, Gompers had begun to frame his policies in Mexico within the wider context of Latin America. The Wilson administration's sponsorship of the Pan American Financial Conference underscored the importance of organizing Latin American workers to combat the growing regionalization of capital. The close ties between the AFL and the Wilson administration and Gompers's growing concern over the European situation meant, however, that the promotion of regional labor ties would have to take place within a framework that did not jeopardize American geopolitical interests. Strategic concerns had already cast a shadow on the nascent movement to forge Pan-American labor solidarity.

Gompers would also soon discover that supporting an anticlerical movement in Mexico and linking up with a labor movement that was more radical than the AFL exposed him to considerable criticism from conservative, Catholic elements within and outside the AFL. He would also shortly find that the growing force of revolutionary nationalism defied the efforts of President Wilson to dictate the ideological boundaries of the Revolution. A second military intervention would test the AFL's support for Wilsonian foreign policy and the depth of its commitment to the Constitutionalists and the Mexican labor movement.

2

Labor Diplomacy and the Pershing Expedition

Although Gompers was pleased with President Wilson's de facto recognition of Carranza, developments in Mexico quickly strained relations with the United States and threatened to undermine AFL support for Carranza. The increasingly nationalistic, anticlerical thrust of the Revolution hampered Gompers's pursuit of reform and stability. Spawned by escalating American fears about the possibility of oil nationalization by Carranza after January 1916 and increased mining taxes, tensions sharpened between the United States and Mexico.[1] The atmosphere of crisis, exacerbated by press reports and rumors of persecution of the Catholic church in Mexico, became even more highly charged when Gen. John J. Pershing led troops into Mexico on March 15, 1916, to pursue Pancho Villa after his attack on Columbus, New Mexico. Gompers took advantage of his budding relationship with Mexican workers to play an important role in efforts to defuse the diplomatic crisis when the U.S. invasion of Mexico nearly led to war that summer.

As church officials launched a strident campaign against Carranza, dissension over Gompers's policies in Mexico surfaced on the AFL executive council. Msgr. Francis Kelley complained to Frank Duffy, council member and head of the Carpenters' Union, about numerous alleged acts of persecution in various Mexican states and urged the AFL to repudiate its endorsement of Carranza.[2] Duffy openly challenged Gompers's support for the Constitutionalists and prompted the executive council to authorize Gompers to conduct an investigation into Carranza's clerical policies through Secretary of State Robert Lansing. In the meantime, Duffy tried to pacify Kelley by telling him that the AFL backed Carranza instead of Villa as the lesser of two evils in an effort to ensure "a stable government in that poor, unfortunate, war-ridden and war-devastated country." He assured Kelley that the AFL would withdraw its support for Carranza if allegations of religious persecution were confirmed.[3]

Gompers met with Lansing and Leon Canova of the State Department's Division of Mexican Affairs to discuss the Mexican situation. Canova told him that an official investigation into Carranza's clerical policies was unnecessary. Dismissing Canadian Archbishop Cloutier's allegations that *carrancistas* were terrorizing priests and nuns, Lansing and Canova stressed that most of the charges were gross exaggerations. Although there had been some reprisals against the church, they informed Gompers, these actions stemmed from the church's political activities and opposition to the Constitutionalists' reforms.[4]

Gompers also sought information from Mexico. In a stern letter to Carranza, he warned that the horror stories of religious persecution jeopardized future AFL support. He asked Carranza about the authenticity of these allegations. He also emphasized that the AFL had been instrumental in preventing full-scale U.S. military action against Mexico.[5]

The State Department's assurances did not mollify Monsignor Kelley, who complained to Duffy that since they were based on official *carrancista* interpretations and lies, such assurances were meaningless. Requesting that he be allowed to appear before the executive council to substantiate his charges, he added that the AFL's endorsement of Carranza was a mistake not only because of the Mexican government's anticlerical policies, but also because it was tantamount to "an endorsement of both Socialism and the I.W.W. in Mexico." Kelley singled out the reform movement in Yucatán as socialistic and denounced numerous *carrancista* governors for providing church buildings for radical meetings.[6]

Duffy suggested that Kelley be invited to address the executive council. He also warned Gompers that supporting Carranza was damaging the AFL's image: "Nothing that I know of has stirred up such feelings generally against the American Federation of Labor as the action of the council in endorsing Carranza as head of the Mexican government last year. However, our last action in deciding to have an investigation made on account of complaints lodged has somewhat righted us, but we are expected to do still more at our next meeting."[7]

Carranza's clerical policies were not Gompers's only concern.

He was disturbed by the intensifying force of Mexican nationalism. He lectured Carranza that it would be ill-advised to tolerate "anti-Americanism" in his government and warned that AFL support was not unconditional. Urging him to purge his cabinet of those who harbored anti-American feelings, he pointed out that the AFL's endorsement of the Constitutionalists was formulated in part on the assumption that Carranza would cultivate friendly relations with the United States.[8]

Although Gompers criticized advocates of a more jingoistic policy toward Mexico, his theoretical position can hardly be called "anti-imperialist," notwithstanding his repeated assertions that the AFL played a key role in defending the Revolution against outside interference. He refused to criticize the Pershing expedition or repudiate the right of the United States to intervene in Mexico's internal affairs. On the contrary, he assured Lansing that he was "greatly pleased" with President Wilson's handling of the Mexican situation. He told Canova that he hoped "that Villa would not be captured but rather that he would die," since "his capture would create a new political problem of what should be done with him."[9]

Assisted by John Murray, a socialist member of the Typographical Union, Gompers began to carve out a more active role in Mexican-American affairs. Murray arrived in Washington from California with information intended to discredit corporate interests that demanded a more vigorous interventionist policy toward Mexico. Along with T. C. Parsons, another member of the Typographical Union, he visited Gompers on May 5, 1916, to present documents which purportedly exposed the direct involvement of Harrison Gray Otis of the *Los Angeles Times* in efforts to launch a counterrevolution in Baja California. According to Murray, William Randolph Hearst was also interested in these plans to send expeditions into Mexico to protect American propertied interests. Having already met with John I. Nolan, a California Congressman and member of the Molders' Union, Murray wanted to present this information to the Wilson administration and knew that Gompers could arrange the proper contacts. He accused the *Los Angeles Times* of being pro-German and charged that some of the expeditions from California into Mexico had the backing of the German government. Gompers arranged a meeting for him with Secretary of Labor Wilson later that afternoon.[10]

On May 10, 1916, Gompers met with Nolan to discuss the Mexican situation. Before tackling the pressing issues, Nolan wanted assurances about Murray's political affiliations. He told Gompers that although impressed with Murray's sincerity, he "wished to know whether or not he was of the radical type of Socialist." According to Gompers's secretary, Florence C. Thorne, Gompers "expressed confidence in Mr. Murray and said that he had known him for considerable time and felt that his purpose in this matter, as in former times, was for the best interests of all concerned, and not for the furtherance of radical propaganda."[11]

Mindful of the broader strategic interests of the United States in Latin America, Gompers stressed to Nolan that full-scale intervention in Mexico would undermine American influence in the region and discredit the concept of Pan-Americanism among all Latin Americans. Such a shortsighted move, he pointed out, would also complicate the negotiations under way to secure U.S. rights to build a canal in Nicaragua, which was then under American occupation. He and Nolan decided to hold a conference with Secretary Wilson to discuss Mexico more fully.[12]

Anxious for information on Carranza's policies, Gompers received assurances from Murray that the allegations of religious persecution in Mexico were generally overblown. Murray said that the internationalist spirit of organized labor prevented the rise of anti-Americanism among Mexican workers; only among the elites was there a strain of anti-Americanism. He gave a vote of confidence to Carranza, who, he said, did not really understand labor but had younger advisors with a more solid grasp of the labor movement. After reading Gompers's last letter to Carranza, he warned Gompers not to expect a reply.[13]

Gompers also wanted to know more about Carranza's growing conflict with the labor movement. In response to increased labor unrest in the spring of 1916, Carranza used Federal troops to break up a strike in Tampico and imprisoned labor leaders in April after a general strike had been called against the oil industry. Other labor conflicts, including a general strike in Mexico City in May, deepened the cleavage between Carranza and organized labor.[14]

Although concerned over Carranza's repressive response to these strikes, Murray refused to attack the Mexican government. Emphasizing that Carranza had faithfully honored many of his commitments to labor reform, he told Gompers that all of the facts surrounding the strikes were not yet known. In reference to a recent printers' strike in Veracruz, Murray suggested that the strike occurred without the backing of the workers, and he downplayed the jailing of strikers.[15]

Amid escalating tensions caused by the presence of American troops in Mexico, Gompers moved to strengthen contacts with Mexican workers by writing to the Casa to suggest a joint labor meeting in El Paso. He expressed support for the organizational efforts of Mexican workers and praised the determination and bravery of Mexican miners who had cooperated recently with "Brother Americans" in a strike in Arizona. The letter indicated that Gompers was also mindful of U.S. strategic objectives. Against the backdrop of war in Europe, AFL-style international working-class solidarity could not ignore the fundamental relationship between the United States and Latin America. The proposed labor conference with Casa leaders would forge greater unity among workers in the Western hemisphere and be a vehicle for promoting more stable relationships between the governments of Mexico and the United States. As Gompers explained, "Matters for the mutual welfare of the sister republics could then be discussed and a future cooperative policy outlined."[16]

Gompers wrote to Carranza again on May 23, 1916, and enclosed a copy of his letter to the Casa. He informed him that Murray and Judge Charles A. Douglas, Carranza's legal representative in Washington, had joined him to discuss the Mexican situation that day and that it was Douglas who suggested that he provide Carranza with a copy of his letter to Mexican labor leaders. Copies also went to Ignacio C. Enriques, Plutarco Elías Calles, and Salvador Alvarado (governors of Chihuahua, Sonora, and Yucatán), and to General Álvaro Obregón, Juan Tudo (secretary of the Escuela Moderna in Mexico City), and Dr. Atl (editor of *Acción Mundial*). Gompers also sent copies to the White House and State Department.[17]

Anticipating a storm of executive-council opposition to his proposed conference with Mexican labor leaders, Gompers complained to Murray that Carranza had still not responded to his request for information on conditions in Mexico. He asked Murray to contact friends who might be able to provide useful information. The acquisition of such information, he stressed, would be crucial to the defense of AFL policies in Mexico: "You can readily realize that if the American Federation of Labor is not in position to give information in regard to charges and questions that are made, that it will be assumed that we are unable to make answer."[18]

The expected opposition came quickly. Issued without the executive council's approval, Gompers's call for a joint labor conference ruffled the feathers of Duffy, who complained that he found out about the proposed conference in the *New York Call*, a newspaper which he denounced because of its "socialistic tendencies." Upset by Gompers's high-handed insistence on formulating international policies without consulting the council, Duffy rebuked him: "I admit you have the right . . . to call conferences, to settle disputes, difficulties and misunderstandings but when these conferences are to be held with other nations then I think the members of the Executive Council . . . should be considered."[19]

The rift between Gompers and Duffy involved more than simply a dispute over parliamentary procedures. Gompers's decision to work with the Casa, which had a more left-wing orientation than the AFL, reflected his willingness to accept what he regarded as temporary ideological impurities in the Mexican labor movement on the assumption that radical tendencies would diminish under his tutelage. Although the reform movement in Yucatán, for example, contained socialist tendencies, Gompers tolerated those forces as a temporary outgrowth of the repressive, slavelike conditions that had prevailed before the Revolution. The hope prevailed in AFL headquarters that "a labor movement of natural growth will develop and finally break through the present temporary system."[20]

Duffy did not display such tolerance. He complained to Gompers that the Casa del Obrero Mundial was "nothing more or less than the Industrial Workers of the World," and he said that he could not "conceive how the American Labor Movement can hitch up with such parties."[21] In Duffy's view, exposing the AFL to domestic criticism over its support for such movements was risky. Contacts with Mexican workers, he reminded Gompers, had yielded no practical benefits for his union: "The United Brotherhood of Carpenters and Joiners of America claims Mexico under its jurisdiction, but so far we have not a single Local Union in that Country and you know we spend more money for organizing purposes than any other organization affiliated with the American Federation of Labor."[22]

The proposal for a joint labor conference enjoyed a much friendlier reception among the United Mine Workers. Frank J. Hayes, the international vice president, and Ed Doyle, secretary of District #15 in Denver, Colorado, sent letters of support to Murray. Doyle had told Murray earlier that he intended to learn Spanish in order to organize Mexican miners in Colorado, New Mexico, and other parts of the United States. He also underscored the need to organize miners regardless of national boundaries. Confident that Gompers could expect the UMW's wholehearted endorsement of the conference, Murray stressed the pragmatic benefits to be gained by carving out a more internationalist policy: "And the Miners without doubt will see that although this is an international and fraternal approachment, it is of great local value because it will aid them in organizing the Mexican miners in the United States."[23]

Gompers also received encouraging news from Mexico regarding the proposed conference. Having written to Col. Edmundo Martínez for information on Carranza's alleged anticlericalism and anti-Americanism, he received a wire from Martínez, who was then in Mexico City. Martínez had been courting Gompers since August 1915 in an effort to have a favorable interpretation of the Constitutionalist movement presented to President Wilson. In a thinly disguised gesture designed to flatter Gompers, Martínez informed him that he would be returning soon to the United States to award him a medal from the "Mexican Federation of Labor" to commemorate the upcoming union of Mexican and American workers.[24]

The Casa wired its acceptance of the proposed joint labor conference but asked to change the site to Eagle Pass. The date of June 25 set by Casa leaders was not convenient for Gompers, who sent a telegram expressing hope that a mutually convenient time could be arranged. "In the meantime," he said, "you may rest assured I shall do everything to prevail upon those in authority to avoid conflict. The men of Mexico must also exert their influence for the same purpose."[25]

Amid press reports that the United States was considering the appointment of an international commission to review the growing crisis with Mexico, Murray urged Gompers to lobby for labor representation on the commission. Gompers used Secretary Wilson to relay his request for representation to the White House. He made it clear that he did not want to serve on the commission; he simply asked to be consulted regarding the appointment.[26]

A rapid deterioration in U.S.-Mexican relations in June 1916 brought the nations to the brink of war. Carranza's insistence on the withdrawal of American troops piqued the U.S. government, which pressured Mexico for guarantees of protection for American investments. Concern over Mexico's mining, banking, and oil decrees prompted Secretary Lansing to warn Carranza that failure to guarantee the safety of American capital would produce "the gravest consequences."[27] President Wilson approved of the hard-line approach. "They might as well know at once," he told Lansing, "all that they will be up against if they continue their present attitude."[28]

Frustration with Carranza also mounted in AFL headquarters, where there was some consideration given to assuring the White House that the AFL's policies aimed to promote cooperation with the Mexican labor movement and did not favor Carranza or any other political faction.[29] Even Douglas, Carranza's legal advisor, was losing patience with his client. On June 16 he summoned Murray for a conference and asked how much influence he believed the Mexican labor movement had. Increasingly pessimistic about resolving the crisis through formal diplomatic channels, Douglas now concluded that only the AFL and the Mexican labor movement could save Carranza and prevent war. He viewed Gompers as "the one person in the two countries to whom the people could look for any hope in the situation."[30] The conversion of Douglas to prolabor views did not go unnoticed by Gompers's secretary. "Either in this conference or in another conference," she noted, "Judge Douglas had expressed the opinion that the labor movement was about the only thing that had developed out of the Mexican Revolution and situation. Such an expression on the part of Judge Douglas is extremely significant, for he is a conservative lawyer of a southern family, and has until experiences with the Carranza government had very little understanding of the labor movement."[31]

As American socialists, anarchists, pacifists, and other peace groups mobilized to prevent war,[32] Gompers encouraged Mexican labor leaders to look to the AFL as the chief vehicle for preserving peace. Shunning peace rallies, petition drives, and demonstrations, he used his official contacts with the Wilson administration and his friendship with Judge Douglas to try to resolve the crisis. Casa leaders viewed closer ties with the AFL as a means to pressure the United States for the removal of troops from Mexico, but Gompers made clear that he favored a more circumscribed brand of international working-class "solidarity." When Carlos Loveira and Baltazar Pages, labor representatives from Yucatán, arrived in New York to rally workers against war, Murray hurried there to "direct them along right lines." Murray persuaded them to revise their appeal, which appeared in the *New York Call* on June 13, 1916, to tone down suggestions of radicalism. Loveira and Pages deleted references to the Haymarket martyrs and attacks on the Catholic church and promised to edit carefully all future press statements.[33]

On June 19, Douglas held a conference with the State Department's Frank Polk, who was receptive to a proposal to withdraw American troops to a neutral zone along the border which the U.S. Army could then patrol to prevent raids against the United States. Polk believed that Gompers was the only person who could effectively present the proposal to President Wilson and suggested that William Jennings Bryan, Wilson's former secretary of state, might also be helpful in the matter. Gompers opposed the suggestion to include Bryan in the discussions. He told Douglas and Murray on June 21 that Bryan's resignation as secretary of state was a blessing, since it allowed the president to adopt a more aggressive policy with regard to the European problem. Already an advocate of military preparedness, Gompers feared that involving Bryan in Mexican affairs might encourage a more pacifist direction for the United States in world affairs. When Douglas urged the formation of a commission to arbitrate the dispute with Mexico while Pershing's troops withdrew to a neutral zone, Gompers expressed concern that this move might be construed by Mexico as a sign of weakness and thus encourage an attack on American forces. Nevertheless, he agreed to present the proposal and set up a meeting for the following day with President Wilson.[34]

Meanwhile, news from Mexico intensified the atmosphere of crisis. American forces engaged Carranza's troops at El Carrizal on June 21, 1916; the skirmish resulted in casualties on both sides and the taking of American prisoners.[35] The clash also imparted an added sense of urgency to the AFL's efforts to ease tensions. If successful, these efforts might encourage Mexican labor leaders to accept Gompers's tutelage, overshadow the antiwar activities of the American left, dramatize the AFL's internationalist commitments, and impress upon the Mexicans that President Wilson's policies aimed to benefit their revolution. The last objective proved the most difficult to achieve.

Even before the clash at Carrizal, Gompers had learned that his overtures toward the Mexican labor movement were paying domestic dividends. James Lord, the head of the AFL's Mining Department, who had overseen the efforts of American labor organizers to organize Mexican miners, reported that Gompers's efforts were gaining converts among socialists and others who had previously criticized his conservative philosophy and practices. Chester M. Wright, the controlling director of the *New York Call*'s editorial policy, also supported the AFL's actions in Mexico. He told Murray that he was relieved that it was Gompers who was directing efforts to unite American and Mexican workers. "A careful reading of the editorials and an understanding of the way the *Call* news has been edited," noted Florence Thorne, "will show that Mr. Wright is using his influence for constructive efforts for practical reform."[36]

Gompers refused to support the public activities of peace groups and tried to minimize the role of socialists in the campaign to prevent war with Mexico. Arguing that he opposed manipulation of the crisis by an organization that had ulterior motives, he refused to endorse a peace rally in El Paso sponsored by the American Union Against Militarism (AUAM).[37] He and Murray impressed upon Mexican labor leaders that the AFL was the driving force of the movement to ensure peace. When Loveira and Pages, the Yucatecan labor representatives, apparently arrived late at a meeting, Murray reminded them that Gompers waited patiently for them, "that it was significant of the fact that he would not do anything until the representatives of labor were present; that he considered the labor movement the important agent in the situation, and that labor representatives should be given the first information."[38]

Upon learning that Loveira was on his way to New York to attend a rally on June 24, 1916, called by socialists and peace groups, Gompers pointedly reminded him to "talk organized labor, not Socialism." Hoping to ward off attacks by the radical community on the AFL's collaboration with members of the Wilson administration, he warned Loveira not to mention that he and Murray were working with U.S. officials.[39]

Secretary of Labor Wilson joined Gompers for a meeting in the White House on June 22 to push for arbitration. Gompers assured the president that Douglas's first loyalties were to the United States, and he left a copy of the proposal to create a neutral zone and an arbitration commission. Although Douglas agreed that the Carrizal incident now made it senseless to consider an immediate withdrawal of American troops to the border, Gompers left a copy of the proposal in case future developments might cause the president to consider the plan. When Douglas asked Gompers after the meeting if he believed that the White House would be amenable to arbitration, Gompers said yes but asked Douglas not to use his name in a telegram to Carranza. Douglas agreed. Apparently reluctant to be identified as officially representative of the Wilson administration's position, Gompers added that Douglas could use his discretion about mentioning his name in a private letter.[40]

On June 23, Gompers also conferred with Roberto V. Pesqueira, one of Carranza's financial experts, and Victor Rendón, a representative of Yucatán's Sisal Commission. He furnished them with copies of letters between Secretary Wilson and the president concerning the AFL's efforts to ease tensions, and reported on his conference in the White House the day before. Carefully avoiding any reference to the strategic and economic designs of the United States in the area, Gompers suggested that the Monroe Doctrine should no longer be the linchpin of U.S. policy in Latin America. This statement, which aimed to assure the Mexican representatives of his anti-imperialist views, clearly contradicted Gompers's previous position on the Monroe Doctrine, a position he had invoked at the AFL Convention in November 1913 to block an anti-interventionist resolution. In an effort to soften Mexican opposition to U.S. policies, he expressed hope to Pesqueira and Rendón that a Pan-American labor movement and friendlier relations among all Latin American nations would result from the AFL's efforts to resolve the Mexican-American crisis peacefully.[41]

Colonel Martínez, who had just returned from Mexico, went to AFL headquarters on June 24 to present Gompers with a medal from the "Mexican Federation of Labor." He did not see Gompers, who was out of town, but went with Murray to meet Secretary Wilson and other top officials in the Labor Department. Secretary Wilson gave Murray and Martínez the impression that the Administration was "standing like a stone wall against a fratricidal war" and assured them that the president sympathized with the basic aims of the Mexican Revolution. The Labor Secretary's assurances impressed Murray, who noted, "I cannot lay too much stress on the fact that he desired with extreme emphasis to make us understand the kindly and peaceful attitude of the Administration toward the Mexican people."[42]

The efforts by Martínez to court Gompers revealed the deteriorating relationship between Carranza and the Casa and the divisions within the Mexican labor movement. To ingratiate himself further with Gompers, Martínez told him that the workers he represented favored sending a diploma with the medal for the AFL president, while the Casa objected to lavishing such awards on him until the AFL did more to prove its commitment to peace. Stressing his own conservative labor philosophy, Martínez characterized members of the Casa as "anarchists, impossibilists, and the I.W.W. of Mexico," and he attacked Luis Morones and Dr. Atl—especially the latter—who were also coming to see Gompers. He warned Gompers that Casa leaders were still suspicious of the AFL.[43]

When pressed by Gompers on Carranza's failure to answer his letter, Martínez replied that the letter never arrived. He assured Gompers that Carranza fully appreciated the AFL's efforts on behalf of peace. According to Martínez, Carranza was unaware of anti-Americanism in his Cabinet and would fire anyone suspected of harboring such sentiments. Martínez denied that the Carranza government was violating freedom of religion, and he underscored his personal efforts to encourage Mexican workers to link up with the AFL.[44]

By the time Casa representatives and other members of a Mexican peace delegation arrived in the United States to meet with Gompers and the AUAM, the possibility of war seemed even more likely. In an ultimatum on June 25, the U.S. government demanded release of its prisoners. Dr. Atl and Morones sent Gompers a telegram requesting a meeting with the executive council "for the realization of our pacifist program."[45] After meeting on the evening of June 26 with Loveira, Pages, and Murray, Gompers drafted a reply instructing the Mexican subdelegation to head for Washington as soon as possible.[46]

AFL leaders did not take kindly to the suggestion of the Mexican delegates that they had come to hammer out a "peace program." Murray said that he would make it clear to the Mexican representatives that the upcoming meeting would be a "labor," not a peace conference. Urging Gompers to explain this carefully to the executive council, he noted that he had already straightened out Pages and Loveira on this point.[47]

To publicize the conference, Gompers stressed the need for a Pan-American federation of labor to counteract the growing influx of American capital into Latin America. "Such a movement," he explained to an AFL organizer in Tacoma, Washington, "is of increasing importance with the policy on the part of the United States government for closer cooperation between all of the two Americas in a Pan-American Union. This closer political alliance is based upon economic interests and foreshadows closer commercial relations."[48]

Despite Carranza's indication that he would be open to every effort to resolve the diplomatic crisis, the U.S. government hardened its position as President Wilson considered delivering a message to Congress that would have placed the blame squarely on Mexico and asked for broader powers to deal with Carranza. Wilson's increasingly aggressive policy received a setback, however, when the AUAM, relying on eyewitness evidence that American troops had initiated the hostilities at Carrizal, put the public on guard against any effort by Wilson to deceive Congress about the details of the skirmish. The AUAM took out full-page advertisements in the *New York Times* and other leading newspapers to inform readers that Captain Lewis C. Morey, a survivor of the clash at Carrizal, affirmed that American troops caused the exchange of fire.[49]

The publication of this information contributed to the search for a peaceful resolution of the crisis as the Wilson administration retreated from its hard-line position. Secretary of State Lansing suggested the creation of a joint commission to arbitrate the dispute. "If the Carrizal incident was a clear case of Mexican aggression," he conceded to the president, "I doubt if I would be favorable to this policy, but it appears to me that Captain Boyd was possibly to blame."[50]

Murray went to AFL headquarters on June 28 with a message from Douglas suggesting that Gompers send a telegram to Carranza requesting the release of American prisoners. The message from Douglas contained a note of urgency, and Gompers immediately dictated the following telegram to Carranza: "In the name of common justice and humanity, in the interest of a better understanding between the peoples and governments of the United States and Mexico, for the purpose of giving the opportunity to maintain peace and avoid the horrors of war, upon the grounds of highest patriotism and love, I appeal to you to release the American soldiers held by your officers in Chihuahua."[51]

Murray took copies to Douglas and the Mexican embassy, and Gompers gave a copy to Secretary Wilson. When news reports later that evening announced that Carranza had ordered the release of the American prisoners, Gompers summoned Murray and released to the newspapers the telegram that he sent to Carranza. Murray sent a telegram to the *New York Call,* and rejoicing began in AFL headquarters over labor's role in breaking the diplomatic deadlock. Gompers received a telegram from Carranza the following evening: "In replying to your message dated yesterday I would state that the government in my charge has ordered the liberty of the American soldiers whom the Mexican forces took as prisoners in Carrizal."[52]

The release of the American soldiers laid the basis for a peaceful resolution of the crisis, and Gompers quickly wrote an article that touted his consistent anti-interventionist position on the Mexican Revolution.[53] Although Gompers encouraged others to believe that he played a key role in preventing war, historians disagree over whether or not he influenced Carranza's decision to free the prisoners. Noting that Carranza decided to release the soldiers before the arrival of Gompers's telegram, Harvey Levenstein dismisses the notion that Carranza acted at Gompers's behest.[54] William G. Whittaker suggests, however, that enough time elapsed between the dispatch of Gompers's telegram and the announcement that the

American prisoners would be freed to make a plausible argument that the efforts of Gompers, Murray, and Douglas were primarily responsible for Carranza's release of the captives. Impressed by Gompers's alleged philosophical opposition to war, Whittaker underscores the AFL president's longstanding anti-imperialist orientation and praises him for almost singlehandedly preventing war with Mexico in the summer of 1916.[55] Philip S. Foner provides a more balanced assessment of the AFL's role in the campaign to prevent war with Mexico. On the one hand, he criticizes Levenstein for minimizing Gompers's contributions to the peace efforts. On the other, he stresses that to give all the credit to Gompers, as Whittaker does, "is to mix fact with fantasy."[56]

Whittaker's analysis suffers from an idealistic conception of Gompers as an anti-imperialist who was completely divorced from the strategic objectives of the Wilson administration. To cast Gompers in such terms is as distorting as to describe Woodrow Wilson as an anti-interventionist. At no point did Gompers challenge the interventionist prerogatives of Wilsonian policy in Mexico. He supported the Pershing Expedition and the American occupation of Veracruz in 1914. It is true that he and Murray worked to avoid an all-out war in June 1916, but these efforts did not reflect a firm anti-imperialist commitment on the part of Gompers. Strategic concerns were uppermost on his mind. Gompers worried about getting the United States bogged down militarily in Mexico at a time when he supported military preparedness for possible U.S. entry into the European war. In crediting AFL leaders for the maintenance of peace, Whittaker ignores other sources of public opposition to war and the economic and strategic concerns of the Wilson administration as factors in the decision to avoid war with Mexico.[57]

The emergence of the AFL as a force in Mexican-American diplomacy did have significant implications, however. By supporting Wilsonian policy in Mexico and keeping the White House fully apprised of his efforts to shape the Mexican labor movement, Gompers demonstrated that his brand of labor internationalism could be useful as an instrument of American foreign policy. His involvement in discussions to break the diplomatic impasse over the Carrizal incident strengthened his contacts with the State Department and the White House and highlighted the role of the Labor Department as a participant in the construction of foreign policy.

AFL headquarters became an important informal conduit for the exchange of information between the governments of Mexico and the United States.

While the U.S. government found it expedient at times to take advantage of Gompers's contacts with Mexican labor leaders and representatives of the Mexican government, Carranza likewise made at least a half-hearted effort through his representatives to enlist the AFL as a lobbying influence against the further escalation of hostilities. Martínez flattered Gompers whenever possible in order to promote a more favorable view of Carranza. Hoping to sway American public opinion, Carranza also sent Dr. Atl, Luis Manuel Rojas, and Modesto C. Rolland to El Paso to participate in labor and peace protests against U.S. policy.[58]

Since Carranza first decided to release the American prisoners on June 24,[59] it is unlikely that Gompers's telegram prompted him to free them. Given Carranza's fierce nationalism, it is possible that working through Douglas, he allowed the AFL to take some credit for the prisoner release rather than appear to have yielded to the formal U.S. ultimatum. Douglas, who kept in close touch with the Mexican embassy in daily attempts to resolve the crisis, perhaps had some knowledge of the impending prisoner release when he suggested that Gompers send the telegram to Carranza.

We must examine more critically Whittaker's portrayal of the AFL as a vigorous anti-imperialist force and his description of labor's role in defusing the Carrizal crisis as "an intriguing example of international working class solidarity."[60] That Gompers worked hard to promote a peaceful resolution to the diplomatic crisis is undeniable. His overtures toward the Mexican labor movement and his diplomatic efforts represented the expression of an internationalist tendency that was missing from Duffy's chauvinistic, parochial view of the Mexican Revolution. Whittaker is correct, therefore, when he calls attention to the progressive, humanitarian commitment which informed the AFL's efforts to prevent war with Mexico in June 1916.

Gompers made clear from the beginning, however, who would chart labor's course in diplomatic waters. Labor's efforts to resolve the crisis would have to be conducted on his terms. Since it was their country that had been invaded by foreign troops, Mexican labor leaders urgently desired a forthright expression of proletarian internationalism. In an executive council meeting on July 1, 1916, attended by Luis Morones and Salvador Gonzalo García, Gompers was evasive and refused to deny the right of the United States to interfere in Mexico's internal politics. Instead, he attacked Villa for attempting a "counterrevolution." "I am not going to discuss the right of the United States to send soldiers into Mexico to capture the chief marauder, Villa," he said. "I suppose American history will say Mexico is responsible for the situation, and Mexican history will say the United States was responsible." [61]

Mexican labor representatives thus hurried to conferences with Gompers with a set of expectations that did not always mesh with the AFL's. They did not seek out Gompers for ideological inspiration or tutelage. It was clearly U.S. military intervention which prompted them to come to AFL headquarters for help in removing American troops from Mexico. Although some Mexican labor leaders, especially Morones, were already becoming more pragmatic and less attached to radical theories, others preferred friendship with the IWW but recognized that Wobblie leaders were unwelcome at the White House and were thus not as influential as Gompers in shaping U.S. policy. As Ricardo Treviño, a Mexican labor leader, later pointed out, "in defense of our own interests and in defense of our own sovereignty and of our own independence we are forced, it is our duty, to recognize as the organized labor movement of the United States the American Federation of Labor, without consideration of its characteristics." [62]

As Whittaker points out, the working relationship which Gompers established with socialists John Murray and Chester Wright was an important development that would assume even greater significance after the United States entered the First World War. [63] Wright used his editorial position at the *New York Call* to praise the anti-interventionist and internationalist commitments of Gompers. This support of Gompers's practical efforts to ease tensions between Mexico and the United States encouraged Wright—soon to become one of Gompers's most trusted aides—to endorse the AFL's broader Pan-American activities. Wright praised Gompers's determination to unite American and Mexican labor in the interests of peace during the Carrizal crisis. "There was something fine and strong," he remarked to Gompers, "about the little group of workingmen down there in Washington in fraternity and amity—men of two nations—talking for the workers, while all about were the vultures screaming for blood in a voice that seemed for the moment likely to drown out all sanity."[64]

Just as President Wilson's peaceful rhetoric weakened the opposition of many radicals and progressives to his intervention in Mexico,[65] so Gompers disarmed some of his socialist critics by condemning the jingoistic activities of corporate interests in Mexico and cultivating Pan-American labor solidarity. An increasingly pragmatic Murray overcame Gompers's earlier suspicions and served as one of his chief assistants on Mexico until Murray's suicide in 1919.[66] Gompers's liberal defense of the Mexican Revolution enhanced his popularity among American mineworkers and wedded key socialists to his policies at a critical time in international affairs.

The favorable publicity that Gompers received as a result of his diplomatic efforts in June 1916 also weakened criticism from the right wing of the AFL. Duffy, who had been the most persistent, outspoken critic of Gompers's policies in Mexico, experienced a change of heart. He praised Gompers in a letter and noted in a postscript, "Sam, you've changed me on this question."[67]

Despite its decision to seek a peaceful resolution to the Carrizal crisis, the Wilson administration did not immediately withdraw Pershing's troops or abandon efforts to shape Mexico's internal political and economic affairs. In the immediate aftermath of the Carrizal crisis, U.S. officials decided to explore how much influence Gompers had with Carranza. Charles Ferguson, a special agent in the Bureau of Foreign and Domestic Commerce who worked to expand American trade in Latin America,[68] tried to involve Gompers in a proposal to convert northern Mexico into some type of "neutral zone" to be controlled by representatives of the United States, Mexico, and other Latin American countries. Ferguson suggested the possible involvement of England, Germany, and France in the creation of a zone for "the carrying out of an ideal for democracy in Mexico, reorganizing society upon a basis of real values, giving the people control over the land and over financial agencies."[69] Given the war in Europe, however, it is unlikely that he entertained serious thoughts of bringing European powers into the arrangement.

Ferguson believed that Gompers was the person most likely to get Carranza to agree to the proposal, but Gompers doubted that Carranza could agree to the plan and still retain political power. Although Gompers stressed that such an arrangement must have the consent of the Mexican people, he "expressed his approval of the fundamental principles which Mr. Ferguson had advanced, and said that he would be willing to cooperate . . . to get the plan before General Carranza."[70] There is no indication, however, that Gompers ever tried to lay the plan before Carranza.

Meanwhile, Murray presented to the executive council a proposal from the Mexican labor delegates to establish a different kind of supervision over a neutral zone. This proposal, which may have had some input from Murray, called for the appointment of a commission consisting of the governors of four Mexican and four American states along the border, and three labor representatives from each country to supervise the neutral zone. Murray also showed the proposal to Secretary of State Lansing and Secretary of War Newton D. Baker. The Mexican delegates were clearly trying to enhance labor's role on both sides of the border, but this study has found no evidence to suggest that any serious effort was made to implement the plan.[71]

The executive council and the Mexican labor leaders did call for the appointment of a commission to resolve the conflict.[72] When the United States and Mexico agreed to form a joint commission to adjust their differences, Gompers pressed for labor representation and suggested that Secretary Wilson be included as organized labor's representative. Apparently wary of Gompers's efforts to involve labor officially in government affairs that did not pertain directly to labor, President Wilson replied that the commission would be too small to be fully representative and thus unable to accommodate labor representation. Undaunted, Gompers urged the president to enlarge the commission, but he was told that the chief obstacle was Carranza's refusal to empower the commission to deal with broader issues. At issue were Carranza's economic reforms, and on July 27 Gompers sent a telegram urging him to grant the commission full authority to discuss the wide range of issues that divided the two nations.[73]

Although unable to secure labor representation on the commission, Gompers continued to press for a seat on other government commissions. As Harvey Levenstein observes, "His special position with regard to Mexican labor and the importance of organized labor in Mexico were now being used by Gompers as a means of gaining entry for the AFL into the charmed circle of government in Washington."[74]

The agreement signed by the executive council and the Mexican labor leaders called for keeping two Mexican labor representatives in Washington until the threat of war subsided, but Murray reported on July 6, 1916, that the Mexicans believed that because the immediate crisis had seemingly passed this was no longer necessary. Gompers insisted that Murray get this in writing and prepared a letter for Loveira and Pages to take with them on their mission to Latin America. Sent by Salvador Alvarado, the socialist governor of Yucatán, to the United States and other parts of Latin America to rally support for the Mexican Revolution, the Yucatecan labor representatives now also became publicists for Gompers's proposed PAFL.[75]

They caused a stir in AFL headquarters, however, when they asked if the proposed federation would welcome the IWW and other unions not affiliated with the AFL. Gompers retorted that he would not yield AFL leadership of the trade union movement to anyone, and he emphatically rejected an IWW presence in the Pan-American labor movement. He stressed that the PAFL must be based on the AFL's philosophical guidelines and structure. Loveira tried to calm him with an apology, saying that he was simply gathering information. Murray later blamed the question from Loveira on Dr. Atl, who had just attended a conference with American intellectuals and radicals.[76]

Gompers wrote Governor Alvarado to publicize his call for a PAFL to counteract the organized thrust of corporate capital into Latin America. He emphasized that the lack of organization among Mexican workers also hurt the American labor movement. The battle against the big capitalists would have to be fought on AFL terms, however; Gompers urged acceptance of pure and simple unionism as the ideological basis of Latin American labor organizations. He sent copies of the AFL's constitution, bylaws, and convention proceedings to Latin American workers and representatives. Latin American unions, he emphasized, should exclude intellectuals and avoid manipulation by politicians: "A fraternalistic or a socialistic organization will not have the same force and value as a bona fide labor movement, developing out of the needs of the workers and in accord with their concepts of their own best interests."[77]

Mexico was the key variable in Gompers's plan to establish a Pan-American labor organization, but divisions within the Mexican labor movement and Carranza's repressive labor policies frustrated his efforts. Carrying letters of introduction from Edmundo Martínez, three men claiming to represent the Confederacíon de Sindicatos Obreros met with Gompers in Washington. They tried to discredit the Casa, underscore Carranza's willingness to accept the findings of the joint commission, and impress Gompers with the strength of their more conservative and, in reality, relatively obscure labor organization in Veracruz.[78]

Their organization, they boasted to Gompers, was the only national labor federation in Mexico and claimed a total membership of about 500,000 from affiliated unions. They attacked the radicalism of the Casa and stressed that the anarchist organization was confined mainly to the Federal District. Although Gompers received copies of Dr. Atl's *Acción Mundial,* which claimed that at least one of the three delegates was not a genuine labor representative, he complied with their request for a letter and other AFL publicity materials to take with them back to Veracruz. He was skeptical of the membership figures which they offered but stressed to the executive council the surprising strength of their organization. Promising to provide a list of "bona fide" Mexican unions at the next council meeting, he told Duffy that the "Mexican Federation of Labor" had at least 250,000 members.[79]

On July 24, 1916, shortly after Gompers met with the three Mexican delegates, a man claiming to be a labor representative from Sonora also arrived at AFL headquarters. Coming by way of Chicago, where he impressed local AFL leaders with his efforts to persuade Mexicans not to act as strikebreakers, A. A. Ravola favorably described reforms being implemented by Sonoran politicians. Emmet Flood, an AFL organizer in Chicago, set up a meeting for him with Gompers, who discovered upon questioning Ravola that he was not a true labor representative but a newspaperman with ties to Adolfo de la Huerta, the governor of Sonora.[80]

Ravola compared Mexican workers to children and underscored the efforts of Sonoran leaders to insulate them from radical doctrines. He stressed the prolabor sympathies of Governor de la Huerta. Later that fall, Ravola notified Gompers that the Sonoran legislature had enacted an impressive array of labor reforms, including the eight-hour day, a minimum daily wage, elimination of labor for children under fourteen years of age, and the creation of a special labor chamber to study labor-capital problems and recommend legislation.[81]

Neither Gompers nor Murray believed that Ravola was a genuine spokesman for organized labor, and Gompers told him to bring authentic credentials if he hoped for another conference in the future.[82] Gompers may have been troubled by Ravola's brash characterization of Mexican workers as children in need of paternalistic guidance from "prolabor" politicians, but he continued to make optimistic assessments of the Mexican labor movement. In a letter thanking Flood for sending Ravola to AFL headquarters, he did not mention the Sonoran's misrepresentation of himself. Instead, he noted the ongoing struggle against socialism in Sonora and interpreted Ravola's connections with Sonoran officials "as additional proof of the strength of the labor movement."[83]

Gompers notified the Arizona State Federation of Labor about his conference with Ravola. He suggested a possible meeting between Sonoran governor de la Huerta and George Hunt, the governor of Arizona who had praised the AFL's role in preventing war between the United States and Mexico. Pointing to the increased flow of American capital into Mexico, Gompers stressed the need to organize Mexican workers in order to protect the American labor movement.[84]

Although Gompers's contacts with Mexican labor leaders diminished during the fall of 1916 as a result of Carranza's attack on the Casa, future developments would confirm the importance of the communications between the AFL and Sonoran Constitutionalist reformers. The latter's support for labor reforms, opposition to socialism, and desire to keep U.S. troops out of Mexico made them receptive to the AFL. Despite his advice to Mexican workers that they avoid manipulative politicians, Gompers would later find the Sonorans' approach to labor relations quite appealing.

In August 1916 the shaky alliance between Carranza and the Casa finally collapsed. Their earnings ravaged by inflation, workers affiliated with the Casa and other unions in Mexico City organized a general strike that shut down public services in the capital between July 31 and August 2. Carranza unleashed troops against the ninety thousand strikers, and he imprisoned leaders of the committee that organized the strike. He also ordered the death penalty for anyone involved in fomenting or carrying out a strike in the public-service sector and responded to the workers' request for payment of wages in specie by denouncing them as unpatriotic counterrevolutionaries. Acting upon the advice of Álvaro Obregón, one of Carranza's chief military men with ties to organized labor, the Casa shut down to escape further repression. Carranza eventually released the jailed labor leaders, but one of them, Ernesto Velasco, remained in prison until early 1918. The crackdown meant the end of the Casa. Those unions that survived were generally much less militant and headed by more pragmatic leaders such as Morones and others who displayed a greater willingness to collaborate with the government.[85]

Although troubled by the repressive turn of events in Mexico, Gompers was reluctant to denounce Carranza's no-strike directive publicly. This reluctance stemmed from the fact that the Mexican-American Joint Commission, which held its first session on September 6 in New London, Connecticut, was engaged in sensitive discussions to resolve diplomatic differences and remove American troops from Mexican soil. Led by Secretary of the Interior Franklin K. Lane the American commissioners had objectives which went beyond obtaining tighter security arrangements along the border. The United States sought to use the negotiations to squeeze out concessions regarding Mexico's domestic economic policies.

Alarmed by the Revolution's nationalist economic reforms, the Wilson administration wanted guarantees for American capital in Mexico and linked the withdrawal of Pershing's troops to the settlement of these broader issues. A new wave of nationalist mining regulations in September 1916 and Carranza's refusal to discuss other issues until American forces withdrew irked American policymakers. Chairman Lane complained to his brother that "Carranza is obsessed with the idea that he is a real god and not a tin god, that he holds thunderbolts in his hands instead of confetti, and he won't let us help him."[86]

By early October 1916 the frustrated efforts of the American peace commissioners to put Mexico's internal economic and political matters on the table for discussion prompted Lane to involve Gompers informally. Hoping to exploit the AFL's growing influence in Mexico to encourage the Mexican commissioners to become more pliable, he sent Gompers a letter suggesting that he might be helpful in breaking the deadlocked negotiations. Gompers responded quickly. He went to Atlantic City, the new site of the conferences, and had a two-hour conversation with Lane, who complained that the Mexican commissioners—Secretary of the Treasury Luis Cabrera, Ignacio Bonillas, and Alberto Pani—stubbornly refused to discuss broader issues until Pershing's forces were evacuated.[87]

Gompers met with Cabrera, Pani, and Bonillas on October 10, 1916, in an effort to change Mexico's negotiating position, and he huddled with the American commissioners the next day. He told Lane that while he was waiting at the hotel desk to see the Mexican commissioners, a man arrived and asked the clerk to announce his presence to Pani over the telephone. The man then got on the phone and told one of the commissioners that he was a representative of the German government and desired to speak with them. On receiving this information from Gompers, Lane requested the dispatch of Secret Service agents to investigate.[88]

Gompers took advantage of the meeting with the Mexican commissioners to express his concern over Carranza's no-strike decree. The Mexican commissioners assured him that Carranza supported labor unions, but they emphasized that the strike which prompted the decree was a purely political act designed to topple the Mexican government. They said that only one man involved in the strike had been sentenced to death and that the decree would probably be modified or rescinded. Payment of wages in specie, they stressed, was an impossible demand on the government. They also added that Carranza had tried to resolve the conflict through negotiations but could find no labor representatives or organizations who would meet with him.[89]

Gompers hinted that the AFL might withdraw its support for Carranza if he did not reverse his repressive policy toward labor. He stressed to the Mexican commissioners that the AFL was trying to steer the Mexican labor movement away from radicalism. "The effort which we were making here," he insisted, "was to endeavor to instill the thought into the minds of Mexican workmen to organize upon a constructive, consistent, continuous, voluntary basis. . . . it can not be expected that the Mexican workmen would escape errors in course of action when their efforts have been frowned down upon so long, suppressed for centuries, denied the opportunity for self-expression and independence."[90]

Despite the obviously biased source of the information, the International Relations Committee offered the same apologetic version of Carranza's handling of the strike to the AFL convention in November 1916.[91] Although careful not to attack Carranza publicly, Gompers revealed privately that Mexican revolutionary nationalism had worn his patience quite thin. In a conference with Murray and Wright on November 12, he reviewed his policies in Mexico and expressed disillusionment over the direction of the Revolution. Perturbed by Carranza's refusal to bend at the bargaining table, he lamented Mexico's lack of appreciation for the paternalistic efforts of President Wilson and the AFL to determine what was in the best interests of the Revolution. "We were aiming to help the President of the United States," Gompers complained to Murray and Wright, "in carrying out his policy *in the interests of the Mexican people* so as to jointly work out the problems for peace and reconstruction (emphasis mine)."[92]

The nationalistic ferment spawned by the Revolution proved increasingly hard to contain and caused Gompers to have second thoughts about the movement unleashed by Madero. Reflecting on his simultaneous pursuit of reform and stability in Mexico, he candidly expressed to Murray and Wright his disenchantment with the direction the Mexican Revolution had taken. "You could not change Mexico from a state of absolutism on the one hand and sovereignty on the other to a great democracy," he said. "The people were not ready for it."[93]

It is clear that by the end of 1916 Gompers hoped to reverse both Carranza's harsh no-strike policy and his refusal to link the withdrawal of Pershing's troops to Mexico's acceptance of U.S.-dictated changes in domestic economic and political matters. Gompers arranged for Murray and Wright to meet with Judge Douglas, and Murray also went to Atlantic City to confer with Cabrera, one of the Mexican members of the joint commission. Although Gompers was still bothered by Carranza's repressive labor policy, foreign-policy objectives were uppermost on his mind. The Mexican labor movement would have to wait! Gompers stressed to Murray and Wright that Carranza's position at the bargaining table must be changed immediately. Mexican workers could simply wait, even if it took a long time to reverse Carranza's antilabor position. "Having suffered injustice for so many centuries," he added callously, "a year, a few weeks longer will be immaterial."[94]

Gompers recognized that the inability of the United States to achieve a favorable resolution of the Mexican crisis through negotiations and a limited military presence in Mexico threatened to undermine U.S. influence in Latin America and had serious implications for the world conflict. He defended President Wilson's refusal to withdraw Pershing's forces, and he expressed fears that those who favored old-style colonialism with regard to Mexico would prevail if Wilsonian policies failed. In his view, other Latin American nations would probably support Mexico in the event of a war with the United States. He also feared that Japan might enter on the side of the Latin Americans. Besides resulting in heavy losses of lives and property, a war between the United States and Mexico might provoke widespread opposition among German Americans. "So that quite apart from purely Democratic humanitarian . . . and our justice loving viewpoint," Gompers explained to Murray and Wright, "the fact remains of what would ensue from such a conflict."[95]

Despite Murray's assurances to Cabrera that since American labor leaders had no financial stake in Mexico, they could approach the Mexicans with "clean hands,"[96] Gompers's candid expression of his top priorities in November 1916 revealed a primary commitment to President Wilson's Mexican policy. It also underscored concern over the strategic problems that an unharnessed nationalist revolution might present if the United States declared war on Germany. Gompers did not urge the withdrawal of Pershing's troops; instead, he tried to persuade the Mexican commissioners to agree to proposals that would have granted the United States a voice in Mexico's internal political and economic affairs, including the right to re-enter militarily, if necessary, to provide protection for American capital.

Now a member of the advisory commission to the recently created Council of National Defense, he increasingly viewed the

Mexican Revolution within the strategic context of the European situation. Consequently, foreign policy objectives took precedence over the interests of Mexican workers. AFL leaders complained about Carranza's antilabor policy but did not call for the Casa's resurrection—perhaps a reflection of the AFL's relief at the death of the more radical labor organization.

Gompers urged the American commissioners to be patient at the bargaining table, but Carranza's refusal to cave in to U.S. demands forced the unilateral withdrawal of the Pershing Expedition at the end of January 1917. The Wilson administration's preoccupation with European developments allowed the Mexican Revolution a temporary breathing space. As the United States prepared to declare war on Germany, Gompers became absorbed in the difficult task of delivering labor support for the Allied cause. However, he did not abandon efforts to shape a reformist labor movement and government in Mexico that would be friendly to the United States. American entry into the First World War and escalating diplomatic tensions over Mexico's new nationalist constitution would influence those efforts.[97]

3

Carranza's Nationalism, World War, and the Pan American Federation of Labor, 1917–1920

Mexico scored a major victory over U.S. efforts to throttle the Revolution when President Wilson ordered the recall of Pershing's forces without having extracted economic and political concessions from Carranza. Even as American troops were evacuating Mexico in February 1917 the promulgation of a new, progressive constitution with an advanced labor code and a bourgeois nationalist orientation brought a new Mexican challenge to the United States. Of particular concern to large American mining and oil interests was Article 27, which vested in the state ownership of all natural resources in Mexico. These corporate interests mobilized a campaign to pressure the State Department to adopt a militant, confrontational position toward Carranza to ensure that Article 27 not be applied.

Chandler P. Anderson, Judge Delbert J. Haff, Frederic R. Kellogg, Frederic N. Watriss, and Harold Walker lobbied the State Department on behalf of oil, mining, and landholding companies. These lobbyists discovered, however, that department officials, although sharing the same fundamental objective of safeguarding foreign capital in Mexico, often had their hands tied by conditions related to U.S. involvement in the world war. A general unanimity of opinion prevailed among U.S. policymakers that the Mexican "problem" should be put on the back burner until after the war. Fear of German influence in Mexico forced the adoption of a somewhat less belligerent approach toward Carranza.[1]

U.S. entry into the First World War lent an added sense of urgency to Gompers's efforts to establish tutelage over the Mexican and other Latin American labor movements. Shortly after President Wilson severed diplomatic relations with Germany on February 3,

1917, Gompers wrote a letter to William G. McAdoo, secretary of the treasury, again requesting labor representation on the High Commission of the Pan American Union. Attacking the "ruthlessness" of American corporate interests in Latin America, Gompers complained that Latin Americans would be suspicious of the United States as long as big business selfishly used the American military to protect investments in the region. In his view, the shortsighted interventionist policies encouraged by segments of the American business community threatened to undermine U.S. influence in Latin America.[2]

In the letter to McAdoo, Gompers stressed that Pan-American cooperation might be critical to the survival of the United States, given the international situation, and that labor could perform a valuable patriotic service by showing Latin Americans a more democratic, humanitarian side. He pointed to his growing contacts in Mexico and emphasized that the AFL's objectives included more than the narrow interests of labor. National strategic concerns, he made clear, were involved in his plans for a Pan-American labor federation, and he tried to convince McAdoo that the AFL's patriotic commitments should earn organized labor a place on the high commission.[3]

American officials continued to frustrate Gompers's efforts to secure representation on the commission, which he believed necessary to protect labor in the face of corporate capital's organized drive to penetrate Latin America. The AFL's reformist approach to the Mexican Revolution, however, caught the attention of corporate liberals who recognized that Gompers's contacts with Mexican workers might be exploited to achieve a favorable nonmilitary resolution of the ongoing crisis with Carranza. The Mexican Property Owners Non-Intervention League of Oakland, California, an organization founded to re-elect Woodrow Wilson in 1916 and defeat the campaign of the oil companies and other large interests to force military intervention in Mexico, sent Gould Harrold, one of its members, to see Gompers in February 1917. Harrold told Gompers that the League, in an effort to promote greater understanding between the United States and Mexico, intended to send a group of goodwill ambassadors representative of American small farmers, women, and workers. These representatives would then submit written reports of their fact-finding mission to American and Mexican legislators. Harrold hoped that such efforts would generate favorable publicity for Mexico and counter the interventionist demands of the oil companies.[4]

After discussing the League's plans with Gompers, Harrold, who owned a large sugar plantation in Sonora, tried unsuccessfully to see President Wilson. John Murray then took Harrold to Judge Douglas, Carranza's Washington attorney, who briefed Harrold on the main issues dividing the United States and Mexico. In a matter related to the war in Europe, Douglas also explained the negative implications of Carranza's recent suggestion that Mexico might place an embargo on all exports to belligerent countries.

Douglas then called AFL headquarters to suggest that Gompers arrange an interview for Harrold with the White House. Gompers took Harrold with him to the next joint meeting of the advisory commission of the Council of National Defense and prevailed upon Secretary of War Newton Baker to arrange a meeting between Harrold and the President. After explaining to Gompers that even he had been unable to see the president recently, Baker said that because of Gompers's recommendation and the critical international situation, he would try to set up an interview for Harrold. On February 14, 1917, Harrold met with President Wilson, who expressed approval of the League's plans. In this meeting, the president suggested that an agreement regarding the U.S. arms embargo could probably be reached if Carranza were to designate a port through which arms could be shipped without the danger of falling into the hands of Mexican rebels.[5]

Harrold, who was about to go to Mexico, hoped to take advantage of the AFL's favorable image with the Constitutionalists. He suggested it might be useful for him to take to Mexico a letter from Gompers to Carranza affirming AFL support for the activities of the Mexican Property Owners Non-Intervention League. Gompers agreed, and he provided Harrold with a letter to Carranza that endorsed Harrold's mission.[6]

The failure of the U.S. government to blunt Mexico's revolutionary nationalism and the critical international situation encouraged corporate liberals and even "not-so-liberal" officials to recognize the importance of labor-capital cooperation in foreign policy. As the United States declared war on Germany, policymakers counted on Gompers to ensure the support of American workers on the domestic front and involved him in efforts to prevent social revolutions abroad.[7]

The rupture in U.S. relations with Germany encouraged Gompers to step up his efforts to establish a hemispheric labor organization. The Pan American Federation of Labor Conference Committee, whose creation had been authorized at the AFL Convention in November 1916, called upon Latin American labor organizations to send representatives to Washington or at least provide the names and addresses of those whom the committee could contact. Gompers became chairman of the committee, and John Murray acted as the secretary. Other members included Santiago Iglesias, an AFL organizer in Puerto Rico, and Carlos Loveira, who represented the labor movement in Yucatán. The committee issued a manifesto that called for a regional labor federation to counteract the growing penetration of Latin America by corporate capital and spread a "humane" influence throughout the Western Hemisphere. In an added note to the manifesto, the committee assured Latin Americans that plans to create a Pan American Federation of Labor (PAFL) had nothing to do with the deteriorating relationship between Germany and the United States, but it pointed out that the international situation made Pan-American cooperation even more imperative.[8]

Mexico's Edmundo E. Martínez, Cuba's Antonio Correa, and Cardenio González, a Chilean, later joined the conference committee, but their actual role involved little more than simply allowing the use of their names to give the committee greater credibility. Martínez, who had become the Mexican consul in Chicago, assured Gompers that his primary allegiance was to the Mexican labor movement and said that he would resign the consulship if the AFL doubted that he was a bona fide representative of Mexican workers. He emphasized that his official government position did not compromise his effectiveness as a representative of the Mexican labor movement. As we shall see, however, his discussions with Gompers in the summer of 1917 focused on the outstanding financial and diplomatic issues that divided Mexico and the United States.[9]

The initial response of Latin American workers to the PAFL manifesto was disappointing, and another plea went out in July 1917 for Latin Americans to give their views on the proposed regional labor organization.[10] In a speech welcoming Correa as a member of the conference committee on August 20, 1917, Gompers spelled out his foreign policy objectives in Latin America: "In addition to the world war in which Cuba and the United States have entered it is perhaps likely that before its termination many of the other countries of Pan-America will also enter in that great war because it is realized that after-all it is a world-war against autocracy; it is a world-war, as President Wilson said, 'to make the world safe for democracy.'"[11]

In a letter to Salvador Alvarado, governor of Yucatán, Gompers explained that a PAFL could "inject liberal ideas into international relations," and he asked Alvarado to provide Loveira with enough funds to underwrite his future work on the conference committee. After thanking Alvarado for helping to make Loveira's work possible, Gompers hinted that Mexico's nationalism, expressed in its independent foreign policy, was especially unpalatable to the United States, given the international balance of forces. "The critical situation that confronts the countries of the Western Hemisphere," he warned Alvarado, "makes us all anxious that nothing shall interfere with the constructive efforts that will make the whole world safer for democracy."[12]

As Harvey Levenstein points out, securing Latin American participation in the PAFL depended on the response of Mexican labor. The low level of industrialization in Latin America generally made for small, weak labor organizations that were often headed by intellectuals. This relative weakness of other Latin American labor movements made Mexico the focal point of Gompers's efforts.[13] The development of the Mexican labor movement in a revolutionary nationalist context made it especially important for Gompers to form a relationship with Mexican workers in order to shape their philosophical orientation and perspectives on the United States.

Following the Casa's destruction, however, no national labor organization existed in Mexico with which Gompers could cement a formal alliance. Government repression and philosophical differences within the labor movement hampered the formation of a centralized labor organization. Unions in Tampico called a labor congress in October 1917, attended by representatives from twelve states and the Federal District. However, sharp conflicts broke out between anarchists, syndicalists, and the more conservative local unions, thus preventing the rise of a national organization.[14]

For more than a year after the United States entered the First World War, the PAFL committee did little more than send out questionnaires and information urging Latin American workers to endorse the AFL's philosophy. Union activities took Iglesias to Puerto Rico, and Murray went to Arizona in the summer of 1917 to investigate the conditions that triggered a strike by Mexican miners in that state. The task of mobilizing domestic labor support for the Allied war effort absorbed an increasing amount of Gompers's time.[15] Thus plans to create a PAFL that would accept Gompers's leadership and U.S. hegemony, attractively packaged in a reformist framework, had to await more favorable conditions.

Gompers continued to involve himself in diplomatic issues concerning Mexico. Col. Edmundo Martínez visited him in July 1917 after returning from a meeting with Carranza in Mexico City. According to Martínez, Carranza had asked him to deliver an important message to Gompers. Martínez assured Gompers that Carranza did not harbor pro-German feelings, and he relayed a complaint that the Hearsts and other corporate interests were providing Pancho Villa and other rebels with arms while the American government embargoed the sale of arms and munitions to the Carranza government. Martínez complained that the refusal of American officials to allow the minting of Mexican gold in the United States was undermining Carranza's attempt to stabilize the Mexican currency.[16]

Gompers escorted Martínez to a meeting with President Wilson on July 18, but the White House became upset by Martínez's report to Carranza of what had occurred at the conference. Martínez apparently told Carranza that Wilson promised to lift the arms embargo and allow the coinage of Mexican gold, and that Mexico should provide evidence against those who were allegedly supplying Villa and other rebels with arms. Criticizing the Mexican consul for misrepresenting the White House's position and placing him in an embarrassing position, Gompers scolded Martínez and told him not to expect further access to Wilson.[17] Nevertheless, he tried to smoothe over the incident by telling the president that Martínez's egotistical tendencies should not obscure his good intentions:

"He evidently, in his guileless way exaggerated the importance of his 'achievements' and was too impetuous to permit time for you to work out a solution of the problem." [18]

Despite his rebuke of Martínez, Gompers apparently believed that he had some basis for concluding that the president would end the arms embargo and allow the coinage of Mexican gold in the United States. In a memorandum dictated after the meeting, Gompers noted that Wilson encouraged Martínez to believe that early action would be taken on these two issues. [19]

Carranza resented American restrictions imposed on the export of gold, machinery, food, and other products. He also balked at U.S. efforts to link the granting of new loans to guarantees for foreign investments in Mexico. Although the United States granted de jure recognition of Carranza in September 1917, after Ambassador Henry Fletcher received assurances from him that foreign capital need not fear the nationalist provisions of the constitution, the "cat and mouse" game with Mexico continued amid growing U.S. concern over German postwar economic influence in Mexico. Corporate lobbyists for the big oil, mining, and landholding companies criticized the granting of full diplomatic recognition of Carranza and urged the State Department to step up the pressure on Mexico to repudiate Article 27. Chandler P. Anderson, for example, tried unsuccessfully to persuade Thomas W. Lamont to encourage American bankers to refuse to participate in the Liberty Loan program until the U.S. government forced Carranza to scrap the Mexican Constitution. [20]

Among those who opposed these corporate lobbyists was Douglas, Carranza's attorney, who believed that a less confrontational policy toward his client was the best way to ensure American economic and political dominance in Mexico. Even as he provided legal counsel to Carranza, he advised U.S. officials to seek less abrasive ways of containing the Mexican Revolution and securing the broader, long-range strategic objectives of the United States in Mexico. This pursuit of a more flexible policy brought him into conflict with corporate representatives who wanted to tighten the screws on Carranza. Despite this conflict, Douglas shared with these lobbyists the fundamental objectives of securing protection for foreign capital and getting Carranza to support the Allied war effort. Since his relationship with Gompers shaped and, in turn, was shaped by his diplomatic efforts, it is instructive to examine his activities in greater detail in order to get a clearer view of the AFL's policies in Mexico.

In a meeting with Secretary of State Robert Lansing on May 5, 1917, Charles Anderson and Delbert Haff complained about a proposal by Douglas and Luis Cabrera, Carranza's secretary of the treasury, to hold a meeting in Mexico City with representatives of numerous American firms doing business in Mexico. At Anderson's suggestion, Haff prepared a memorandum for Lansing that outlined the efforts of Douglas to win the support of foreign interests for the Carranza government. According to Haff, Douglas hoped to get these representatives to endorse Carranza publicly. This would enable Carranza to secure a loan to help rehabilitate Mexico's industries and develop a sound financial structure that would also provide protection for foreign capital. Frederic Kellogg, the Mexican Petroleum Company's chief counsel, and William Loeb, who represented the American Smelting and Refining Company (ASARCO), declined invitations from Douglas to attend the meeting in Mexico City.[21]

Although the State Department listened to these complaints about Douglas, the U.S. Bureau of Investigation provided a more favorable assessment of his activities. A report filed in October 1917 indicated that Douglas was trying to use economic leverage to persuade Carranza to enter the war against Germany. Douglas assured Carranza that abundant financial aid would be forthcoming if he made the necessary guarantees to foreign investors and announced a diplomatic break with Germany. The agent who filed the report noted that Douglas hoped to soften Carranza's nationalism and convince him to "invite and make it possible for the safe investment of American capital in Mexico, to help in developing her resources and creating new industries."[22]

Not everyone in Carranza's government trusted Douglas,[23] but the Bureau of Investigation noted the cooperative relationship between him and Ignacio Bonillas, the new Mexican ambassador. Before presenting his credentials to President Wilson, Bonillas submitted his written remarks for Douglas's approval and even asked him what kind of clothes he should wear. The Bureau of Investigation's report pointed out that Bonillas supported Douglas's plan to use financial inducements to get Carranza to embrace the Allied war effort. Douglas intervened with the U.S. Treasury Department to allow Mexico to export $500,000 in gold from banks in El Paso, Texas, and stressed to Bonillas that this confirmed the "benevolent" intentions of the United States.[24]

Douglas also hoped to convince Carranza that meddling in Central American politics by backing revolutionary movements would only cause more trouble for himself. Douglas's overall approach to Carranza made a good impression on the Bureau of Investigation's agent who compiled the report on him. The agent had no doubts about Douglas's loyalty. "Mr. Douglas is a most interesting gentleman," he wrote, "and there is no doubt in my mind but that he has, and will always consider first the interests of the United States Government, before he will those of the Mexican Government, and if it ever reaches the point whereby it is up to him to participate as legal adviser of the Mexican Government, in anything that would be harmful to the United States that he would refuse to do so."[25]

Douglas kept in touch with Gompers, who became concerned during the summer of 1917 over a bitter struggle with the IWW in the Arizona mining camps. The successful recruitment of Mexican miners by IWW organizers from Mexico encouraged the AFL to strengthen its contacts with Mexican workers. Douglas participated in discussions with Gompers over the mining situation in Arizona, and the Arizona Federation of Labor elected a committee to meet with representatives of the Sonoran Workingmen's Congress.[26]

Developments in early 1918 encouraged Douglas to tap his relationship with Gompers as he worked to defuse an increasingly volatile confrontation between Carranza and the United States. When Carranza ordered the oil companies to pay higher taxes and reregister their titles in February, the U.S. government sent naval units to the waters off the coast of Tampico and threatened intervention unless he rescinded the decree, which provided for confiscation if the oil firms refused to comply. Even as they lodged an official protest on April 2, 1918, U.S. officials dangled the lure of economic incentives to persuade Carranza to abandon his nationalist economic policies.[27]

In a meeting with Gompers, Douglas laid out a flexible proposal that, he argued, would benefit Carranza but still strengthen Mexico's economic dependency on the United States. He told Gompers that Mexico had about $10,000,000 in one of the Federal Reserve banks but could not touch the assets because of U.S. wartime restrictions on the export of gold. The trade balance between the two countries favored Mexico, and Carranza insisted that the balance be paid in gold. Douglas stressed that the matter could be resolved to the benefit of both nations. Although he believed that the wartime curbs on the export of gold were generally wise, he argued that an exception should be made in Mexico's case because of political and economic considerations:

> If our government should agree to settle the balance of trade in Mexico's favor in gold, say as a temporary arrangement and therefore subject to change in the near future, and assuming that the balance of trade in favor shall in the next five months reach an average of $5,000,000 American money a month, the total of the export of gold during that period of time would be $25,000,000. I am assured that two-thirds or three-fourths of this money would have to be expended by Mexico in the purchase of products and other materials in the United States—this would mean that there would flow back from Mexico at least two-thirds of the gold that we would send into Mexico.[28]

Douglas recognized that despite the nationalist orientation of the Revolution, fundamental economic forces at work during the World War deepened Mexico's dependency on the United States. As Europe's share of trade with Latin America declined, American interests increased their trade and investments in the region. If the United States could accommodate Carranza's nationalism in certain areas, it could reap a more bountiful economic and political harvest in Mexico in the long run. American labor could share in this harvest since increased markets in Mexico meant greater production and more jobs in the United States. Although Carranza's pro-German sympathies irritated U.S. officials (and Douglas), the real bone of contention was his nationalist economic policies.[29]

By April 1918 the inability of the United States to browbeat Carranza into making economic and political concessions forced a more flexible approach. Henry Fletcher, the ambassador in Mexico City, informed Lansing that the latest confrontation with Carranza over the new oil decree was indicative of the broader failure of U.S. policy to achieve its objectives by badgering and threatening Mexico. In fact, he argued, the U.S. embargo on food and gold exports and other war measures aimed at Mexico only strengthened Carranza's nationalism. Fletcher worried that the United States might have to deal with the Mexican "problem" before the war ended. When Lansing relayed these fears to the White House, President Wilson asked him to contact the Federal Reserve Board to explore more innovative, flexible strategies in Mexico.[30]

This shift in strategies included involving the AFL and members of the New York banking community in an attempt to extract concessions from Carranza. President Wilson decided to use the relationship between Gompers, Douglas, Thomas Lill, and Henry Bruére. As Carranza's financial advisors, Lill and Bruére, acting at Carranza's request and with U.S. approval, had launched a comprehensive review of the Mexican government's financial structure in May 1917. They held a conference with Gompers and Douglas on July 28, 1918, and, in accordance with a suggestion from Gompers, prepared a confidential memorandum which Gompers discussed at length with President Wilson the following day. Douglas concluded that Gompers was the only person who could persuade the president to adopt the course of action suggested by Lill and Bruére. The president told Gompers that Douglas, Lill, and Bruére should come to the White House individually or collectively for more extensive discussions and asked for a formal letter on the plan. Gompers suggested to Douglas that the letter and memorandum be delivered to President Wilson through Herbert Hoover.[31]

Lill and Bruére proposed that the U.S. government help to maintain Carranza by indicating to American financial interests that it would guarantee loans that they might make to the Mexican government. Such guarantees would further U.S. wartime and postwar objectives in Mexico. Lill and Bruére warned that Germans held a large part of Mexico's foreign debt and that German influences were trying to strengthen their economic position. Since Carranza refused to accept a loan directly from the American government, they argued, U.S. bankers could make the loan arrangements if their government would act as the "moral guarantor" of the transaction. Lill and Bruére emphasized that such informal financial diplomacy could ensure a preeminent American economic influence in postwar Mexico. They cautioned that the further deterioration of Carranza's economic and political situation was not in the strategic interests of the United States. "The loan is suggested as an alternative to a more costly undertaking both in capital and principle, with which the United States would seem to be confronted in case of the dissolution of the present Mexican government."[32]

Gompers's involvement in financial diplomacy strengthened the AFL's efforts to play a more dynamic role in U.S.-Mexican affairs, and his relationship with Douglas played a leading role in reactivating the drive to establish a regional labor federation. During the period of tensions between the United States and Mexico in the spring of 1918, Douglas visited his client in Mexico City and expressed grave concern over Mexico's pro-German neutrality. Financial aid would be forthcoming, he told Carranza, if Mexico joined the Allied war effort. Unable to persuade Carranza to renounce Mexico's war neutrality, he returned to Washington and suggested to Gompers that the time was ripe to create the PAFL. Douglas recommended that the AFL send a delegation to Mexico to cultivate support for the organization and discuss a broad range of issues affecting the two countries. According to him, Carranza approved of the efforts to cement relations between American and Mexican workers.[33]

Gompers moved swiftly on the recommendations of Douglas, who believed that formalization of Mexican-American labor relations could accomplish important political objectives for the United States and also save the Carranza government from direct intervention. In a telegram charged to the Council of National Defense, Gompers told Santiago Iglesias, who was in Puerto Rico at the time, to take the next boat to Washington. He wanted Iglesias to be a member of the AFL commission to Mexico.[34] Gompers provided the White House with a memorandum submitted by Douglas, in whom he expressed complete confidence. "The American Federation of Labor, as you know," Gompers told the president, "has in the past been of some assistance in re-establishing better relations than existed at a few of the critical periods . . . between the Government of Mexico and the United States and I am constrained to believe that the subject matter presented herein can be helpful again to meet, not only the immediate solution—first with Mexico, and soon thereafter, with all the Pan-American countries."[35]

Gompers sought government financing for the PAFL. He pressed the White House for over a month before learning that such aid would not be forthcoming. President Wilson favored the convening of a Mexican-American labor conference but refused in May to subsidize it. He urged Gompers to avoid official government involvement in order to make the project more effective.[36]

The most obvious obstacle to the formalization of ties between the AFL and Mexican labor in early 1918 was the absence of a national labor organization in Mexico following Carranza's attack on the Casa in August 1916. However, internal developments in the spring of 1918 made formal contacts between the AFL and the Mexican labor movement possible. Sponsored by Gustavo Espinosa Mireles, governor of Coahuila, a labor convention opened in Saltillo on May 1, resulting in the birth of La Confederación Regional Obrera Mexicana (CROM). Although they paid lip service to the theory of anarchosyndicalism, Luis Morones and other emerging CROM leaders guided Mexican labor away from revolutionary syndicalism. "In place of the 'direct action' of anarchism," Harvey Levenstein writes, "it [CROM] advocated 'multiple action'—which meant the combined use of the strike, to obtain better working conditions from the employers, and direct political action, in the matter of the unions of Britain—to achieve a change in the whole socioeconomic system."[37]

Radicalism retained a considerable vitality in sectors of the CROM, but the ideological orientation of the newly formed federation foreshadowed its soon to be consummated marriage with the AFL. Nevertheless, many leftists in the Mexican labor movement opposed collaboration with the AFL, which they denounced as an instrument of U.S. imperialism. To win Mexican labor's support for American war aims would not be an easy task for Gompers, for Mexican workers backed Carranza's policy of neutrality.[38]

It is not altogether clear if Carranza actually suggested sponsoring the national labor convention in Saltillo, but there were men around him who recognized the utility of having an officially sponsored labor movement. Creating a captive labor movement could help to stabilize Mexico's economic situation by providing concessions to labor while the government retained control through the cooptation of leaders and organizations. A reformist labor movement under the government's tutelage could also use its ties with the AFL to mobilize anti-interventionist forces in the United States.[39]

Chief among those revolutionary leaders who had important contacts with Mexican labor leaders and favored the incorporation of labor into a ruling coalition was General Álvaro Obregón. Obregón, then in poor health, resigned as Carranza's secretary of war to return to his home state of Sonora in May 1917 and visited the United States later that year on a trip that combined business and political interests. He developed a personal friendship with Ambassador Fletcher, who suggested that the United States accord him a very friendly reception during his visit. Lansing agreed that it would be wise to lavish special attention on Obregón, and the State Department provided the money to have a Spanish-speaking American army officer accompany him in the United States. The War Department assigned Harvey Miller to this position. The Justice Department shadowed Obregón for awhile but later called off the surveillance.[40]

While in Washington in the spring of 1918, Obregón met with the Federal Reserve Board, the War Trade Board, high officials in the War Department, the State Department's Frank Polk, and Gompers. Obregón concluded successful arrangements with U.S. officials for the marketing of garbanzos, or chick peas, from his estates, and he won many friends in the U.S. by selling most of the 1918 harvest to Herbert Hoover's Food Administration for shipment to Europe. He recommended that other chick-pea producers also support the U.S. Enemy Trading Act by refusing to conduct business with Germans. On April 16, the day Gompers submitted Douglas's memorandum to the White House and asked for government funding of the PAFL, Obregón met with Gompers. He later provided letters to facilitate the rapidly unfolding plans of Douglas and Gompers to set up the PAFL.[41]

Undaunted by President Wilson's initial refusal to subsidize the project, Gompers pushed ahead with efforts to cement a formal relationship with the Mexican labor movement. In a telegram again charged to the Council of National Defense, he and John Murray notified Morones on May 10, 1918, that an AFL delegation would leave soon for Mexico City. Accompanied by Iglesias and James Lord, head of the AFL's Mining Department, Murray visited the Mexican ambassador, who communicated his support and enthusiasm for what the PAFL might accomplish in the area of inter-American relations. Ambassador Bonillas urged the AFL delegates to visit Governor Espinosa Mireles in Saltillo on their way to

Mexico City.[42] Gompers warned Murray, Lord, and Iglesias that real problems could develop if they were found to be carrying official letters from the Mexican ambassador (who must have offered to provide official endorsements of their mission). "Let Bonias [sic] write as ambassador to all whom he wishes," Gompers stressed, "but not carrying any letter from him."[43]

The AFL mission apparently caught the State Department off guard. Pointing out that the mission had President Wilson's approval, Gompers contacted Secretary Lansing on May 10, 1918, to request his assistance in facilitating the issuance of passports to Lord, Murray, and Iglesias, who visited the Division of Mexican Affairs and received their passports on May 13. Frank Polk, counselor for the State Department, asked Leon Canova of the Division of Mexican Affairs about the AFL mission after learning about it in an intercepted cable from Consul General Adolfo de la Huerta in New York to General Cándido Aguilar, Mexico's secretary of foreign relations. The Division of Mexican Affairs telephoned AFL headquarters about a week later to ask if any other labor representatives would be going to Mexico at that time.[44]

Murray, Lord, and Iglesias stopped in Saltillo on May 19 and visited with labor leaders and representatives of the governor. According to the AFL delegates, Coahuilan officials told them that the time was ripe for Mexican labor to achieve a "complete, thorough organization on constructive, progressive lines," and expressed enthusiasm over the possibilities of the PAFL. Urged by officials to address some public meetings in Saltillo, Lord, Murray, and Iglesias decided that it would be wiser not to do so until they talked to Carranza in Mexico City, where they arrived on May 23. They went immediately to the U.S. embassy and were then escorted by Ambassador Fletcher to a meeting with Carranza, who granted them a rather lengthy interview. In the report on their trip to Mexico, the AFL delegates noted, "President Carranza listens carefully and speaks deliberately, and after a comprehensive discussion he appeared convinced of the power for good a Pan-American International of Labor Centers would be, and wished us every success."[45]

While in Mexico the AFL representatives assured labor leaders that the PAFL would be a federation of equals and that the AFL would not try to impose its will on Mexican workers. Although the secret aim of the PAFL was to use Mexican labor to secure Carranza's support for the Allied war effort, Lord, Murray, and Iglesias carefully avoided talking about the war during their stay in Mexico. They carried a letter from Gompers that stressed the need for inter-American labor cooperation to check the growing threat of corporate capital in the region.[46]

Despite their efforts to camouflage the real purpose of the PAFL, the AFL representatives found themselves under heavy fire from leftists in the Mexican labor movement and pro-German newspapers. They faced tough questioning about the AFL's role in the wartime persecution of the IWW and its links to the White House.[47] As the AFL delegation's report later noted, Iglesias was especially effective in disarming Mexican critics of the AFL: "He is conversant with their history and wrongs, speaks their language, and succeeds in bringing the most radical to agree with him on programs and methods."[48]

The willingness of CROM leaders to cooperate with Gompers intensified ideological warfare in the Mexican labor movement. Morones came under fire for opening discussions with the AFL without the authorization of the CROM's rank and file. Having emerged from the labor convention in Saltillo with growing power, he refused to allow internal opposition to prevent him from proceeding with arrangements to head a CROM delegation to a joint labor conference to be held in Laredo, Texas, on November 13, 1918.[49]

Lord, Iglesias, and Murray returned from Mexico optimistic. Several Mexican senators from mining and industrial states had also promised cooperation, and employers in the mining industry, which was dominated by foreign capital, expressed a willingness to pay higher wages if Mexican labor would change its philosophical orientation. The AFL commission's report complained about the destructive influence of radical syndicalism among Mexican workers, especially its "demoralizing effect on both operations and workers" in the mining industry:

> We were told by a mine manager that the managements had given up fighting the unions, and were now hoping for some steadying influence to appear, whereby equitable agreements could be negotiated by localities or districts that would insure some measure of industrial peace at least during the life of such agreements. He told

us recently they had been compelled to close down their mill for repairs, which automatically closed the mine. The syndicate demanded the wage for this period of idleness, claiming that machinery and ore could very well wait a week but their stomachs would not. He was compelled to grant their demands. He admitted that wages were too low, but said that if the unions were to go into negotiations in a business-like way with the companies, with a view of establishing a joint agreement peacefully handling disputes, a much better wage and working situation could be arrived at. We cite this instance because we found considerable of this sentiment among employers and others who have probably not been too considerate of the conditions of toil heretofore.[50]

This report suggests that what concerned Lord, Iglesias, and Murray most was not the lack of organization among Mexican mineworkers, but rather the philosophical basis of their unionism. The AFL delegates noted the strong presence of unions in the mining industry but underscored the need to eradicate Mexican radical syndicalism. Blaming these tendencies on years of prerevolutionary repression and subsequent manipulation by left-wing intellectuals, they concluded that the time was ripe to move the Mexican labor movement decisively away from its anarchosyndicalist roots. They also noted that many Mexican labor leaders, disappointed in the failure of their movement to achieve substantial benefits, expressed a greater willingness to organize along the structural lines of the AFL: "They realize that cooperation and helpfulness from the north will be fully assured in a general way and more available, by their participation in the Pan-American Federation of Labor."[51]

President Wilson overcame his reservations to provide covert funding for the PAFL. George Creel's Committee on Public Information (CPI) and the American Alliance for Labor and Democracy (AALD), an organization headed by Gompers to combat pacifism among American workers and socialist intellectuals, became conduits for government money to underwrite the upcoming joint labor conference and a newspaper to promote the strengthening of inter-American labor relations. A virtual appendage of the CPI, the AALD extended its activities to Mexico. Chester Wright, the former editorial director of the *New York Call*, headed the news department of the AALD and directed the publicity activities of the CPI's Labor Publications Division. He also became involved in the project to establish the Pan-American Labor Press, whose publication was the responsibility of a committee officially headed by Murray, Iglesias, and Lord.[52]

During the summer of 1918, as U.S. officials considered more flexible strategies to deal with Carranza, President Wilson received encouragement from corporate liberals who had investments in Mexico to reconsider his refusal to fund the PAFL. The corporate liberal wing of American investors in Mexico showed a greater willingness to incorporate the AFL into foreign policy in order to stabilize the Mexican situation and ensure continued U.S. economic and political hegemony. Thus, it is useful to examine the views of two such individuals who advised the President that a broader strategy, one that involved the AFL, was crucial to containing the Mexican Revolution and checking German influence there.

At the same time that Gompers was working with Lill, Bruére, and Douglas in financial diplomacy, a representative from the *Washington Post* visited AFL headquarters to report that John R. Phillips, the president of the San Lorenzo Sugar Company, which was based in Los Angeles and had extensive interests in Mexico, had notified the White House that he had enough influence over Carranza to sell the president's policy objectives to him. In accordance with instructions from the president, Phillips prepared a memorandum to be delivered to the White House by Gompers. Phillips wanted to circumvent the State Department, since he believed that hardliners there were too heavily influenced by interventionists like the Otises and Chandlers in Los Angeles, who attacked his views on Mexico and, according to him, tried to ruin him financially.[53]

Phillips offered to use his contacts with members of the Carranza Government to open unofficial negotiations intended to achieve a thorough rapprochement between the United States and Mexico. He emphasized to President Wilson that the political solution to the Mexican problem depended on the restoration of domestic peace through the rehabilitation of Mexico's finances and productive capabilities. Stressing that "old time methods and formulas" would be ineffective in dealing with Carranza, Phillips set forth a detailed loan proposal, one that would take account of Carranza's domestic political needs. He made clear that he would undertake negotiations with the Carranza government on the premise that Mexico must change its constitution "to eliminate the portion which might seem to be inconsistent with most friendly relations with her sister nations or which might impose undue hardships upon alien residents and property owners."[54]

Phillips concluded that the United States had to demonstrate a more creative approach, one that took into consideration the needs of the Mexican masses. Here the AFL could play a valuable role. He admitted that he was only a recent convert to corporate liberalism, that the World War and the Mexican Revolution had caused him to rethink his earlier views against organized labor. "Mexico's problems are so closely related to those of Labor," he argued, "that it is very fitting that the labor leader should be one of the instruments for the solution of those problems."[55]

Phillips recognized that containing class conflict would be the greatest postwar challenge to American policymakers. He stressed that Gompers and Franklin Roosevelt, who had promoted harmonious labor-capital relations in his capacity as the assistant secretary of the Navy, could cooperate to resolve the "labor question." Any differences between Roosevelt and Gompers, he noted, stemmed from methods, not fundamental aims. Phillips also believed that the AFL could help to resolve the labor question south of the border: "Just as we need Mexico's food stuffs and natural products, so are the laboring classes in Mexico in need of the guidance of constructive labor leadership from the United States."[56]

Lewis Warfield, a transportation engineer who owned a silver mine and had interests in Mexican timber and iron ore, also encouraged President Wilson to endorse a formal role for the AFL in Mexico. Warfield carried a letter of recommendation from Pastor Rouaix, Carranza's secretary of fomento (economic development), to the Mexican ambassador in Washington. The Bolshevik Revolution increased Warfield's fears that the Mexican Revolution might deepen if the United States did not devise more creative strategies to ease the economic and social distress that underlay Mexico's political turmoil. "A departure from the customary diplomatic forms in negotiations," he told President Wilson, "seems to me to be worth while trying right now with the Mexican government."[57]

Warfield recommended an economic policy that would rehabilitate American industrial enterprises in Mexico, and he complained that American finance capital catered to the oil companies and virtually froze out other entrepreneurs who needed financing. He worried that a continuation of this shortsighted investment strategy would only exacerbate Mexico's social, economic, and political maladies and pose problems for the United States. He also pointed out that the perception that the U.S. government had imperialistic designs on Mexico and Central America could only benefit America's competitors. A recent statement by Hipólito Yrigoyen, the president of Argentina, that trade contacts and relations between Mexico and Argentina were improving underscored to Warfield that an alternative version of Pan-Americanism threatened to undermine U.S. hegemony in Latin America.[58]

After underscoring the massive unemployment problem in Mexico, Warfield told the president that he had talked to one of the AFL representatives who went to Mexico to drum up support for the PAFL. Warfield emphasized that AFL leaders had softened their earlier insistence that American capital be invested as much as possible at home. According to him, the AFL was receptive to the idea of rehabilitating industries in Mexico, since most of these enterprises produced only for the Mexican market and did not threaten to be competitive in the world economy. He also emphasized that the AFL hoped that the more effective employment of Mexico's productive resources and labor would check the postwar influx of cheap Mexican labor. Finally, he told the president that AFL leaders hoped to profit from the greater use of Mexico as an outlet for American surplus goods.[59]

As William Appleman Williams writes, "With the Mexicans already providing what seemed to be radical leadership for the entire area, the Bolshevik Revolution hit American policy in Latin America like a Caribbean hurricane."[60] Phillips and Warfield emphasized that World War I and the Bolshevik Revolution widened the implications of the Mexican Revolution and thus challenged U.S. policymakers to develop a more creative strategy that included the AFL. Of course, Gompers shared their concerns about the possible growth of Bolshevism in Latin America. Although the war ended before the PAFL conference convened in Laredo on November 13, 1918, he pressed ahead with his efforts to shape the

Mexican labor movement. Other Latin American labor representatives participated in the conference, but the Mexican labor movement was the chief concern of AFL leaders.

Although invited, neither President Wilson nor Carranza attended the labor conference in Laredo but sent Secretary of Labor William B. Wilson and General Pablo de la Garza as their respective personal representatives. At a public gathering in Laredo, Gompers urged the crowd to ignore rumors that the AFL had suspicious motives in sponsoring the conference. Nevertheless, the conference proceedings quickly revealed that the Mexican delegates brought with them an agenda that provoked AFL leaders—an agenda that included a desire to improve conditions for Mexican workers in the United States, secure the release of IWW members who were jailed during the war, and avoid voting on any matters related to U.S. foreign policy. Since the Mexican delegates wanted the conference to focus exclusively on labor matters, they collided with Gompers, who was bent on winning their support for President Wilson's peace proposals.[61]

Irked by Mexican complaints that the AFL's racist practices excluded Mexicans in the United States from union membership, William Green of the United Mine Workers grew tired, he said, of responding to the introduction of resolutions that claimed the AFL discriminated against even those Mexicans who were allowed to join its unions. Gompers became especially aroused when Mexican delegates attacked the AFL's cooperative role in jailing Wobblies for their opposition to the war. The Mexicans called for AFL action to secure the release of those persecuted for their antiwar views. This exhausted the patience of Gompers, who unleashed a venomous attack on radicalism and upheld the AFL's role in the war:

> The I.W.W.'s in the United States are exactly what the Bolsheviki are in Russia, and we have seen what the I.W.W. Bolsheviki in Russia have done for the working people of Russia, where the people have no peace, no security, no land and no bread.
>   I did not expect . . . that the A. F. of L. would be put on its defense before this conference. The A. F. of L. has stood from the first day of its existence until now in defense of every right denied to the people and in opposition and protest against every wrong inflicted upon any people. The American trade union movement . . . stood 100 per cent in this world's struggle for freedom, and now the war has come to an end. . . . I ask you men what do you think the

chance for democracy would have been if Germany could have won the war.[62]

As head of the conference's Committee on Resolutions, Green squashed a Mexican proposal to avoid issues related to the war and the internal politics of Mexico and the United States. This set the stage for the introduction of an AFL resolution that called on conference members to approve what President Wilson intended to lay on the table at the Paris peace conference. Particularly offensive to the Mexicans were those sections of a resolution that called for a League of Nations and condemned economic nationalism. In a conciliatory speech, Morones explained that blanket support for U.S. foreign policy objectives and failure to display concern for workers of all ideological "stripes" would expose Mexican labor leaders to left-wing criticism at home. Nevertheless, Gompers scorned the Mexican delegation's reluctance to vote on Wilson's peace proposals. The PAFL delegates worked out an acceptable compromise after a lengthy, spirited debate.[63]

Despite bitter disputes during the sessions, Gompers emerged from the Laredo conference with the Mexican labor movement more firmly in tow. Although Morones had raised objections to AFL proposals, the conference nurtured a growing personal relationship between Gompers and Morones. Unhappy with the CROM's weakening commitment to radicalism and its budding romance with the AFL, disaffected elements within the CROM broke ranks to form El Gran Cuerpo Central de Trabajadores (great Central Body of Workers) at the end of 1918. However, Gompers could count on the growing power of CROM leaders to move that organization into a formal alliance with the AFL. The Laredo conference left no doubt as to the locus of power in the infant PAFL; the CROM would be a junior partner. AFL delegates outnumbered Mexican labor representatives by more than two to one and used their numerical superiority to elect Gompers, Murray, and Canuto A. Vargas, a representative of the AFL's Mine, Mill and Smelter Workers' Union of Morenci, Arizona, as officers of the PAFL. Not surprisingly, Washington became the site of the new organization's headquarters. The conference laid the basis for the PAFL's first annual congress in New York City on July 7, 1919.[64]

The AFL emerged from the First World War optimistic that the gains made as a result of wartime corporatist arrangements would lead to further advances for organized labor. Wartime labor shortages had led to higher wages, improved working conditions, and shorter hours for organized and unorganized workers. The intervention of the federal government in industrial relations had encouraged an impressive increase in AFL membership. Perhaps the most important governmental agency that acted as an arbiter of labor-capital conflicts during the war was the War Labor Board, which consisted of five AFL representatives and five representatives from industry. Co-chaired by Frank P. Walsh and former President William Taft, the board established guidelines to ensure uninterrupted industrial production for the Allied war effort. It regulated working conditions and wages and recognized workers' rights to organize and engage in collective bargaining. It also provided that strikes and lockouts were illegal, that unions could not coerce nonunion workers into joining, and that organized labor must accept the status of existing nonunion shops. Under the supervision of the War Labor Board, employee representation plans were initiated in nonunion firms.[65]

The corporatist pact that governed industrial relations during the war increased the stature of Gompers as a statesman and representative of labor's patriotic commitments. In addition, the wartime repression of Wobblies and socialists weakened forces that had challenged his leadership of the labor movement. Buoyed by the AFL's acceptance as an important force in wartime planning and strategy, Gompers hoped that "making the world safe for democracy" would bring greater domestic benefits after the war and strengthen his efforts to carve out a larger international role for the AFL.

Although Gompers was unable to persuade President Wilson to allow official labor representation at the Peace Conference in Paris, he received the president's backing to chair a separate conference to discuss labor's agenda for postwar reconstruction and create an international labor organization linked to the proposed League of Nations. Urging immediate adoption of "the first international charter for the rights of labor," Gompers defended the labor articles in the Covenant of the League of Nations: "The world needs to be made safe for labor as well as for democracy. The world cannot be safe for democracy until it is safe for labor. . . . Labor must be safe in all lands or it is safe in none."[66]

Gompers's growing influence in Mexico encouraged him to view the PAFL as an instrument to reconstruct a world order that upgraded the living conditions of workers everywhere. Of course, his concern for the safety of labor extended only to nonradical working-class organizations. Furthermore, Latin American labor organizations would have to accept U.S. hegemony in the region. Gompers viewed the PAFL as a supplement to the Monroe Doctrine.[67] As Harvey Levenstein notes, "In the same way as the United States was assured at Versailles that it would continue its paramount influence in Latin America, the formation of the PAFL, supplementing the League's International Labor Organization and the new international labor organization being created in Amsterdam, would ensure the dominant role of the AFL in the international labor relations of the Western Hemisphere."[68]

AFL leaders thus hoped that the end of the First World War marked the dawning of a new era of political stability and economic progress at home and abroad. Gompers, who lobbied tirelessly for the ratification of Wilson's peace proposals, argued that the rehabilitation of the world capitalist economy required an early resolution of the political crisis. Problems related to industrial production, finance, and markets could not be addressed effectively until Europe's immediate postwar political settlements were arranged. Only then could a more progressive order be constructed—an order that fostered cooperation between nonradical workers and employers, granted employees the right to unionize, and derived its moral strength from an underlying principle "that Labor is not a commodity but is inseparable from human life."[69]

AFL leaders moved quickly to mobilize Latin American labor's support for President Wilson's peace proposals and to improve the material conditions of those in the region who would endorse the AFL's brand of Pan-Americanism. While in Paris in February 1919, Gompers received a letter and draft of a proposal from Murray to be submitted to President Wilson pending Gompers's approval. The proposal, which had been approved by Lord and Morones, called for a Pan-American economic conference to discuss a range of issues, including labor conditions in Latin America, stabilization of wages, and the eight-hour day. Murray pointed out that besides advancing labor's agenda, the proposed conference could also be very useful in promoting a favorable view of the League of Nations.[70]

The AFL executive council directed Gompers to inform Latin American ambassadors in Washington that the PAFL conference in July 1919 authorized him to represent the Latin American labor movements at a meeting of the International Federation of Trade Unions in Amsterdam later that summer. Gompers kept the State Department posted of his efforts to increase American labor's stature with the workers and governments of Latin America. He also persuaded Morones at the second PAFL congress to support the Treaty of Versailles with its League covenant. Morones initially refused to endorse the AFL's position, but he reversed himself after getting Gompers to put the PAFL on record in favor of opening membership in the League of Nations to all countries.[71]

On June 13, 1919, Secretary of Labor William B. Wilson reminded delegates to the AFL's annual convention that postwar radicalism posed a serious threat to the world. In a speech that focused almost exclusively on the need to combat Bolshevism, Secretary Wilson praised Gompers's leadership during the war. "Upon him," Wilson said, "has devolved not only the direction of your forces and associated forces in the great struggle against the military autocracy of Germany, but there has also fallen upon his shoulders . . . the great burden of conducting the battle against the other insidious forces that would endeavor to utilize violence for the destruction of democracy, the powers of Bolshevism as expressed in some of the countries of Eastern Europe."[72]

Secretary Wilson believed that labor's patriotic contributions to the war and its commitment to democracy proved that more harmonious industrial relations could prevail in the postwar era. Arguing that employer repression encouraged radicalism, he stressed the commonality of interests between labor and capital:

> The employers and employees have a mutual interest in securing the largest possible production with a given amount of labor, having due regard to the health, the safety, the opportunity for rest, recreation and improvement of the workers. These being safeguarded, the larger the amount that is produced, the larger will be the amount that there is to provide. . . . Their interests will diverge only when it comes to a division of what has been mutually produced, and if

they are wise in their generation in these modern times, with labor realizing its importance in the defense of the country and the maintenance of the country, instead of solving the problem by the use of the economic power on the part of the employer, imposing his will upon the worker, or the use of collective power on the part of the employees imposing their will upon the employers, they will sit around the council table and endeavor to work out the problem on a democratic basis that will secure to each all that he is entitled to receive.[73]

Despite Secretary Wilson's confidence that more enlightened attitudes would harmonize social relations and discourage radicalism, the postwar attacks on organized labor, irrespective of its theoretical orientation, indicated that the wartime corporatist pact had splintered. In the atmosphere of the Red Scare, Gompers complained that the AFL's campaign against radicalism had not spared it from postwar repression, and he condemned the lack of appreciation for the AFL's role during the war. He expressed his bitter disappointment over the postwar assault on organized labor at an executive-council meeting in 1920:

The normal activities of the American labor movement are not appreciated by the men in charge of big affairs and in affairs industrial and political of our country. On the contrary, instead of receiving the support which we do not ask but receiving the consideration to which we are justly entitled, without respect to this soviet attempt to overthrow our cause and destroy our movement. We are entitled to that consideration instead of which our organizations are persecuted and prosecuted, our efforts to exercise the normal activities are outlawed or sought to be outlawed. It is not encouraging for us who are trying to do our level best for our country, our people and our movement to find that we are hunted and haunted by our own people in the United States. . . . We are in such a state that we are compelled to be engaged in fighting for our own existence in our own country than to take up constructive propositions that may be helpful in a more advanced cause for us all.[74]

Under attack domestically, Gompers also found that his approach to the Mexican Revolution put him in sharp confict with those who urged armed intervention. Aided by Senator Albert Fall's subcommittee investigation of conditions in Mexico, big oil interests whipped up a campaign of anti-Bolshevik hysteria to mobilize public support for intervention and pressure the White House into severing ties with Carranza. Some State Department officials who tolerated Carranza's nationalism during the war now joined the chorus of voices demanding a forthright resolution of the Mexican "problem."[75]

The dissolution of the corporatist wartime social contract prompted the AFL to attack the reactionary forces on domestic and international issues. Demonstrating a more independent posture in relation to capital and the state, the AFL sharply criticized the strident calls for intervention in Mexico. After conferring with Morones in New York, Murray told Gompers that the *New York Tribune, The New Republic, The Nation,* and *The Survey* pledged their editorial support in the campaign to block intervention. Morones attended the AFL convention in June 1919 as a fraternal delegate and sent a telegram later that summer to Gompers requesting help to prevent intervention. The executive council issued a declaration of concern over the Mexican crisis and criticized the use of force to resolve the problems between the United States and Mexico.[76]

Despite reports from the U.S. War Department that stressed the political links between Carranza and Morones, an "extreme radical and a Bolshevist,"[77] a deteriorating relationship with Carranza encouraged CROM leaders to form the Partido Laborista Mexicano (PLM) to promote the candidacy of Álvaro Obregón in the presidential election of 1920. CROM officials signed a secret agreement with Obregón, who challenged the candidacy of Ignacio Bonillas, Carranza's ambassador in Washington and hand-picked successor. Carranza's inability to control organized labor led him to adopt more repressive measures that cost him what little support he enjoyed in that sector. Always strained, the relationship between Carranza and labor disintegrated as the PLM provided important support for Obregón, who toppled Carranza in a military coup in the spring of 1920.[78]

Despite their criticisms of interventionist forces in 1919, AFL leaders had also lost patience with Carranza. After receiving information from Morones that Carranza intended to restrict the right to strike, the officers of the PAFL protested to the Mexican government and wrote articles in support of the CROM. Prior to Obregón's coup, a CROM representative had briefed the AFL on what was about to occur, and Gompers quickly endorsed the movement after Carranza's fall. After receiving a letter from Obregón through Morones, Gompers gave a swift vote of confidence to the new government. He urged Obregón to disavow any involvement in the killing of Carranza, who was surprised in a mountain village and slain by local guerrillas as he tried to reach Veracruz.[79]

The overthrow of Carranza marked the rise to power of Obregón Adolfo de la Huerta, and Plutarco Elías Calles—the so-called Sonoran Triangle—who dominated the politics of national reconstruction in the 1920s. All recognized the need to grant concessions to labor and the peasantry in order to broaden the social base of economic development within a capitalist framework. Their social origins and experiences in the northern state of Sonora imbued them with a pragmatic capitalist mentality and put them in closer contact with the masses. They cultivated ties with CROM leaders in an effort to defeat the radical wing of the labor movement and incorporate the officially sanctioned body of organized labor into a ruling coalition. They viewed CROM unions as mechanisms to keep labor on a leash and provide important political support in the struggle against reactionary landowners, rapacious military chieftains, and clerical forces. Despite radical rhetoric and cries of "Mexico for the Mexicans," Obregón entered office on December 1, 1920, with only a mildly reformist, nationalist agenda for economic and social development.[80]

Optimism prevailed in AFL headquarters that the assumption of power by the Sonoran revolutionaries would contribute to the success of American labor's policies in Mexico. The Sonoran blueprint for national reconstruction included a role for a nonradical movement that would encourage friendly relations with the AFL. Greater AFL-CROM cooperation would facilitate Gompers's efforts to extend AFL-style unionism throughout Latin America in order to combat radicalism and improve labor's bargaining power in the face of growing penetration by American capital.

AFL leaders concluded that Obregón would bend enough on Article 27 to accommodate the United States and remove a major source of diplomatic friction. James Lord believed that Obregón would exploit his close ties to labor and peasant organizations to garner support for diluting economic nationalism. Lord viewed Obregón as more malleable than Carranza on this issue, and he argued that a more flexible position on Article 27 would be forthcoming if the United States provided Obregón a breathing space. In a speech at Clark University, he expressed confidence that Obregón was "big enough" to "convince the people that the constitution wants changing, that some of their idealism should be set aside, and that they should do the very necessary work that needs doing." Lord also noted with approval that the Mexican labor movement had become less hostile toward foreign capital: "The Mexican worker is beginning to realize that he has unnecsarily [sic] wasted a lot of time shouting, 'salute the revolution sociale,' and 'capital is internationale,' and he is beginning to feel that the only thing that is international is labor and that if it is intelligently organized, the worker has nothing to fear, no matter from what country capital comes."[81]

The AFL did not lament the passing of Carranza, whose strong nationalist convictions and quarrels with the Mexican labor movement repeatedly irritated Gompers. Gompers was confident that the CROM would benefit from its relationship with the Obregón regime and that the new Mexican government would be friendly to the United States. Gone were the days in which he urged Mexican workers to stay clear of manipulative politicians. Gompers was convinced that Obregón, de la Huerta, and Calles would safely steer the CROM into calm ideological waters. "They are progressive, anxious to proceed as rapidly as conditions will permit toward the improvement of the life of the Mexican people," he said. "However, they give no indication of being swept off their feet by false teaching and vain hopes."[82]

4

AFL-CROM Relations and Mexican Reconstruction, 1920–1923

The overthrow of Carranza in May 1920 marked the end of the military phase of the Mexican Revolution and enabled the Sonoran architects of the coup to lay in place a corporatist infrastructure to promote national reconstruction. Deep social and political problems confronted Álvaro Obregón, Adolfo de la Huerta, and Plutarco Elías Calles, who recognized that the Revolution had politicized social forces, previously inert, whose emergent self-consciousness and aroused expectations could not be ignored. Despite the assassination of Emiliano Zapata a year earlier, a militant peasantry still pressured the government for land reform and joined Mexican workers in demanding a vigorous implementation of the Constitution of 1917. In short, the Sonorans faced a challenge from below to advance the social goals of the Revolution.[1]

Poised on the right were regional military chieftains, reactionary large landowners, and a bitter Catholic church hierarchy resentful of the Revolution's encroachments upon its power and prestige. A popular spirit of anti-imperialism complicated matters for the new leaders, who had to contend with a northern neighbor that stood perched to intervene, if necessary, to remove the threat of the Mexican Constitution's economic nationalism. Given nationalist sensitivities, Obregón, who became president in December, 1920, following the interim presidency of de la Huerta, could ill afford to appear to knuckle under to U.S. demands. Plagued by slumping silver and copper prices, massive disruptions in agriculture and industry, growing unemployment, peasant demands for land, workers' demands for higher wages, a depleted public treasury, and an international postwar recession, he could not allow the quest for political stability to alienate his social base of workers and peasants.

99

The United States withheld official diplomatic recognition in an attempt to extract written concessions exempting foreign capital from Article 27 of the Mexican Constitution. In desperate need of Amercian financial assistance, goods, and assurances that his domestic enemies would not receive support from the United States, Obregón assumed power within the context of a devastated economy, intense social conflict, American diplomatic pressure, and a world still shaken by the war and the Bolshevik Revolution. He could not ignore his northern neighbor. "In twentieth-century Mexico," writes Ramón Ruiz, "no regime stood a ghost of a chance of surviving without Washington's embrace. Until the pope in the White House conferred his benediction, no Mexican president could look to God for help."[2]

Obregón quickly capitalized on the CROM's friendship with the AFL to assure the "pope in the White House" that his movement posed no threat to the United States. He sent Morones to AFL headquarters for help in arranging a meeting in the White House to calm fears that foreign capital might be jeopardized by his government. Myron M. Parker, Obregón's legal attorney in Washington, assured the State Department's Division of Mexican Affairs that his client would provide adequate guarantees to American capital, and he escorted Morones to a meeting with the division's C. M. Johnston on May 22, 1920. Parker requested a meeting with Secretary of State Bainbridge Colby, but it was Gompers who was able to make the proper arrangements. Gompers set up an interview for Morones with Joseph Tumulty at the White House. Canuto Vargas, secretary of the PAFL, accompanied Gompers, Morones, and the latter's secretary to the White House, where Tumulty also arranged a meeting between Gompers, Morones, and Colby on May 25.[3]

Despite Obregón's assurances, the creation of a new climate that encouraged Mexican workers to organize unions and strike without fear of official repression concerned the United States. A wave of strikes during de la Huerta's brief presidential tenure prompted the U.S. government to send fourteen diplomatic notes protesting government decisions that favored labor over capital.[4] The State Department received reports from Mexico that labor militancy and radical influences threatened to unleash social revolution. The American consul at Nogales, Sonora, reported that American railroad and mine workers had visited the consulate to warn of labor unrest and growing demands for nationalization of the Southern Pacific Railroad of Mexico and the firing of American workers. Labor demonstrators in Mexico City and other industrial areas demanded enforcement of Articles 27 and 123 of the Mexican Constitution and the imposition of price controls on basic food necessities. Article 123 guaranteed the right to unionize, called for the eight-hour day and a minimum wage, urged the national government to ensure equal treatment for Mexican and foreign workers, and granted numerous other concessions to labor.[5]

The arrival of George K. Davis and other members of the IWW to counteract AFL influence in Mexico also made U.S. officials in Mexico City somewhat edgy. Fed by the interventionist campaign spearheaded by Senator Albert Fall's subcommittee investigation of Mexican affairs, jingoistic interests found a more hospitable climate in the State Department during the summer of 1920. An official in the Division of Mexican Affairs expressed the growing frustration with Mexican developments: "The policy of *laissez faire* with respect to Mexico is not always a wise one. I am convinced that we are not only justified, but morally obligated, at times, to take a direct interest in the internal affairs of our southern neighbor."[6]

AFL leaders attacked those who demanded intervention in Mexico. On the opening day of the AFL convention in the summer of 1920, the executive council criticized the "organized exploiters of the oil, mineral, timber and land values in Mexico" and affirmed support for the president's policies. The council's report charged that Senator Fall's subcommittee had "done much to destroy Latin-American faith in the American government."[7] Speaking as secretary of the Committee on International Relations, Matthew Woll continued the attack, charging that certain capitalists gained their investments through corruption and the active collusion of previous Mexican governments. Woll also pointed out that engaging in corrupt practices and deliberately defying Mexican laws deprived these capitalists of the right to call upon the U.S. government for protection.[8]

The outgoing Wilson administration, despite the fact that it had twice intervened militarily in Mexico, worried that the election of Warren G. Harding signaled a victory for the oil interventionists. President Wilson sent a letter to Secretary of State Colby on the day after the 1920 presidential election, attacking Robert Lansing, his former secretary of state, as a "snake in the grass" for lining up with the oil companies. "These are particularly dangerous interests," Wilson warned, "and are certain to lead us astray if we follow their advice in any particular. . . . Now that an administration is about to come in that will try to upset everything that we have done in Mexico, I feel particularly solicitous lest we should prepare the way for their mischief in any way."[9]

James Lord and Chester Wright went to Mexico City in early September to deliver a message of support from the AFL to de la Huerta and Obregón. They also undoubtedly discussed the upcoming PAFL convention to be held in Mexico City in January 1921. Gompers received an invitation to attend Obregón's presidential inauguration in December but did not go. He named Morones as his personal representative, instead.[10]

Before attending the PAFL convention in Mexico City, Gompers conferred with the State Department about U.S.-Mexican affairs. He later told the PAFL delegates that he urged the United States to recognize the Mexican government. According to Gompers, the State Department affirmed its support for his efforts to improve relations between the governments and the labor movements of Latin America.[11]

While in Mexico City to attend the PAFL Convention, Gompers delivered messages from President Wilson and the State Department to Obregón, with whom he had a meeting that lasted more than ninety minutes. Gompers also had conferences with de la Huerta, Calles, and Antonio Villarreal, Obregon's ministers of finance, interior, and agriculture, respectively. U.S. officials insisted that Obregón appoint a commission to meet with American representatives to draw up a treaty that would then lead to diplomatic recognition of the Mexican government. Gompers emphasized to Obregón that Article 27 was the chief stumbling block to U.S. recognition. Obregón assured Gompers that his administration would declare Article 27 unconstitutional, but he argued that Mexico should not have to formalize these guarantees in a treaty.[12]

Gompers found himself in an embarrassing position as the PAFL convention opened. At Obregón's suggestion a CROM committee had gone to Laredo to meet the AFL delegates and escort them to Mexico City in a special car. The American consul at

Laredo refused to honor the passports of Morones and Robert Haberman,[13] an American Socialist who was working with CROM leaders, and allow the CROM delegation to cross the border. Infuriated by the incident, Morones asked Gompers in his opening speech to the PAFL convention to investigate the matter. Gompers explained that the State Department had already given its approval for the CROM representatives to cross the border but failed to notify the appropriate consulate official. He stressed that the detention of CROM leaders was the work of a petty bureaucrat and not the U.S. government.[14]

Sensitive to criticisms from the Mexican left, Morones used the PAFL forum to deny that his labor organization was an appendage of the American labor movement. Mexican radicals condemned what was becoming a cozy relationship between the CROM and the AFL and derided Morones for failing to get the PAFL conference, held in Laredo in November 1918, to adopt a resolution of support for Wobblies jailed in the United States during the war. Even CROM officials privately poked fun at Gompers after the PAFL convention in Mexico City.[15]

Given the ideological jockeying for position by Mexican radicals and labor elements during the early days of Obregón's tenure, Gompers benefitted from the role of AFL socialists in the PAFL. Following the suicide of John Murray in 1919, Chester Wright, the former editor of the *New York Call* who did publicity work to promote the PAFL during the First World War, became the English-language secretary of the organization. Mother Jones also supported the AFL's policies in Mexico and attended the PAFL Convention in Mexico City. Gompers suggested that she be allowed to address the convention, and she recounted her efforts on behalf of the Mexican Revolution. After relating how Madero invited her to help organize Mexican miners at Cananea, she urged the Mexican workers to shun factionalism and focus on organizing to advance their aims within a bourgeois democratic structure:

> You are beginning to pave the way for a stable government of the people, and I want to ask you to do all you can to render all the faithful assistance you can to the noble men you have got in office now. . . . I want to tell you something: Stop this thing of throwing stones at each other; it is a horrible disease today in the labor movement. . . . Now the world was not made in a day. . . . As long as

you permit the capitalists to keep you divided, calling each other names and poisoning each other, you are going to make no progress.

Finally, she urged them to embrace the AFL:

The American Federation of Labor can do more to advance the nations to plant Christianity in the bosom of mankind than all the churches and all your institutions. . . . I know that this institution . . . is the one institution that is leading the nations upward and onward to the final goal. . . . Unite your forces, stand shoulder to shoulder. Come up here and shake hands with Mr. Gompers. Shake hands with the boys.[16]

Mother Jones's endorsement of AFL policies in Mexico flowed from a consistent philosophical position. It stressed the need to organize Mexican workers to prepare for an eventual peaceful transition to socialism while opposing those who advocated the violent overthrow of capitalism. She urged vigilance against reactionary forces, especially clerical counterrevolutionary elements. A genuine sympathy for Mexican workers guided her actions, and she believed that the AFL could play a valuable role in the fulfillment of her dream to see a socialist order in Mexico. By the same token, Gompers found her remarks to the PAFL convention quite useful as he confronted the mobilization of radical forces in Mexico.

To argue, as Philip Foner does, that Mother Jones "does not seem to have realized that one of the motivating forces behind the formation of the PAFL was the growing influence of radical unionism"[17] misses the underlying point of her position. This suggests that Gompers, CROM leaders, and Mexican officials somehow duped her into supporting the PAFL without her full cognizance of what the organization was all about. Without minimizing her contributions to the Mexican Revolution, it is important to point out that she shared the AFL's opposition to radical unionist elements that preached the violent overthrow of capitalism. Although she feared religious fanatics in Mexico, she also worried that Communists jeopardized prospects for a peaceful transition to socialism. She expressed this latter fear in a letter from Mexico to John Fitzpatrick, president of the Chicago Federation of Labor, on May 16, 1921: "we have good many so-called Communist freaks here that want to rule and dictate. God help the day that those fanatics should ever get to the helm." She added that if CROM officials could "only keep their heads level for the next few years, they will give an example to the world of what can be acquired in a peaceful manner instead of by force."[18]

Although Gompers urged Mexican workers to support Obregón's government and guard against the possibility of a reactionary armed movement, he came away from Mexico City convinced that a much more serious threat was imminent—the threat of Bolshevism. Upon returning to the United States he stepped up the campaign against radicals in Mexico. In an effort, perhaps, to put more ideological distance between the AFL and more militant unions in the United States at a time when postwar reaction spawned growing attacks on organized labor, Gompers publicized his fears about the threat of Bolshevism in Mexico in the *American Federationist*:

> The greatest danger to Mexican trade unionism is the doctrine of bolshevism. It is immaterial whether Lenine [*sic*] is actually paying propagandists in Mexico. There are those who are doing the work as well as paid agents could do it. Not the least effective of the agents of sovietism in Mexico are several young draft evaders from the United States who find it more pleasant and profitable to be in Mexico than to be in Leavenworth.[19]

Bolshevism, he warned, posed a grave threat to the Mexican labor movement, but in his view the real aim of the Communists was to subvert the American labor movement by establishing an important beachhead in Mexico.[20]

What especially frustrated Gompers was the refusal of employers to bargain with the conservative wing of the labor movement in the United States. The refusal of open-shop advocates to recognize the AFL as a legitimate representative of labor simply bred radicalism. Gompers argued that the attitudes of "autocratic employers" were synonymous with those of Lenin. "Indeed no effort is more flourishing than the hostile employers," he complained, "in the manufacture of radicals and bolshevists."[21]

Although one might be tempted to dismiss Gompers's version of falling dominoes in the Western Hemisphere as an opportunistic effort to publicize his anticommunism, labor unrest and radical ferment during the early months of 1921 did put pressure on the Mexican government and alarm U.S. officials and AFL leaders. Opposition to the CROM's conservative drift and collaboration with the Mexican government led to the formation of the Confederación

General de Trabajadores (CGT) in February. Sponsored by the Communist Federation of the Mexican Proletariat, the CGT embraced revolutionary notions of "class struggle," "libertarian communism," "rationalist education for the working class," and "direct action" to achieve "the complete emancipation of the workers and peasants." The founding anarchosyndicalist convention in Mexico City attacked the CROM's relationship with the AFL as an accommodation to U.S. imperialism. Many CGT members had formerly belonged to the Casa, and IWW elements from the United States also supported the new labor organization. The badly divided Mexican Communist Party (PCM) allied with the CGT, but ideological disputes soon prompted it to withdraw.[22]

The CGT, which had perhaps forty thousand members, was comprised mainly of streetcar and textile workers. It endorsed agrarian reform and called for an alliance of peasants and workers. CGT leaders urged a militant, uncompromising struggle against employers at the point of production and rejected cooperation with the government. They bitterly complained to Obregón about reprisals against their syndicates by military authorities. Despite government repression, the CGT maintained its commitment to revolutionary ideals and refused to sacrifice its independence in the early 1920s.[23]

Other independent unions competed with the CROM, which probably had eighty thousand members. Catholic unions enjoyed only marginal success, but they sometimes undercut CGT influence in the textile industry. Some railroad and electrical workers also remained outside the CROM. Like the CGT, however, these and other independent unions found it difficult too compete against a rival organization that enjoyed the government's blessing.[24]

Obregón doled out key political jobs to CROM leaders, who converted their organization into a pliant instrument of support for the new government. He put Morones in charge of the Ministry of Factories and appointed Celestino Gasca as mayor of the Federal District. The appointment of a CROM official to head the labor section within the Ministry of Industry, Commerce, and Labor gave the CROM considerable influence in shaping the outcome of labor-capital disputes brought to the government for resolution. It also put the CROM in an advantageous position relative to the disbursement of government funds.[25]

The CROM could count on official support for its efforts to recruit workers and defeat its rivals. Under Obregón, the state expanded its role as a referee of labor-capital disputes. Arbitration boards set up in the states to resolve industrial conflicts often ruled in favor of CROM unions. In struggles with rival unions, the CROM also benefitted from crucial state intervention on its behalf, although Obregón preferred to entrust the resolution of strikes to the CROM and local officials unless broader political and economic interests were threatened.[26]

The government expected favors in return. In their movement to win greater material benefits for workers, CROM leaders did not intend to become mere servants of the state or capital, but they did play an important role in keeping industrial peace. For example, they cooperated with Obregón to halt a strike by railroad workers in February and March of 1921, refusing to support a CGT call for a general strike. In the view of one American capitalist observer, the outcome of the railroad strike augured well for the eventual defeat of bolshevism in Mexico.[27]

Obregón used the CROM to consolidate his power at home, and he took advantage of its friendly relations with the AFL to gain an ally in the campaign to secure U.S. recognition. The Harding administration insisted on written guarantees that American property was exempt from Article 27, but Obregón devised a strategy to mobilize American public support for his government and pressure the Republican administration for recognition. He told Texas governor Pat M. Neff that he was trying to convince the Mexican masses that they had nothing to fear from American labor and other progressive groups in the United States.[28]

In the early days of his administration, therefore, Obregón adopted a policy to court the AFL, the American socialist community, and others who supported his reform efforts. A sizable segment of the American business community, eager to cash in on the opportunities for increased trade and investment, recognized the pragmatic capitalist orientation of Obregón and lobbied for U.S. recognition.[29] It was this wing of the American capitalist class whose point of view Obregón hoped would influence Harding's policies. In desperate need of financial aid and manufactured products, especially machinery and capital goods, the Mexican government thus included the AFL in a coordinated strategy to sway the Harding administration.

After Carranza's ouster, the International Association of Machinists (IAM) began to play a more prominent role in Mexico. Attracted by the reformist goals of Mexican officials—some of whom were members of the Machinists' Union—E. C. Davison and William Johnston, respectively general secretary-treasurer and president of the IAM, also recognized that the economic reconstruction of Mexico had material implications for American workers suffering from the postwar glut of goods. Mexico was heavily dependent on the importation of machinery and capital goods to advance its industrial development, and if union firms could fill the Mexican orders, overall American economic prosperity would increase. Furthermore, the bargaining position of AFL unions would improve if labor leaders brought home the orders.[30]

In a move to solidify AFL support for Obregón, Robert Haberman, who by this time had developed an important role as a liaison between the CROM and the AFL, visited AFL headquarters, where he stressed the successful efforts against communism in Mexico. He also relayed a proposal from Mexican officials to establish an industrial bureau to ensure that contracts for American goods would be negotiated only with firms endorsed by the AFL. On July 26, 1921, he told members of the PAFL executive committee that four million pesos' worth of contracts were being held up pending the conclusion of arrangements with the AFL. Citing the recent purchase of a fire apparatus from an American firm that had been endorsed as a union establishment, Haberman pointed out that the Chamber of Commerce complained to the State Department because the written order for the purchase mentioned that the agreement had been concluded with the recommendations of organized labor. He also suggested that the AFL send unionists to teach in Mexican trade schools.[31]

Intrigued by these proposals, Gompers suggested that another meeting be held at which Davison and Johnston could be present to discuss how to implement the arrangements. He also promised to solicit recommendations from Charles Moyer, president of the Mine, Mill and Smelter Workers, regarding the sending of a dependable union representative to teach scientific and applied mining in Mexico.[32]

Davison and Johnston attended the next meeting of the PAFL executive committee on August 1, 1921, to hear Haberman explain that the Mexican government had decided in January to buy in the United States only those goods bearing the union label or produced in factories and shops approved by the AFL. Haberman emphasized Mexico's dependence on imported factory goods, and he said that the proposed industrial bureau would have an advisory board to determine whether those factories bidding on Mexican contracts were fair to organized labor. The bureau would then relay this information to the Mexican government for use when placing orders in the United States.[33]

Haberman reported that an agreement to buy locomotives from the Baldwin Locomotive Company in Philadelphia had been scrapped by the Mexican government because of that firm's non-union orientation, and that Baldwin's president was on his way to Mexico in an effort to save the deal. Other lucrative contracts awaited the determination of bidding firms' attitudes toward organized labor. According to Haberman, de la Huerta, the secretary of the treasury, had control over the purchasing of goods and would appoint someone—perhaps Morones—to supervise this work.[34]

Mexican labor was clearly trying to strengthen its clout with the Obregón administration, which, in turn, was experimenting with ways to take advantage of the CROM's connections with Gompers. The proposal offered to strengthen the AFL's domestic bargaining position and enhance its role in shaping U.S.-Mexican relations. Of course, the Mexican government and top CROM officials expected the proposed bureau to encourage AFL support for U.S. recognition of Obregón. Haberman emphasized that the offer to work hand in hand with AFL leaders rested on the assumption that the AFL would continue its friendly attitude toward the Mexican government.[35]

Davison sounded a note of caution about the possibility of corruption in the proposed industrial bureau. He stressed that no commissions should be paid on the contracts. Gompers, confident that Haberman's proposal was mutually beneficial, promised that AFL leaders would conduct themselves in a way that would benefit workers and the government of Mexico. Mexican officials, he assured Haberman, would get "a dollar's worth of material for a dollar paid." Gompers added that "the service will be performed as far as possible by men who have the conscientiousness and the intelligence to organize for their own and for the mutual protection of themselves and the people of our country and Mexico."[36]

These discussions came at a time when the Harding adminis-

tration was reaching out to AFL leaders in an effort to institutionalize a working relationship between national policymakers and
American labor. Despite tensions between Republicans and the
labor movement, there were elements in the Republican Party that
did not want to alienate the AFL altogether.[37] On July 18, 1921,
Gompers held a conference with President Harding to discuss unemployment, amnesty for political prisoners, the upcoming Washington Conference on the limitation of naval armaments, and the
appointment of William J. Burns as director of the Bureau of Investigation. Gompers urged the president to grant political amnesty
to Eugene V. Debs, stressing that political prisoners in other countries involved in the world war had been released and that the free-
ing of Debs would eliminate the socialists' most effective propaganda tool, since Debs was a symbol of martyrdom to the Socialist
Party. Gompers requested labor representation on the American
delegation to the Washington conference and later received an appointment to the advisory committee.[38]

On the day of Gompers's conference in the White House, Davison and Haberman met with the Bureau of Investigation's J. Edgar
Hoover to provide information on Mexico and the AFL's policies
there. Davison had just returned from Mexico, where he attended
a CROM convention in Orizaba and met with Obregón, de la
Huerta, and other Mexican officials. He told Hoover that one of
Haberman's chief duties as a member of the IAM was to provide
American labor leaders with information on radicals in Mexico. Although Davison offered to put the IAM's services at the bureau's
disposal whenever needed, he attacked the moral character of
American representatives in Mexico, especially consuls and subordinate officials who displayed a fondness for lavish parties and
heavy drinking. He stressed the conservative character of the
Obregón government, which had placed orders through him for
railroad cars and machinery that he hoped to fill through the
IAM.[39]

Attorney General Harry Daugherty, the Harding administration's most outspoken advocate of an anti-union policy, called
Gompers to his office on July 27, 1921. Daugherty told Gompers
that he intended to reorganize the Bureau of Investigation to prevent some of the unwarranted snooping that it had done in the
past. He assured Gompers that he did not want to appoint anyone

to head the Bureau who was antagonistic to the AFL. Although Gompers flatly opposed the appointment of Burns, whom he regarded as a threat to civil liberties, he stressed that his relationship with members of the Harding administration was as cordial, if not more so, than with any previous administration. Gompers assured Daugherty that despite his efforts to prevent Harding's election, he was anxious to serve the new government and see its success. The discussions were cordial, and Daugherty interjected at one point, "I call you Sam and you call me Harry. That's the way I feel."[40]

Thus, despite tensions between organized labor and the Harding administration over domestic policies, Machinists' Union officials offered to cooperate with the Justice Department against communism in Mexico. The material incentives that the Mexican government dangled in front of American labor leaders strengthened an AFL policy that called for change in Mexico within a capitalist framework. AFL leaders were confident that the clientelist relationship between the CROM and the Mexican government would produce material benefits for Mexican workers and diminish the threat of communism. They were also apparently satisfied that Obregón's attitudes toward the United States and his proposed method of dealing with Article 27 offered sufficient protection to foreign capital to make U.S. intervention unnecessary.

Encouraged by top CROM officials, Obregón cracked down on the left and deported several radicals, including some Americans, as the struggle between the CROM and the CGT intensified.[41] Although the Harding administration welcomed the crackdown, it wanted further assurances that Article 27 would not jeopardize American interests. Col. Harvey W. Miller, the acting military attaché at the American embassy in Mexico City, expressed faith in Obregón's position on Article 27 and urged diplomatic recognition. Obregón told Miller that he needed U.S. recognition in order to consolidate his government and that the United States would be partly to blame if Bolshevism made any significant headway in Mexico.[42]

Despite Miller's recommendations and similar advice from various quarters, the State Department resisted pressures to recognize Obregón. Secretary of Commerce Herbert Hoover sent Secretary of State Charles E. Hughes a copy of a letter that he had received from a friend who had done business for many years with mining interests in Mexico and who knew Obregón and Joe Polin, the Mexican president's brother-in-law. Hoover's friend J. B. Rice underscored Obregón's fear that domestic political foes would brand him as "pro-gringo" and topple his government if he signed a treaty to ensure the safety of American capital in Mexico. Rice said that Obregón was unhappy with radical members of his cabinet but was afraid to dismiss them without having first secured recognition and moral support lest a revolution should break out. Rice told Hoover that withholding U.S. recognition could spark a revolution in Mexico and possibly usher into power someone less friendly to the United States. In response to the message Hoover sent, Hughes stood firm: "I have read the letter with interest, but I should say to you that there are a large number of persons of importance who have had for many years intimate acquaintance with affairs in Mexico and large interests in Mexico, and they hold diametrically opposite views with regard to what should be done." [43]

The Obregón administration appealed to American capitalists who favored a more progressive investment and trade policy in Mexico. Mexican officials emphasized that increased American trade and investment could help solve problems of overproduction in the United States, create jobs, and enhance American economic prosperity. Luis Montes de Oca, the Mexican consul general in El Paso, addressed a meeting of the Tri-State Association of Credit Men and pointed out how closer economic ties with Mexico would benefit the United States. "If the stability of the immense American manufacturing industries is to be preserved, and if the surplus of American capital is to be given generous and profitable investment," he said, "the United States must face the problem of her foreign trade, and see that it is developed to the fullest extent through the creation and fostering of new markets. . . . In Mexico you can sell almost anything that your industries manufacture and buy whatever raw materials your factories need." [44]

Montes de Oca stressed that the United States should seize the opportunity to capture important Mexican markets that might otherwise be grabbed by England or Germany. "The construction of railroads in Mexico would furnish work for your factories in the making of locomotives, cars, rails and other necessary material," he said. New railroad lines in Mexico would also open up new markets for the United States and facilitate the importation of Mexican raw materials. Mexican oil would supply American industries, and Mexican gold and silver would benefit American mints. Montes de Oca noted that these developments would "insure work to thousands of workmen and employees in the United States, would safeguard the salaries of executives and office forces all over your country, would keep your railroads occupied with freight movements and would swell your banking transactions, all going to increase and preserve the prosperity of the American people."[45]

Sharing the podium with Montes de Oca was Zach Lamar Cobb, a former U.S. customs collector at El Paso and advisor on Mexico with the War Trade Board, who urged the United States to break the diplomatic deadlock with Mexico. He emphasized that greater understanding of Mexican people and customs would benefit American exporters, and he recommended better cooperation to develop progressive investment strategies that would expand American trade with Mexico. "There has been a tendency for American investment interests in Mexico to be considered to the exclusion of our commercial interests," he complained. "This is wrong in principle. The two should go hand in hand. American investments in that country should increase trade between the two countries. There should be no rivalry between the two."[46]

Obregón hoped that a more enlightened view of Mexican nationalism would shape U.S. policy toward his government, but he faced a serious challenge in the summer of 1921 from disgruntled oil barons who resisted the imposition of higher export taxes and feared radicalism in the oil fields around Tampico. Calles had toured the oil region that spring and complained about the deplorable living conditions of oil workers. In an interview with the English-language newspaper *The Mexican Post*, he pointed out that despite the seemingly high wages, the plight of workers in the oil region could not be worse because of the high cost of living and unsanitary conditions. He alleged that at least thirty thousand workers were disabled every six months, and he urged oil workers to organize. He called on the companies to pay the new export tax and provide better living quarters, schools, and medical facilities for their workers. Calles also complained about the activities of lawyers and individuals known as *coyotes* who used unscrupulous means to gobble up land in the oil region. He emphasized that he intended to revise the titles of all the oil companies and land-owners, since the existing contracts violated Article 27.[47]

The new oil decree, which Obregón issued on June 7, 1921, set an export tax of 25 percent and triggered a swift confrontation be-tween the oil companies and the Mexican government.[48] The American consul in Tampico notified the secretary of state on June 30 that the oil companies had ordered the suspension of shipments beginning July 1 on account of the new tax. Expecting labor unrest and agitation, the consul urged "reasonable precautions" against anticipated reprisals against American interests.[49]

The appearance of two American warships off the coast of Tam-pico heightened U.S.-Mexican tensions and provided an opportu-nity for the AFL to lobby against American intervention. Gompers received a telegram from E. C. Davison and John (José) Kelly, who were attending a CROM convention in Orizaba as representatives of the IAM. Davison and Kelly asked him to protest the dispatch of ships to intimidate labor unions in Tampico. Gompers complied with their request. He wrote to Secretary of State Hughes asking that he or the secretary of the navy issue a statement that the ships were not sent to interfere in a labor dispute. "It is a fair inference that the fact that the warships of our navy are now at Tampico," Gompers complained to Hughes, "is being exploited by the em-ploying interests there to the effect that these war vessels are at Tampico for the avowed purpose of overawing the workers who are now engaged in a lockout imposed upon them."[50] Hughes assured Gompers that "the presence of the ships has nothing whatever to do with labor unions to which Mr. Davison refers in his telegram or with disputes between employers and employees, but is simply a precautionary measure for the purpose of assuring adequate pro-tection to the lives and property of American citizens."[51]

Although Hughes quickly ordered the withdrawal of the ships, it is unlikely that Gompers's letter influenced the decision. A more likely explanation emerges from a letter in which Hughes told Pres-ident Harding that the presence of the ships off the coast of Tam-pico risked entangling the United States prematurely in a conflict that could have been avoided. Hughes stressed that the ships could always return, if necessary, and he warned that elements in

Mexico might be tempted to provoke an incident and force American intervention.[52]

Gompers sent a telegram to Orizaba transmitting Hughes's reply to the AFL's request. The CROM convention greeted the reading of his telegram with applause and cheers of "Viva Gompers." It is important to note, however, that Gompers had not pressed Hughes for an unqualified renunciation of the right of the U.S. government to intervene in Mexico—a fact that did not go unnoticed in Mexico. Editorials in the Mexico City newspaper *El Heraldo* on July 9 and 12, 1921, pointed out that the secretary of state's response to Gompers did not go far enough to repudiate the use of American troops to protect American capital. Although *El Heraldo* noted the AFL's limitations as an anti-interventionist force, it praised the role of Davison, Kelly, and Gompers and acknowledged that such working-class solidarity would make U.S. policymakers reflect before acting in the future.[53]

Morones urged Gompers to publicize the CROM's protest over Mexico's exclusion from the Washington Conference on Disarmament, which opened on November 11, 1921. Insistent that discussions relative to Mexico's economic affairs, especially the petroleum issue, should not be conducted without formal Mexican representation at the conference, he told Gompers that Mexico feared becoming another Belgium in the event of a war between the United States and Japan. Gompers and other PAFL officers had earlier urged CROM members to conduct a demonstration showing support for world disarmament, but Morones was apparently more concerned with what Gompers could do as a member of the conference's advisory committee to protest the slight against Mexico. IAM officials also received copies of Morones's letter of protest. The CROM's unhappiness prompted Davison to urge Gompers to inform Morones of the AFL's support, "as well as to relieve his mind from the element of suspicion that seems to dwell therein regarding the intent and purposes of the Limitation of Armaments Conference."[54]

Gompers, Lord, Vargas, and Wright met with Harding on December 2, 1921, to relay the CROM's protest. Gompers told Morones that the president described his speculation about a war between the United States and Japan as "very farfetched." Gompers said that Harding assured him that the point of conflict between Obregón and the U.S. government was simply a procedural one. However, the president reiterated the official position, demanding that Obregón sign a treaty to provide the necessary guarantees to American interests.[55]

Throughout the early 1920s the Mexican government took steps to placate foreign capital without putting these concessions in the form of a treaty. As Mexican officials had assured AFL leaders, the Supreme Court issued five consecutive rulings in favor of the oil companies by 1922. De la Huerta, as Minister of Finance and Public Credit, also negotiated an agreement with the International Bankers Committee on Mexico to renew service on Mexico's foreign debt in September 1922.[56]

Despite these accommodations, Obregón still could not secure formal U.S. recognition. Pressures mounted, nevertheless, for a change in American policy. Even President Harding became impatient with the State Department. He told Secretary of State Hughes that "unless we make some progress in the near future . . . we ought to contrive to let Latin-America and the world know, simply and definitely, why there is no resumption of former friendly relations with the Mexican Republic."[57]

The State Department refused to change course, but the AFL had developed enough confidence in the Obregón administration by the summer of 1922 to pass resolutions endorsing U.S. recognition and attacking capitalists for trying to mold U.S. policy in Mexico to suit their narrow interests. Gompers sent Secretary of State Hughes copies of the resolutions adopted by the AFL Convention. The resolutions praised the Mexican government's compliance with the basic precepts of international relations, its commitment to protect American property and lives, and its sponsoring of progressive social welfare and humanitarian legislation. Gompers stressed to Hughes that withholding U.S. recognition only played into the hands of Obregón's domestic enemies.[58]

In contrast to the AFL's optimistic assessment of the Mexican government, State Department fears about the spread of radicalism intensified during the summer of 1922. Department officials were more skittish about the Mexican government's efforts to incorporate workers and peasants into the political structure, even if those efforts involved social concessions that were often more rhetorical than real. Fears of Calles were especially acute. The American chargé d'affaires in Mexico City told Matthew Hanna, chief of the Division of Mexican Affairs, that reports led him to believe that "possibly there is something in the reported Soviet intent of Calles."[59]

Numerous reports that linked Calles to bolshevism stressed the weakness of the Obregón government, and compared conditions in Mexico to those in Russia during the spring and summer of 1917 came across desks in the State Department. So alarmed were some American consuls in Mexico that they lost faith in the will of Mexican businessmen to protect their own class interests and face the radical threat squarely. This frustration occasionally degenerated into a bitter denunciation of Mexicans in general. Thomas Bowman, the consul in Monterrey, made no effort to disguise his profound disgust with wealthy, educated Mexicans:

> I have often observed in my reports that this class of Mexicans invariably submitted supinely to abuse of their just rights; in forced loans, exorbitant taxes and other forms of robbery by use of official authority, without making any effort in opposition. But I had believed that enough patriotism existed among them to impel them to exhibit disgust, in private at least, at an insult to their national flag and personal resentment at attacks upon their clergy and themselves as a class.
>
> Whenever a revolutionary crisis has occurred in the parts of Mexico where I have been stationed the men of the wealthy class have not failed to appeal to my office for help in protecting them against summary action and their property against reprisals. But I have never known one of them to exhibit a modicum of courage in defending his rights not even to the extent of going on record publicly as opposed to such abuse.
>
> I confess to have grown entirely out of sympathy with all classes of Mexicans. The *peon* has at least the mitigating fact of ignorance for an excuse of his folly; the revolutionist at least risks his life and liberties in obtaining his spoils; but the men of the educated class, the business element, have neither ignorance, courage nor patriotism to their credit.
>
> If the lower classes are favorably impressed by communistic ideas there is no reason why they cannot repeat the history of Russia here if they can but find competent leaders.[60]

The American consul general in Mexico City became so distraught over conditions that he suggested to Hughes that the U.S. government encourage a coup to oust Obregón. In his view, foreign diplomatic recognition of Obregón would simply accelerate the sovietization of Mexico. A coup, he concluded, was the only way to forestall the triumph of Mexican communism.[61]

The AFL's policies in Mexico often came under fire from the same elements in the State Department that regarded Obregón's government as a transitional stage to communism. The consul general in Mexico City criticized Gompers's backing of the Obregón-Calles forces,[62] and William Blocker, the consul at Piedras Negras, condemned the growing CROM-AFL alliance. Blocker complained to the secretary of state that AFL and CROM representatives were discussing plans to organize workers on both sides of the border. The labor leaders were investigating the possibility of locating railroad shops in Piedras Negras and Eagle Pass that would provide opportunities to workers from both countries. The implications of such efforts were unpalatable to the American consul. Blocker complained that the AFL and the CROM were "dictating to the National Railways of Mexico, as to just where such shops are to be placed and proposed sizes thereof."[63]

When railroad workers went on strike in the United States in August 1922, Mexican workers staged demonstrations in the capital to express solidarity. George Summerlin, the American chargé d'affaires, reported that numerous red and black flags and banners hailing the Third International were unfurled by demonstrators. He also noted that employees of the Mexican National Railways in Nuevo Laredo launched a strike in support of the striking American railroad workers. Gompers wrote a letter asking CROM leaders to discourage Mexicans from going to the United States to act as strikebreakers. The Mexican consul general in San Antonio issued a plea to Mexicans there not to "scab" on the American railroads, and Mexican railway unions sent money to aid the strikers.[64]

By the summer of 1922, Obregón's strategy of using the AFL to influence American public opinion had drawn criticism from conservative quarters in Mexico. An editorial in the Mexico City newspaper *Excelsior* praised Obregón's desire to promote economic development by coming to terms with the United States, but it disagreed with the methods that he was using to try to win diplomatic recognition. The editorial criticized Obregón for shunning traditional diplomatic procedures to work out international agreements, and it complained that efforts by Mexican officials to court American labor were based on the misguided notion that a powerful wave of "socialistic" opinion would sweep the United States and force diplomatic recognition. It questioned whether the AFL's commitment to the Mexican government was, in fact, genuine. It noted that the "Yankee socialists" were too weak to confront their own government or respond effectively to the repression of workers and radicals in the United States. "There you have our allies of yankee land," the editorial concluded. "There you have those who defend us against the imperialism of Harding and the capitalism of Wall Street. Has it not been fully demonstrated that we have nothing to hope for from the labor organizations of the United States?"[65]

CROM leaders and the Mexican government also tried to cultivate support in Europe. Ricardo Treviño visited Italy, France, and Switzerland as a CROM representative in 1922, and contacted leaders of the International Federation of Trade Unions (IFTU) in Amsterdam. Commissioned by the Mexican government, Morones attended the IFTU congress in 1922 and urged European labor leaders to visit Mexico as CROM's guests. However, the CROM did not enter into a formal relationship with the IFTU.[66]

It is likely, as suggested by Nick Buford, Morones's biographer, that the CROM would have joined the IFTU had the AFL endorsed such action. There was concern in AFL headquarters over the CROM's contacts with European labor organizations. At a meeting of the PAFL executive committee on April 25, 1923, Chester Wright read a clipping from the *New York Call* which stated that IFTU officials from Amsterdam planned to meet with CROM leaders in Mexico City in September. Gompers instructed Canuto Vargas to write the CROM's secretary for more information on the proposed conferences.[67]

Morones also tried to visit the Soviet Union in late 1922 but was refused a passport by the Soviet embassy in Berlin. The CROM's ties with the AFL were a factor in the Soviet Union's snubbing of Morones. Articles critical of the CROM appeared in *Pravda*, and the Third International circulated literature in Mexico that attacked the PAFL and the AFL as instruments of American imperialism.[68]

In the spring of 1923 Calles proposed launching a campaign in conjunction with the AFL to generate favorable publicity for Mexico. He asked John Kelly, an organizer for the Machinists' Union who was working in Mexico, to discuss the subject with

Gompers and William Johnston, president of the IAM. In April meetings with Gompers and PAFL secretaries Vargas and Wright, Kelly discussed plans for the campaign and recommended that Mexico establish a fund in the United States to underwrite labor's publicity efforts. He said that Gompers and Johnston would be in charge of the campaign and that Gompers should appoint a board of trustees to supervise the fund if the Mexican government agreed to provide the money. Vargas suggested that in order to pressure Obregón for swift action on the matter, the plan should mention a specific sum of money. The AFL leaders decided that the campaign, if launched, should not mention the current diplomatic impasse between the United States and Mexico. They drafted a letter to Calles and enclosed the suggested plan, which contained the signatures of Gompers, Wright, Vargas, Johnston, Kelly, and E. C. Davison.[69]

Before such plans could be implemented, however, AFL leaders learned that the United States and Mexico had agreed to hold formal talks in Mexico City in an effort to break the diplomatic deadlock. In another conference on April 25, 1923, Gompers, Wright, Vargas, and Kelly discussed whether the publicity campaign was still necessary in light of these developments. They decided to send the previously drafted letter to Calles, since the object of the campaign was to promote a greater understanding of Mexico among American workers, regardless of the formal diplomatic status between Mexico and the United States. Kelly assured the others that Calles agreed that political recognition was secondary to the need to foster the good will of American people. Wright suggested that the AFL lobby for representation on the U.S. commission to Mexico. Gompers agreed to try to arrange a meeting with Secretary of State Hughes to request the appointment of a labor representative to the commission.[70]

Hughes refused to grant Gompers an interview and told him on the phone that a labor representative would not be appointed to the commission. At Vargas's suggestion the PAFL executive committee sent a telegram to Calles suggesting that the Mexican government invite James Lord to Mexico City during the Mexican-American negotiations and subsidize his trip. The telegram stressed that Lord's presence would be beneficial to the Mexican and American commissioners. Gompers then notified Lord to expect an invitation from Mexico City and enclosed credentials for the trip.[71]

Domestic political considerations encouraged Obregón to reach an accommodation with the United States. The campaign to determine his successor was about to get underway, and diplomatic recognition would pave the way for loans to buy weapons if an armed rebellion occurred. The assassination of Pancho Villa on July 20, 1923, suggested that the upcoming presidential campaign might be turbulent.[72]

Despite continuing gloomy reports from American consuls in Mexico regarding the alleged radical drift of the Mexican government,[73] the State Department adopted a more flexible position to resolve outstanding differences and grant diplomatic recognition to Obregón. The Bucareli Conferences, which ended on August 15, 1923, led to U.S. recognition of Obregón, who gave verbal assurances that Article 27 was nonretroactive. According to the agreements reached in Mexico City, Americans who lost lands in Mexico would receive compensation, and the Mexican government would create a special commission to determine claims submitted for such losses. Although denied formal participation in the Bucareli Conferences, James Lord went to Mexico City, where he met with top officials of the Mexican government to discuss ways to promote greater understanding between American and Mexican workers. His efforts to promote labor's viewpoint informally to the Mexican and American delegates to the conferences ended, however, when he suffered a nervous breakdown in Mexico City around the middle of June.[74]

William Appleman Williams has written that "it took a great deal of fancy footwork on the part of Obregón before he could get close enough to whisper the difference between Mexican nationalism and Marxist socialism into Washington's ear."[75] Such "fancy footwork" included assurances that foreign capital would enjoy a stable political climate that guaranteed property rights. National sensitivities dictated, however, that such assurances be given in a manner that respected Mexico's sovereignty. Although labor-capital cooperation in the formulation of U.S. policy toward Mexico had weakened with Republicans in the White House, Obregón calculated that Gompers and progressive sectors of the American capitalist class could persuade the Harding administration to develop a more enlightened conception of his policies.[76]

By September 1923 Gompers could look upon his Mexican policies with a great deal of satisfaction. His support of the Sonoran wing of the Revolution rested on the belief that Obregón would nurture a conservative labor movement friendly to the AFL, promote progressive economic policies, check the threat of radicalism, and dilute revolutionary nationalism enough to eliminate Article 27 as a source of friction with the United States. Gompers recognized that political pressures and nationalist sensitivities made it difficult for Obregón to repudiate Article 27 in a formal treaty. To do so would expose Obregón to charges from Mexican radicals that he had knuckled under to American pressure. The United States finally accepted Obregón's promise that Article 27 was nonretroactive, and shortly after granting recognition to Obregón, the State Department sent Gompers a message thanking him for his efforts to promote the establishment of diplomatic relations. Gompers received similar messages from Obregón and CROM leaders.[77]

American business interests recognized Gompers's role in the campaign to improve relations with Mexico. The El Paso Chamber of Commerce invited him as the chief honored guest to address a meeting in late October 1923. Sharing the speaker's platform with Gompers was Enrique D. Ruiz, Mexico's consul general in El Paso. In the audience were twenty-one businessmen from Norway, Sweden, Finland, and Denmark, who had been invited by the Obregón government to visit Mexico to explore investment opportunities. They listened to welcoming addresses from the president of the local chamber and Consul Ruiz and then heard Gompers introduced as the "man who saved the labor movement of Europe from going red."[78]

Gompers briefed the business audience on what to expect in Mexico. He warned them to banish any thoughts about exploiting "slave" or "peón" labor. He underscored the progressive views of Mexican government officials and stressed that the partnership between organized labor and "forward-looking" businessmen heralded a new era for Mexico. Any capitalist who wanted to invest there must realize that to take advantage of the tremendous opportunities required the adoption of fair standards that recognized the dignity of Mexican people. Gompers noted that since the Revolution had brought many improvements, he could now endorse the flow of foreign capital into Mexico. "There was a time under my observation, in Mexico," he said, "when I should have advised any man who respects himself and those he represents in any European country—I would have advised him to keep away from Mexico, which was under a regime that was practically a dictatorship and under which the people in that then unhappy country labored. God Speed the men in this mission now!"[79]

5

Labor's Role in the de la Huerta
Rebellion and Election of Calles

Following the Bucareli Conferences, the AFL and the Republican administration found their official policies toward Obregón in harmony for the first time. Diplomatic recognition of Obregón, however, did not eliminate the lingering fears of U.S. officials about labor militancy and radicalism in Mexico. Recognizing that AFL leaders were working to defeat Mexican radicalism did not erase skepticism about the AFL-CROM relationship. In a "Special Report on Mexico," Louis DeNette, an agent from the Bureau of Investigation, acknowledged Obregón's successful campaign to promote political stability, but he worried that the Revolution's politicization of the masses could yet present problems for the United States. He pointed out that agrarian reform laws, minimum wage statutes, and other reform measures implemented in various Mexican states had helped to unleash "a reign of strikes, labor wars, lockouts, destruction of property and general lawlessness."[1]

Obregón's use of "placating phraseology" to win the support of some landowners and industrialists did not erase DeNette's fears about the close relationship between the CROM and the Mexican government. DeNette worried that Mexican officials, by supporting organized labor, might inadvertently encourage Mexican workers to demand deeper change that was unacceptable to the United States. AFL leaders backed Calles as Obregón's successor, but DeNette shared the skepticism about Calles that was prevalent within the administration. "It has been stated by some competent observers," he noted, "that Calles' apparent bolshevik attitude is not his real sentiments, and that if he is ever elevated to the presidency he will be found to be an ultraconservative. This may be a fact, but his history and more recent actions do not so indicate."[2]

Obregón's ability to gain U.S. recognition and the backing of the

AFL paid off as the campaign to determine his successor heated up in the fall of 1923. When Obregón picked Calles over Finance Minister de la Huerta to follow him into the National Palace, he discovered the fragility of the unity within the Sonoran Revolutionary family. Obregón accepted the resignation of his minister of finance about a month after the Bucareli Conferences and stepped up his attacks on de la Huerta's alleged mismanagement of the treasury when de la Huerta accepted the presidential nomination of the Partido Cooperatista Nacional (PCN) on November 23, 1923.[3] The bitter presidential campaign, which gave birth to a military uprising led by de la Huerta in December 1923, had important implications for the Mexican labor movement and AFL leaders.

Following the establishment of diplomatic relations between the United States and Mexico, Gompers had two pressing objectives in Mexico: to forestall a CROM alliance with the IFTU, and to mobilize support for the election of Calles. At his suggestion, the PAFL executive committee held conferences with CROM leaders in El Paso in late October 1923. During those meetings Gompers discussed these topics and plans to hold a PAFL convention in 1924.

AFL leaders had been concerned over the relationship between the IFTU and the CROM since Morones attended the IFTU's Congress in 1922. The PAFL executive committee expressed concern in April 1923 over press reports that Amsterdam officials planned to hold discussions with CROM leaders in Mexico City later that year. John W. Brown, an IFTU representative, attended the AFL convention in October 1923 and increased this concern when he told Gompers that he was on his way to Mexico. After arriving in Mexico City, Brown sent Gompers a letter indicating that tentative arrangements had been made for a party of European trade union leaders to arrive in Mexico at the end of January 1924. Suggesting that Gompers join them for discussions, he said that the AFL could communicate its reply through Robert Haberman.[4]

Gompers put CROM members on the defensive at the El Paso conferences in October 1923 by immediately raising the issue of the IFTU's efforts to cultivate friendly ties with Mexican labor. He began by explaining why the AFL refused to affiliate with the IFTU after the First World War. The principle that a majority vote would be "sufficient to enforce in all countries whatever action was taken" infringed upon the AFL's autonomy within the IFTU. Gompers complained that the IFTU was spending too much money to promote general strikes on May 1 of each year. "The A.F. of L.," he told CROM members, "rather than furnish money to propagate general strikes will spend it for the benefit of the American labor movement." [5]

Haberman and the other Mexican labor representatives expressed surprise when Gompers produced Brown's letter. Samuel Yúdico assured Gompers that the CROM agreed with his analysis of the European labor movement, and he downplayed the significance of IFTU overtures toward the CROM:

> I want to report that Mr. Morones on his trip to Europe visited Spain, France, Germany, Austria and England. During all the talks he had with the leaders of the labor movements of those countries Mr. Morones arrived at the conclusion that no one had any idea of what was going on in the American labor movement. That is why he asked them to come as observers. That was the only and sole object, to come here as tourists. All they know about Mexico is Villa. In spite of all that ignorance they attempt to be the leaders of labor of the entire world. Only after an explanation of the Mexican labor movement by Mr. Morones did they take any interest. Mr. Morones because of close connection with the Mexican and American Federation of Labor extended the invitation to include the Pan-American Federation of Labor. We lament the letter of Mr. Brown. It is premature. The Mexican Federation of Labor had in hand the matter of meeting the European labor officials. It would be a very sad thing if Mr. Gompers would not be there. We must have him there. [6]

In response, Gompers thanked Yúdico for the invitation to attend the meetings with European labor leaders in Mexico but said that he would not call a special meeting of the executive council to consider the invitation. He sharpened his attacks on the IFTU. Irritated by what he regarded as an intrusion by the IFTU into the AFL's sphere of influence, he denounced the "faulty" conceptions that European labor leaders had of the Western Hemisphere. He noted the great strides made by Mexican labor without the help of European labor leaders, who, he said, had "dissipated their energies by trying to gain control of the state." He complained that Brown and others were trying to undermine the labor movements in the Western Hemisphere, and remarked that it was "presumptuous for a man to come from another part of the world and seek to call a convention of labor on this continent." Accusing European labor leaders of trying to poison relations between the AFL and the CROM, Gompers sneered, "They think that they will be able to induce the labor movements of Mexico, Central America and the United States to go along with them and make them believe they can benefit them by putting a ballot in the ballot box once in three or four years."[7]

The CROM members responded by also criticizing European labor movements and Europe in general. Fernando Rodarte commented that European conditions were deplorable and told Gompers that during a trip to Europe he discovered that European labor leaders simply wanted to make the CROM a "satellite." This, he explained, prompted Morones to tell the Europeans that they had little to offer the Mexican labor movement. Rodarte stressed that Morones told these men that they could not give speeches or call conferences while in Mexico, that they were nothing more than tourists![8]

Gompers emerged from these conferences confident that the IFTU would not gain a foothold in Mexico. Especially gratifying were the assurances given by the CROM's Reynaldo Cervantes Torres, who promised that no action would be taken to undermine the AFL's relationship with the Mexican labor movement, that the CROM would continue to be, in effect, a satellite of the AFL. He emphasized that the CROM would not align with any other labor movement without first consulting the AFL. "We send an observer to the International Federation of Trade Unions to let them know what we are doing," he said, "but we would not affiliate with Amsterdam, Moscow or any other movement."[9]

The subject of Calles's presidential candidacy surfaced during the conferences. Yúdico conveyed a complimentary message from Calles to Gompers, who left no doubt as to which Mexican presidential candidate he endorsed. Gompers stressed that it was the CROM's "duty" to work for Calles. "If I were a citizen of Mexico," he told the CROM representatives, "if I had the right, I would enter the campaign with every energy to help in his election."[10] Asked by Cervantes Torres to endorse Calles in writing, Gompers wrote a letter to Morones in which he expressed his support for Calles and noted that arrangements had been concluded at the conferences to hold the next PAFL convention in Mexico City in

December 1924. He told Morones that he looked forward to being in Mexico City to witness the inauguration of Calles.[11]

CROM leaders and local officials hosted a social gathering in Juárez, Mexico, after the conferences in El Paso. Gompers, who had been invited as the guest of honor to sit in the mayor's chair in the city hall of Juárez, addressed a mass meeting to praise the Mexican labor movement. "The development has been not only in the economic power which the Mexican people have brought about," he said, "but the exercise of their political power to bring into the presidency such a man as Obregón." Underscoring his own contributions to the Mexican Revolution, Gompers emphasized the PAFL's commitment to the struggle for freedom and democracy and urged the audience to elect Calles to preserve the political gains made under Obregón:

> People who know me know I am an evolutionist rather than a revolutionist. But I take this opportunity to say on Mexican soil, as I have said in the United States, that I am against tyranny, brutality and autocracy. Rather than those I would encourage revolution. . . . If you fail in your duty, if you forget your own responsibility and reactionaries get in the saddle, where do you think your rights will go? When reaction is in the saddle men who believe in freedom and justice must retire to the background. In private only may they aspire for freedom and justice. When freedom loving men are in office reactionaries must conspire in secret to destroy justice.[12]

Gompers's endorsement of Calles on Mexican soil stirred controversy in the Mexican presidential campaign. The Mexico City newspaper *Excelsior* attacked his meddling in the campaign and scolded Calles for denouncing the activities of oil interests in the campaign while failing to repudiate American labor's actions. Gompers defended his policies and reaffirmed his support of Calles, emphasizing to the American press that Mexican workers backed Calles wholeheartedly.[13]

The assassination of Pancho Villa in the late summer of 1923 foreshadowed the turbulent course of the campaign to determine Obregón's successor. Opposition to Calles came from different quarters. Many critics charged that Calles had masterminded the assassination to prevent Villa from coming out of retirement to support de la Huerta's presidential candidacy.[14] Nationalists complained that the Obregón-Calles regime undermined Mexico's sovereignty by capitulating to American oil interests in the Bucareli

Agreements. Many wealthy landowners and Catholic leaders who feared a more radical drift under Calles backed de la Huerta, who also received the support of regional military chieftains whose prerogatives were threatened by federal budgetary cutbacks. Several former members of Obregón's Cabinet endorsed de la Huerta. Within two weeks after de la Huerta accepted the presidential nomination of the PCN, his advisors convinced him that a military revolt was necessary to prevent the "imposition" of Calles. Overcoming his earlier opposition to a military struggle, de la Huerta fled to Veracruz, where he assumed the title of "Supreme Chief of the Revolution."[15]

Although many reactionary elements joined the de la Huerta Rebellion, which broke out on December 7, 1923, the complexities of the movement, as Barry Carr points out, suggest that it was more than simply a "putsch." Salvador Alvarado, Rafael Zubarán Capmany, and Antonio Villarreal, all of whom had previously friendly contacts with Gompers, were among those rebels who could legitimately tout their commitment to social reforms. The cozy relationship between Obregón and CROM leaders alienated independent labor organizations. Railroad workers and sectors of the CGT, including important leaders such as Rosendo Salazar and José Escobedo, supported de la Huerta's movement. Disaffected labor elements were fed up with the corruption and opportunism of CROM leaders, meager economic gains, and official persecution of independent labor organizations. They hoped to get a better deal from de la Huerta, who had cultivated the support of railway unions since his interim presidency in 1920. The rebellion enjoyed support even among some of the state organizations of CROM affiliates. Although the Mexican Communist Party had received a subsidy from de la Huerta and promised to back him in case of a revolt, the PCM, at the urging of its new president, Bertram Wolfe, changed its position to support the Obregón-Calles organization during the rebellion.[16]

CROM leaders quickly called on the AFL for help. Morones linked the survival of the CROM and the PAFL to the defeat of de la Huerta.[17] AFL leaders interpreted the collusion of anarchosyndicalist forces and counterrevolutionaries in the rebellion as a conspiracy against democracy in Mexico. The PAFL executive council quickly publicized its support for the Mexican government and denounced the "powerful extreme reactionaries and a small group of extreme revolutionists of the communist or bolshevist type, a combination which is curious but not entirely unnatural."[18]

How to reconcile the diverse political tendencies in his movement posed a serious obstacle for de la Huerta, who tried to assure U.S. officials that he would protect American interests and persuade AFL leaders that he was prolabor. De la Huerta and his representatives unsuccessfully appealed to Gompers for aid. Jorge Prieto Laurens, de la Huerta's chief publicity agent, told Gompers that "the object of this movement is the socialization of the land and of the instruments of production."[19]

To underscore the duplicity of *delahuertista* propagandists, Gompers noted that other rebel agents attacked the alleged "Red" tendencies in the Obregón-Calles camp. He provided the State Department and the press with a letter that he sent to Obregón denouncing the rebel movement. He pointed out that the rebels "represent themselves to us as ultra-radicals saying that their movement has the support of the reds, while on the other hand they say to American investors that they stand for law and order and that Articles 27 and 123 of the Mexican Constitution will be made inoperative in so far as the labor and agrarian reforms are concerned." Gompers accused de la Huerta of trying "to deceive investors and employers of Mexico and the United States on the one hand, and to mislead the working people of Mexico on the other.[20]

The AFL did not limit its response to the rebellion to public expressions of support for the Mexican government. Gompers urged Secretary of State Hughes to investigate reports that Americans were furnishing arms and ammunition to the rebels. He also notified union representatives and transport workers along the border to watch for guns and supplies destined for the rebels. The mobilization of labor unions against the rebellion also extended to Europe. Following appeals from the PAFL executive committee, the IFTU promised to put European workers on the alert against the smuggling of supplies to the *delahuertistas*.[21]

The *delahuertistas'* assassination of Felipe Carrillo Puerto, the Socialist governor of Yucatán, further antagonized labor. IAM officials condemned the assassination and declined an invitation from de la Huerta to meet in Veracruz. E. C. Davison wrote a letter to

de la Huerta attacking him for allowing reactionary forces to manipulate him and for letting personal political ambitions destroy a
previously admirable record of public service.[22]

The AFL did not waver in its opposition to the rebellion, despite
appeals from rebels with whom Gompers had previously friendly
contacts. Reminding Gompers of their long friendship, Antonio
Villarreal denounced Calles as a "simulator" and urged the AFL to
reverse its position. He denied that Calles was a friend of labor and
stressed that the de la Huerta movement would safeguard the social advances of the Mexican Constitution. "These cringing solicita-
tions," Gompers told Obregón, "show how desperate is the frame
of mind and the situation of the rebels."[23]

Anxious to establish a stable political climate conducive to capitalist development, the United States gave substantial military aid
that enabled Obregón to crush the rebellion after impressive initial
victories by rebel forces. In response to charges by conservative
congressmen that the United States was providing military supplies to a Bolshevik regime, Secretary of State Hughes stressed that
the rebel movement was nothing more than an attempt to grab personal political power by individuals who were interfering with
American commerce.[24]

The decision to aid Obregón flew in the face of numerous reports filed by American consuls in Mexico who held a more favorable view of the *delahuertistas* and feared the radicalism of Calles.
The American consul in Puebla reported that U.S. aid to Obregón
drew universal fire in his district because of "Bolshevik" support
for the government. Fearing what the election of Calles might
mean for American capitalists in Mexico, he suggested that the
United States try to persuade Calles to withdraw his candidacy as
a condition for aid.[25]

Indicative of the prevailing anti-Calles sentiment among American consuls was the report filed by O. Gaylord Marsh in Progreso,
Yucatán, during the initial stages of the rebellion. After Marsh
noted that Yucatán had fallen to the *delahuertistas,* he added that
"this is the first political movement since the overthrow of Madero
that has attracted the approval and support of the educated, cul-
tured, and propertied classes of Yucatán, there being a feeling that
the movement is against that ignorant, brutal, and unrestrained
radicalism which has practically controlled the Republic for the last

few years."[26] By the end of the rebellion, Marsh had reassessed his earlier enthusiasm for the rebels and acknowledged the wisdom of the U.S. position in support of the Mexican government: "While many people marveled in a way at American assistance to Obregón and his Socialistic followers, it is now generally known and admitted that the United States made no mistake in judging the general and larger issues in Mexico, the rebels being mere boys organized for banditry on a large scale."[27]

Consular officials who feared Calles also criticized the AFL's activities in Mexico. The American embassy expressed concern that the favorable press attention that Gompers was getting in Mexico City suggested a friendship between Mexican and American workers, not necessarily a feeling of friendship for the United States. The embassy noted that local press accounts generally credited Gompers with the U.S. decision to provide military aid to Obregón.[28]

Claude Dawson, the consul general, complained about Mexican radicalism and challenged the AFL's support of Calles. Although Dawson acknowledged that a sincere desire to defeat radicalism underlay the AFL's policies in Mexico, he argued, in essence, that Gompers was being duped by Morones, Calles, and others whom Dawson regarded as spokesmen for the "extreme wing of Mexican labor":

> Charitably minded people have figured that radicalism in Mexico is a temporary phenomenon, doomed to disappear in a comparatively short time because of a generally low level of intelligence, opaque mentality, and flitting constancy of its human element. For these reasons some have argued that Mexican radicalism is mild and inoffensive and therefore tolerable because it can be kept within bounds.
>
> The dream of the charitably minded has had a sudden awakening. It was first shaken by the alliance between the American Federation of Labor and the labor forces of Mexico for promoting the election to the Mexican presidency of General Elias P. Calles. This was inexplicable to sound native and foreign thought in Mexico at the time because so illogical; and the only reasonable interpretation from the American standpoint is that American labor has been persuaded into the belief that the self-confessed extreme radicalism of Calles is a political maneouvre designed to insure his election, after which he can be relied upon as the long-sought 'strong man', successor to Profirio [sic] Diaz, and at the same time safeguard legitimate labor aspirations according to the conservative attitude of the American Federation of Labor under the leadership of Samuel Gompers.
>
> As the exponent of constitutional conservative methods in the

emancipation of the working class, Mr. Gompers probably be-
lieves that General Calles represents the moderate wing of Mexican
radicalism.[29]

An editorial in *Excelsior* on January 16, 1924, also questioned the
White House's view of Mexican "socialism" as something akin to
the philosophy of the AFL. The newspaper concluded that Gompers played a key role in persuading the Coolidge administration
to support Obregón against the *delahuertistas* by successfully describing the CROM's philosophy as similar to the AFL's "moderate" brand of socialism.[30]

Gompers prided himself on having given the White House a
more enlightened view of the Obregón-Calles regime. In a conference with Manuel Gamio, director of Mexico's Bureau of Anthro-
pology, in the spring of 1924, he took credit for having prodded
the Coolidge administration into aiding Obregón against the rebels.
Central to the U.S. decision, he told Gamio, was a proper interpretation of Mexico's social agenda under Obregón and Calles. "Socialism has come to mean in this country," he explained, "a violent
overthrow of all government. This is different in all countries, in
Mexico it means social welfare." He added, "One of the reasons
and this is confidential, for the hesitancy of the American Government to take sides in the recent rebellion, was the charge made
against Obregon and Calles that they were socialists and some of
us had to explain the difference."[31]

The defeat of the de la Huerta Rebellion paved the way for the
election of Calles, and labor's coordinated efforts against the rebels
strengthened the already firm AFL-CROM alliance. There was still
concern in AFL headquarters, however, that attacks on Calles from
the right and the left might destabilize the situation. Frank Bohn,
who had delivered a letter from Gompers to Obregón expressing
continued AFL support, returned from Mexico in the spring of
1924, concerned that divisions in the labor movement might yet
prove disruptive. He warned that textile and clothing workers in
Mexico were demanding ownership of factories. He urged Gompers to write to Calles suggesting that he be careful not to say anything that could be construed by the press as smacking of bolshevism. Gompers sent a letter urging Calles to be very selective
in his remarks to avoid being misquoted in the newspapers.[32]

The AFL executive council hosted a luncheon for Calles in Atlantic City, New Jersey, in August 1924 and heard the president-elect promise that his government would be "eminently construc-tive."[33] While in the United States, Calles also spoke at a dinner arranged in his honor by the American Manufacturers' Export As-sociation, the Mexican Industrial Commission, the Mexican Cham-ber of Commerce in the United States, and the New York Board of Trade and Transportation. He emphasized the material benefits for industry and commerce that would result from "the economic betterment of these 12,000,000 disinherited Mexicans and economic well-being which would create a thousand new needs of produc-tion and consumption."[34]

Expressions of solidarity abounded at the AFL convention that met in El Paso in November 1924. In attendance were numerous Mexican fraternal delegates, who heard Gompers pledge that the AFL would stand "shoulder to shoulder" with the CROM in its fu-ture struggles.[35] The Mexican labor leaders and government offi-cials who addressed the AFL convention assured delegates that radicalism had been defeated in Mexico. Roberto Haberman prom-ised that the CROM would oppose all attacks on the AFL in Mexico. Speaking as secretary of the Committee on International Relations, Matthew Woll praised the CROM for having expelled a communist delegate from its convention. He hailed the expulsion as "the beginning of the Monroe Doctrine of American labor to apply to the western hemisphere."[36]

In speeches that would have been well received by American policymakers and businessmen, Mexican leaders told the AFL con-vention that Mexico's era of revolutions had ended with the defeat of de la Huerta. Antonio Díaz Soto y Gama, president of the Agrar-ian Party (Partido Nacional Agrarista), explained that the need for violent revolution had stemmed from the feudal conditions of the peasantry under Díaz, and he claimed that Mexico's government now represented workers and peasants who no longer needed to revolt. He stressed that Mexico was now "safe" and hospitable to foreign capital.[37]

The Mexicans appealed to the underlying material concerns of the AFL's foreign policy. Mexico's dependent status as a producer of foodstuffs and raw materials meant that national reconstruction in the 1920s offered golden opportunities for American industry. Mexican leaders who courted Gompers recognized that the AFL supported reforms in Mexico as long as they did not threaten Mexico's dependent relationship with the United States. They assured AFL leaders that Mexico's blueprint for national economic development did not upset this fundamental relationship. José Miguel Bejarno, a representative from the Department of Agriculture, enticed the AFL convention with visions of vast markets and jobs that would result from the integration of Mexico's Indian peasants into the national economy. "Of the 16,000,000 people in our country," he said, "there are only three or four million of actual consuming power; only about that number wear shoes. Just imagine, when they come into our system of civilization what buying power they will have." He promised that Mexico would not promote a broader industrialization that would compete with American factories and workers. "It is extremely foolish to try and make Mexico an industrial nation," he concluded. "We are still in the agricultural stage. We should develop agriculturally and get our manufactured goods from those who are much further advanced."[38]

Great pomp and ceremony surrounded the AFL's welcoming of the Mexican delegation to the convention. On November 18, 1924, in accordance with an earlier agreement, AFL delegates left their convention and crossed the international bridge to attend a joint labor session in Juárez. A detail of mounted Mexican police and the uniformed band of the Fifty-Fifth Battalion of the Mexican Army escorted them to the meeting. At the session, the CROM's Juan Rico introduced Gompers, who denounced the de la Huerta Rebellion as "a rebellion against democracy" and defended his support of Obregón: "When we find, as we do find, that the government of your Republic is in harmony with the constructive intelligent progress of the great mass of your people, it is entitled to your constant support."[39]

Calles invited the AFL delegates to attend his inauguration on December 1, 1924. Mexico would provide a train of Pullmans to take them to Mexico City on November 27 and would defray other expenses as well. The PAFL convention was to coincide with the inauguration, so labor could celebrate its role in electing Calles and conduct other business at the same time.[40]

To a certain extent, the AFL's militant celebration of Calles's election reflected the configuration of domestic forces that tried to

push American politics to the left in 1924. Among the most en-
thusiastic supporters of Obregón and Calles were IAM officials,
who endorsed the Mexican government's commitment to organized labor, land reform, education, and other social reforms. IAM
president William Johnston also headed the executive committee
of the Conference for Progressive Political Action (CPPA), which
nominated Robert LaFollette as its presidential candidate in 1924.
Also on the CPPA's executive committee was the Socialist Party's
(SPA) Morris Hillquit, who promoted efforts to build a coalition
with the progressive labor forces that dominated the LaFollette
nominating convention. Like Robert Haberman, who worked in
the Pan-American labor movement to build labor and socialist support for Obregón and Calles, Hillquit endorsed the PAFL and
applauded the AFL's anti-interventionist efforts in Mexico on several occasions. Although it recognized the limitations of LaFollette's nonsocialist agenda, the SPA endorsed the CPPA platform
in an effort to forge a new political coalition.[41]

The effort to construct a progressive coalition on domestic and
foreign issues—including the defense of Calles—received a boost
when the AFL abandoned its traditional "nonpartisan" political approach and endorsed LaFollette. Despite Republican allegations of
communism hurled at the LaFollette camp, the CPPA campaign
denounced the Communists, who rejected LaFollette and tried to
capture control of the Minnesota Farmer-Labor Party. The CPPA
also opposed the formation of an independent political party. In
reality, AFL support for LaFollette was lukewarm, at best. Following his defeat, AFL leaders announced that their decision to endorse an independent candidate was a mistake and that labor
would return to its "nonpartisan" traditions. The disintegration of
the CPPA coalition dashed Socialist hopes—however slight—that
cooperation with nonsocialist progressives might produce a labor
party.[42]

LaFollette's anti-interventionist views had important implications for Mexico, and the CROM courted the progressive coalition that backed his candidacy. Haberman attended LaFollette's
nominating convention to publicize the PAFL as a counterweight
to imperialism and capitalist exploitation. He also attended SPA
conventions and local meetings to praise the growing role of or-

ganized labor in shaping relations between Mexico and the United States.[43]

The CROM invited SPA officials to attend the inauguration of Calles alongside AFL leaders. Although the Mexican Communist Party, under the leadership of Bertram Wolfe, also supported Obregón and Calles during the de la Huerta Rebellion, Wolfe received no such invitation. In fact, Calles expelled him in July 1925 after the PCM criticized the Mexican government for serving the interests of U.S. imperialism.[44]

AFL leaders attended the inauguration of Calles and the PAFL Convention amid great fanfare. Juan Rico addressed the convention to pledge continued CROM involvement in the PAFL, but he warned that Mexican labor would oppose "any attempts to impose upon our own movement tendencies or methods with which we may not be in accord, even though they be acclaimed as an advanced nature."[45] Despite Rico's pledge of future cooperation, his attempt to assert the CROM's independence did not set well with Gompers, who arose to emphasize that the AFL would continue to be the leading force in the inter-American trade union movement. "So far as we possibly can we want to be upon an equality in our congress," Gompers asserted, "but we must understand this,—that the labor movements which are now in the beginning, and those . . . which have had an existence and greater responsibility, can not permit that those who have less experience shall have fullest opportunity of determining the policy of all. You may rest assured of absolute freedom of discussion within the limits of reason and fair dealing, one with another."[46]

Illness cut short Gompers's activities in Mexico City, and on the way home, he died in San Antonio, Texas, on December 13, 1924. His presence in Mexico City had not gone unnoticed by American officials and foreign investors. The AFL's endorsement of Calles received a mixed review in government and private-sector circles. The evidence suggests that some American capitalists in Mexico had a more favorable view of the AFL's activities than did U.S. officials.

Perhaps to encourage including the AFL in efforts to solve the Mexican "problem," Henry Anderson, who was on the Mexican-American Mixed Claims Commission, provided the secretary of state with a copy of a letter from E. R. Jones, president of Wells Fargo in Mexico, to Fairfax Harrison, president of the Southern Railway Company. Also a member of the International Committee of Bankers on Mexico, Jones described the elaborate reception enjoyed by Gompers at the inauguration of Calles and concluded that the late AFL president had exerted a moderating influence on the new government. "I personally talked with him several times during his visit to Mexico," Jones told Harrison, "and must say that I believe his advice to ex-President Obregon, President Calles and Minister of Labor Morones was sound and conservative and will have a very sobering effect on any radical tendencies that might be considered as forming a part of the new administration's policy." Jones also told Harrison that the business outlook in Mexico was good, and he expressed confidence that Calles would give protection to foreign and domestic capital and labor alike.[47]

Other capitalists provided the American consul general in Mexico City with similar reports. They attributed Calles's favorable attitudes to the conservative influence of Gompers. Calles, they noted, was providing "moral support" to employers during the early days of his presidency.[48]

James Sheffield, the American ambassador, was unconvinced. By the spring of 1925, Calles's relationship with organized labor, regardless of the CROM's conservative ideology, intensified embassy fears that radicalism jeopardized foreign capital. Gompers's warm reception at the inauguration of Calles disturbed Sheffield, who worried that Calles would not be able to keep the "arrogant" demands of organized labor in check. Sheffield complained to Secretary of State Frank B. Kellogg about the special attention lavished by Calles upon AFL leaders: "You may recall that Mr. Samuel Gompers attended the inauguration of President Calles and was extended many honors, while the representatives of countries which had sent Special Ambassadors to the inauguration were shown no unusual courtesies or even consideration."[49]

The AFL's endorsement of Obregón and Calles was an expression of the progressive tendencies that had consistently influenced labor's response to the Mexican Revolution. By mobilizing AFL resources against the *delahuertistas*, Gompers displayed a determination to keep Mexico on a democratic course between reaction and radicalism. Defeating the rebels, in his view, would diminish the threat posed by what he regarded as a symbiotic relationship between radicals and reactionaries. Confident that Calles was not a threat to the United States, Gompers quickly condemned the rebel movement that threatened Mexico's stability. He had confidence that Calles would safeguard organized labor's interests but defeat communist and anarchosyndicalist forces. He admired Calles's toughness in dealing with his enemies.

The militant spirit that contributed to the defeat of the de la Huerta Rebellion confronted tendencies within the AFL leadership, however, which limited its fullest expression. The International Seamen's Union, which had mobilized its members to guard against the smuggling of military supplies to de la Huerta's followers, tried to capitalize on the internationalist spirit among American and Mexican delegates at the 1924 AFL convention and commit the AFL to a stronger anti-imperialist position in Latin America. Two members of the Seamen's Union introduced a resolution that would have denied American financiers the right to call on U.S. troops to collect their foreign debts. Unwilling to endorse putting this clear restriction on the activities of American financiers abroad, Matthew Woll used his position as secretary of the Resolutions Committee to kill the resolution.[50]

6

Robert Haberman, the AFL, and Mexican Radicalism, 1917–1924

Since the inception of his involvement in the Mexican Revolution, Gompers had worked with several trade union socialists—especially John Murray, Santiago Iglesias, and Chester Wright—to implement AFL policies. In the early 1920s, he also developed a working relationship with Robert Haberman, an American socialist who became an important figure in the topsy-turvy world of left-wing politics in Mexico and liaison between the CROM and the AFL. Haberman's search for a peaceful transition to socialism in Mexico led him to support the PAFL as a means to promote labor solidarity and better Mexican-American relations. Shadowed by the American intelligence community, often regarded as a dangerous Bolshevik in conservative American and Mexican circles, and once thought to have been a draft dodger and German spy, he worked both sides of the border to promote the PAFL and strengthen anti-interventionist forces in the United States. His prescription for a peaceful socialist transformation in Mexico included a heavy dose of anticommunism, a fact which made collaboration with him more palatable to AFL leaders.

What makes Haberman particularly intriguing, however, is the fact that he not only had important contacts with American socialists, progressives, and AFL leaders, but was a man with impressive connections in Mexico, too. The only foreign member of Grupo Acción, the CROM's small but very powerful policymaking clique, he worked with Felipe Carrillo Puerto in Yucatán, and he played an important role in Obregón's efforts to consolidate his power and reinstitutionalize the postrevolutionary Mexican state in the early 1920s. He also may have been working as a spy for the U.S. government. At the very least, he offered to collaborate with the U.S. Justice Department to weaken radical influences in Mexico.[1]

Controversy followed Haberman, whose alignment with CROM labor bosses enabled him to pursue his own political aspirations and work with the Sonoran politicians who institutionalized the labor movement's client status in the 1920s. Given his high-level involvement in Mexican politics and his contacts with AFL leaders and U.S. officials, we need a more detailed analysis of his role in the Mexican Revolution. The fact that he was attacked as a "labor-faker" and tool of Wall Street, on the one hand, and condemned as a Bolshevik, on the other, suggests that this complex figure and his many-sided activities require careful study.[2]

A native of Romania, Haberman emigrated to the United States on December 6, 1901, and promptly enlisted in the Army Medical Corps. Discharged as a sergeant after three years, he became a naturalized American citizen and earned a baccalaureate from New York University and a law degree from Brooklyn Law School. After practicing law in Fresno, California, from 1912 to 1914, he moved to New York's Greenwich Village and waged an unsuccessful campaign to win a judgeship on the Socialist ticket. The *New York Call* hired him to work on its advertising staff, and the Joseph Ellner Company, Ltd., an advertising firm with leftist connections, employed him to solicit new accounts.[3]

In 1916, Haberman served as secretary of the peace commission organized by David Starr Jordan to mobilize antiwar forces during the crisis provoked by the Pershing invasion of Mexico. His political activities in New York put him in touch with Mexicans who wanted to promote a sympathetic view of the Revolution in the United States. After a conversation in New York's Civic Club with Modesto Rolland, a young publicist for the growing reform movement in Yucatán, he agreed to visit Yucatán to gather material for articles to promote the area and induce colonists to settle there. A large group of Hindus living in the United States hired him to discuss with Yucatecan officials the possibility of establishing a land colony. Rolland arranged for Yucatán's Henequen Commission to underwrite the trip, and Haberman accepted the arrangements, hoping to capture at least part of the commission's advertising account for the Ellner Company.[4]

Haberman applied for a passport on March 27, 1917, but left for Yucatán without one on April 19, after a Bureau of Investigation agent's search of his personal belongings aboard ship failed to disclose "anything of an incriminating nature."[5] The Bureau of Investigation and the State Department conducted an investigation of his passport application,[6] and O. Gaylord Marsh, the U.S. consul in Progreso, Yucatán, kept him under surveillance. Marsh regarded him as a "very dangerous German agent" and complained that he had become involved in numerous labor rallies and socialist political activities in Yucatán. Reporting that Haberman planned to return to the United States in late June, 1917, Marsh recommended that he be detained there until the war ended. Haberman's profession of support for the Allied cause did not convince Marsh, who reported, "He is strongly Pro-Ally in his statements to me but I am informed by several Americans that he is violently Pro-German." In reference to Haberman's painstaking efforts to allay suspicions that he was a draft dodger, Marsh noted that he "shows his [Army] discharge to all Americans he sees."[7]

Complying with a State Department request, the Bureau of Investigation stopped Haberman to examine his papers and belongings when he returned to the United States on June 30, 1917. Immigration authorities in New Orleans seized him because he carried no documentary proof of his citizenship. A Bureau of Investigation agent then questioned him about his activities in Yucatán before allowing him to depart for New York. According to Haberman, the allegations that he was a spy came from a group of younger Americans with whom he had been involved in an altercation in Yucatán. He claimed that they reported him to Consul Marsh as a spy after he accused them of being "slackers."

Describing himself as a socialist "of a constructive type and not a destructive anarchist," he told the Bureau of Investigation agent that Frederic C. Howe, New York's Commissioner of Immigration, could vouch for him. When asked about his affiliation with the Emergency Peace Federation, he said that the Ellner Company handled more than $40,000 worth of advertising for the federation, whose account he had personally supervised. He stressed that this was a purely business matter and that he joined the federation as an act of courtesy after securing the account. To explain why he was carrying $750 in cash and bank drafts from the Henequen

Commission, he claimed that several Yucatecans gave him money to buy items for their personal use and that the rest of the funds covered his expenses for the trip. He also stated that he intended to "do his bit" to help the U.S. war effort.[8]

Although Haberman, who was thirty-three years old when the United States entered the First World War, was once considered in violation of the Selective Service Act, a later inquiry showed that he registered for the draft in accordance with the law. He continued to have problems, however, when he applied for a passport on November 8, 1917, to return to Yucatán. He submitted with his application a letter from Frederic Howe "vouching for him" and a statement from the Russian-American Direct Trade Corporation that he was going to Mexico to extend its export business. His request was denied, but he managed to slip back to Yucatán without a passport, arriving in Progreso on February 1, 1918.[9]

Upon returning to Yucatán, Haberman quickly assumed an important role in local politics, linking up with Felipe Carrillo Puerto, president of the state's Socialist Party (Partido Socialista de Yucatán, PSY). A deepening reform movement, launched by General Salvador Alvarado in 1916 and pushed to the left by Carrillo Puerto, aimed to curb the power of local henequen plantation owners and improve the miserable conditions of the Indian workers. The monocultural character of the Yucatecan economy, which revolved around the export of henequen, a sisal plant used to produce baling twine and other kinds of rope, encouraged Alvarado and later Carrillo Puerto to attempt greater state control over production and marketing and promote land reform and education. Given U.S. strategic wartime concerns and the International Harvester Company's reliance on Yucatán as a major source of henequen, these reforms worried American policymakers.[10]

Carrillo Puerto organized workers, largely agricultural, into armed unions called the Ligas de Resistencia. Haberman provided him with an account of how labor organizations functioned in the United States and encouraged him to call a convention of the Ligas. At the Motul Workers' Congress, which convened in March 1918, Haberman addressed the delegates to promote consumer cooperatives and attack U.S. imperialism. He stressed the need to forge a strong international socialist movement to counter U.S. aggression, but he argued that armed resistance would be futile. "You do not need cannons to fight against the gringo capitalists," he said, "that fight would be like a sheep against a lion." The best course of action, he explained, would be to establish an alliance with American workers and join the Socialist Party: "The workers of the United States are also slaves and as oppressed as you, and they do not want war with Mexico, because when there is war, workers lose their lives and everything. You do not need rifles or cannons, the only thing necessary, my dear comrades, is a socialist party."[11]

Because Haberman opposed the IWW, he was clearly suggesting closer ties with the AFL. By stressing the opposition of American workers to war, however, he ignored the AFL's role in the Allied war effort. Although the AFL recommended that government agents harass the People's Council of America and the Ellner Company, Haberman's employer, because of their socialist affiliations and opposition to the war,[12] the path followed by Haberman in Yucatán led away from the antiwar route traveled by his employer.

An analysis of his activities suggests no fundamental incompatibility with the objectives of the American Alliance for Labor and Democracy (AALD), a government-sponsored organization of prowar socialists and AFL leaders who worked to boost publicity for the Allied war effort. Although no formal link between Haberman and the AALD has been established, his endorsement of an alliance with the AFL and his participation in the Liberty Loan program in Yucatán indicated the philosophical commonality of interests that would later make it possible for him and Gompers to work together.[13]

Carrillo Puerto put Haberman in charge of the cooperative stores, whose purpose was to cushion Yucatecan workers and peasants against the high prices of food and other basic necessities. As G. M. Joseph has shown, the monocultural economy weakened the cooperative movement, since the state had to depend on the import of food and provisions from the United States during the war. Carrillo Puerto promoted a pro-Ally public relations campaign in an effort to convince the American consulate that the U.S. Food Administration should grant export licenses to these cooperatives. The U.S. export policy continued, however, to favor private Yucatecan merchants over the cooperatives.[14]

Although Consul Marsh's recommendation was not followed, he urged that export licenses be granted to the cooperatives. He reported that Haberman and Carrillo Puerto had agreed to distribute pro-Ally literature in branch offices of the Socialist Party. Marsh emphasized that the peaceful success of the Socialist Party depended on the success of the cooperatives, and he argued that it was important to maintain friendly relations with the Socialists. "My British, French, and Italian colleagues and many of my friends including some who are reporting to Washington," he noted, "would apparently black list the co-operatives and the socialist party. I do not favor any such action at present as I feel that we should endeavor to cultivate their friendship if possible but at the same time not allow them to gain more power at our hands than advisable." [15]

Marsh recommended that the United States grant the cooperatives export licenses for foodstuffs not to exceed 15 percent of Yucatán's allowances. "Such action," he explained, "will keep the socialists friendly and hopeful and will allow them no monopoly, and we, I hope but am not sure, may be able to use them to create a better feeling toward us amongst the common people." He indicated that he had not been taken in by Haberman and Carrillo Puerto: "Mr. Haberman and Mr. Carrillo are trying to impress me with their friendly sentiments and they make very elaborate promises and have I am told spoken very highly of the United States in public speeches. I have not a great deal of confidence in them and I think they want merchandise and the backing of the United States in their efforts to gain complete socialistic control in Yucatán." He calculated, however, that American officials could "turn this desire to our advantage without giving them all they want and without their being in a position to say that we opposed them. [16]

Although Marsh regarded Haberman as "poor, sincere, and honest but disposed to place the principles of socialism above the principles of any established government," [17] he recognized that Haberman's links to the Yucatecan masses might be useful to the United States if handled carefully. Despite earlier unsubstantiated reports from the Office of Naval Intelligence that Haberman was a dangerous German spy and member of the IWW, a more favorable assessment of his activities began to emerge in the State Department during the summer of 1918. When his wife, Thorburg, applied for a passport to join him in Yucatán to devise a public health program for the schools and help in the campaign against German propaganda, Marsh voiced no objections. The State Department's Office of the Counselor noted that naval-intelligence allegations about Haberman's links to the IWW and German intelligence operations were perhaps unfounded: "On the whole, Haberman's record in this country, his acquaintance with Frederick C. Howe, his present quiet conduct according to the Consul and the lack of any definite information in reports from the Department of Justice of 6 or 7 months since, made when Haberman previously applied for a passport seem to indicate that the . . . allegations may, after all, not be borne out by facts."[18]

The growing strength of the PSY and Haberman's activities concerned Federal authorities in Mexico City. Sharp conflicts broke out between the PSY and General Luis Hernández, Carranza's chief of military operations, who provided greater military protection to local henequen plantation owners. Haberman's role in local politics became an issue in the tense state of affairs as Carrillo Puerto defended him against expulsion by General Hernández. U.S. military intelligence reported that Haberman, who had a pending passport application, was anxious to return to the United States in January 1919.[19]

Listed in the State Department's "Who's Who in Mexico" and denied a passport in May 1919, Haberman became Carrillo Puerto's inspector general of cooperatives for the Liga Central in June. The cooperative movement collapsed soon thereafter, however, when Carranza used troops to halt the budding reform effort spearheaded by the local Socialist Party. Carrillo Puerto fled to the United States, while Haberman, who had been officially certified as a draft dodger in December 1918 and denied an American passport, left Yucatán for Mexico City.[20]

Some critics accused Haberman of corruption in his handling of the cooperatives. Bernardino Mena Brito, a bitter political rival of the PSY, charged that Yucatecan workers blamed the failure of the cooperatives on Haberman's mismanagement and dishonesty. Haberman's radical reputation was simply a mask, according to Mena Brito, who alleged that the United States deliberately portrayed him as a dangerous radical so that the reform movement in

Yucatán would employ him while, in reality, he was working for henequen speculators on Wall Street.[21]

Although I have uncovered no evidence to prove or disprove Mena Brito's charges, Haberman's commitment to the reform movement in Yucatán did not preclude the simultaneous pursuit of personal financial gain. A combination of personal business and political objectives had guided his actions in Yucatán from the outset. The line between personal financial concerns and ideological objectives apparently blurred on occasions. An acquaintance of his in Yucatán told a friend in a letter opened by U.S. postal censors that Haberman exploited his political connections to his fullest advantage and "ought to be making some money for he has his own way and all the pull he wants with the Socialist Party and consequently the Government."[22] Given evidence in the Bureau of Investigation files that Haberman used his political connections later in the 1920s to profit from graft,[23] perhaps we should not dismiss Mena Brito's allegations out of hand as merely the accusations of a partisan critic.

Haberman's ties to Carrillo Puerto and his endorsement of an evolutionary rather than revolutionary course of development for the Mexican labor movement opened political doors for him in Mexico City following Obregón's overthrow of Carranza in 1920. He believed that national reconstruction under the leadership of the Sonoran revolutionaries meant greater social reforms and more favorable conditions for the peaceful implementation of socialism. As we shall see, the decision to promote the CROM's clientelist relationship with the Mexican government and work with Gompers advanced Haberman's personal political ambitions, but it contributed to the defeat of independent unionism and radicalism in Mexico. The role that Haberman played in the campaign to isolate, coopt, and defeat left-wing forces enabled him to weave his way into the Mexican power structure.

Carleton Beals, an American journalist who moved in left-wing circles in Mexico City, was with Haberman in the latter's apartment on Avenida Juárez when Obregón made his triumphal entry into the capital wearing a blue shirt with red suspenders. As Haberman and Beals gazed out upon the procession, they discussed the implications of Obregón's movement. Specifically, they debated whether

Obregón would promote fundamental change that would benefit the Mexican masses. Beals was skeptical about Obregón's alleged commitment to peasants and workers, but Haberman could
hardly contain his enthusiasm. According to Beals, Haberman's
eyes really twinkled at the sight of Obregón's red suspenders. The
color of Obregón's suspenders had a seductive political appeal to
Haberman, who concluded that radicals would now have a friend
in the National Palace. Beals annoyed him by suggesting that
Obregón was merely an opportunist. "I have seen any number of
cardsharpers in suspenders," Beals insisted, "but I never noticed
any particular love for the people among any of them." [24]

The CROM's special relationship with Obregón aroused Haberman's enthusiasm, for he worked with top CROM officials in support of the new government. He overcame his reservations about
labor boss Morones, whom he earlier regarded as a "shyster," after
he held discussions with him shortly after Obregón's coup. [25] Explaining his conversion to Leon Marvini, an Italian radical who had
also been active in Yucatán's reform movement, Haberman denounced the chronic sectarian bickering among the "so-called
reds" and said that he had decided to work with CROM officials.
He assured Marvini that Morones deserved his support: "I can say
to you honestly and sincerely that he is, to date, the best organizer
in Mexico; also he is one of the most radical." Haberman mentioned that he had been appointed professor in the National University to teach socialism and cooperativism, and he told Marvini
that de la Huerta was "redder than you and I together." [26]

U.S. military intelligence described Haberman's appointment
to the National University as "part of the present Government's
policy of conciliation towards agitators, revolutionists, etc., in order that the short time de la Huerta is in office may be as peaceful
as possible," but noted that "it is also frequently asserted and appears possible that the present President has a certain amount of
sympathy with the radicals." [27] The Mexican government's official
endorsement of the CROM and its willingness to cultivate the support of radicals excited Haberman. He began to organize CROM-
affiliated unions and cooperatives and used his contacts with
leftists in the United States to promote a favorable view of Mexico's
new leaders. Working as a pharmacist and clerk at the American
Drug Store in Mexico City, he organized drug store employees and

lobbied for the establishment of a special pharmacy school. José Vasconcelos, Obregón's minister of education, put him on the payroll as a co-director of an educational institute, and Antonio Villarreal's Ministry of Agriculture employed him as a translator. Haberman also wrote favorable articles on Mexico for radical and liberal publications in the United States, and he signed his letters "To the Red Dawn."[28]

The symbiotic relationship between the CROM and the government afforded Haberman access to top Obregón administration officials as he joined the highly select inner council of CROM leaders. He established especially close ties to Calles, who later gave him an expanded role in his administration. Haberman became a point man in the Mexican government's campaign to win friends among liberals and radicals in the United States while assuring American officials that adequate guarantees would be given to foreign capital.

It is unclear whether Gompers knew Haberman before the PAFL convention in Mexico City in January 1921, but Haberman accompanied Morones and other CROM leaders to the border to escort AFL delegates to the conferences. It was Obregón's suggestion that a CROM committee greet the AFL delegates at the border and bring them to Mexico City in a special car. According to *The New York Times* of January 10, 1921, it was Haberman's presence that created problems for the CROM leaders when the American consul at Nuevo Laredo refused to let them cross the border. The newspaper claimed that Haberman was working for the Third International; meanwhile, a Justice Department report alleged that Morones and Haberman secretly aimed to buy ammunition in Laredo for the Mexican government. Gompers's intervention ended the embarrassing incident, and he assured an irritated Morones on the convention floor that the incident was the work of an arbitrary petty official and did not reflect the State Department's official position. According to Gompers, the State Department assured him in advance that the CROM committee would be allowed to cross the border but failed to relay these instructions to the consul.[29]

If Gompers did not know much about Haberman in January 1921, he must surely have begun to ask questions about the man. Shortly before the PAFL convention, Chester Wright wrote an article in the *American Federationist* which attacked the radicalism of

Carrillo Puerto and "a small number of Americans who sought safety by entering Mexico and thus escaping military service during the war." Although he did not mention Haberman specifically, Wright described Carrillo Puerto as the most radical person he had met on a recent trip to Mexico and complained that these American draft evaders joined him to form the "nucleus of a Bolshevist movement" in Mexico.[30] Given Haberman's close ties to Carrillo Puerto, his work in Yucatán, and persistent allegations that he had evaded the wartime draft, it is reasonable to assume that Gompers regarded him with at least a bit of suspicion. The evidence suggests also that Haberman, who attended the PAFL convention as a fraternal delegate representing the Drug Store Employees' Union in Mexico City, had his own reservations about Gompers. He and other CROM leaders privately derided Gompers after the convention.[31]

The integration of Haberman into the Mexican power structure during the first year after Obregón's coup paralleled the deep splintering of left-wing forces. As socialist, communist, and anarchosyndicalist factions fought each other bitterly, CROM leaders and government officials strengthened their positions by coopting or isolating their left-wing rivals. By November 1920 Morones had concluded a deal with Linn A. E. Gale, an American draft evader who helped to lead a faction out of the Mexican Socialist Party to form the Mexican Communist Party in 1919.[32] In exchange for financial subsidies from the CROM, Gale changed his line on Morones, Haberman, and other CROM leaders. While sharply attacking the anarchosyndicalist forces, *Gale's Magazine* now transformed Morones from a "sleek, well-groomed, pot-bellied agent of Samuel Gompers" to an "out and out Bolshevist."[33] With Haberman's help, Gale's wife, Magdalena, landed a part-time teaching job in the Ministry of Education. According to Diana Christopulos, Haberman was probably the architect of the arrangement between Gale and Morones.[34]

As his activities in Yucatán indicated earlier, Haberman demonstrated a willingness to adjust his radicalism to accommodate the situation at hand. He probably deliberately exaggerated de la Huerta's so-called radicalism to encourage Marvini and other leftists to endorse the CROM's alliance with the new regime. Haberman boasted to Marvini that he would soon contact Ludwig C. A. K.

Martens, the Third International's representative in New York, but the Bureau of Investigation's file on Haberman contains reports which suggest that he deliberately exaggerated his contacts with Martens in order to ingratiate himself with radicals in Mexico City. According to intelligence reports, his failure to see Martens on a trip to New York under an alias passport in late October 1920 caused Haberman to lose the confidence of many Mexican radicals.[35]

Aware that he was constantly shadowed by U.S. intelligence agents, Haberman evidently enjoyed the aura of danger and mystery that enveloped his activities. Regarding him as one of its "pet playmates," the U.S. embassy in Mexico City noted that he "loves to be shadowed and to appear dangerous."[36] His stature among radical elements diminished, however, as he joined the Mexican political establishment, and his involvement in the PAFL in early 1921 further alienated him from left-wingers who denounced him as an agent of Gompers. Perhaps the most perceptive assessment of Haberman came from Gale, who provided the American intelligence community with information after his deportation from Mexico and subsequent imprisonment in the United States. "While Haberman is an active socialist and is sincere," Gale observed, "he is not anti-American but on the contrary is distinctly friendly to the United States in many ways. . . . He helped Luis Morones 'kid' Gomers [*sic*] but is too much of an opportunist to do anything against the United States government."[37]

Radical ferment and increased labor militancy during the early months of Obregón's tenure irritated U.S. officials as well as Gompers, who returned from the PAFL Convention in Mexico City convinced that foreign radicals seriously threatened the Mexican labor movement. Following the founding convention of the CGT in February 1921, communist and anarchosyndicalist groups blasted the Mexican government, the CROM's relationship with the AFL, and Haberman's involvement in the Pan-American labor movement. Radical circulars denounced the PAFL as an organization designed to soften Mexican opposition to American financial interests and threatened death to the followers of Gompers, "the American butcher who sold our comrades of the North to the European slaughterhouse."[38]

The polarized atmosphere in the spring of 1921 did not help Obregón's campaign to win U.S. recognition and ensure the kind of political stability necessary to attract foreign capital. IWW-led May Day demonstrations outside the U.S. consulate and other public demonstrations in Mexico City attacked the government and the CROM's marriage to the AFL. The fears of U.S. officials intensified when unionists in Mexico City paraded through the Chamber of Deputies with red and black flags calling for social revolution. Carlton Jackson, the U.S. commercial attaché, informed the Bureau of Foreign and Domestic Commerce that the incident dismayed conservatives, especially Americans in the capital who had been trying to develop confidence in the stability of Obregón's government but who now questioned whether the president would deal firmly enough with the radicals.[39]

Obregón partially eased these fears when he expelled many foreign leftists. Gale was the first to depart in April, and soon after the disruptions in the Chamber of Deputies, Obregón deported several foreign members of the CGT.[40] Against the backdrop of these deportations, the Mexico City newspaper *Excelsior* reported on May 19 that several students called press attention to Haberman as a "bolshevist" professor at the National University. On July 6, the American consul in Mexico City noted the impact of Obregón's crackdown on Haberman, who was still in the capital: "Since the recent deportation of certain undesirable foreigners from Mexico he has kept himself in seclusion."[41]

Haberman's connections served him well during the roundup of foreign radicals. Although a Justice Department report claimed that Obregón deported him on July 18, 1921,[42] the slippery Haberman actually came to the United States on an official mission for the Mexican government. He arrived in AFL headquarters shortly after Gompers had urged Secretary of State Hughes to declare publicly that U.S. warships off the coast of Tampico did not intend to interfere with labor unions during a confrontation between Obregón and the oil companies. The "deportee" bore a letter from Calles thanking Gompers for prevailing upon the State Department. Referring to Haberman as their "mutual friend," Calles told Gompers that Haberman would "explain verbally our actual situation."[43]

Haberman assured Gompers that the CROM was winning its battle against rival left-wing unions and radical elements. He briefed Gompers on Gale's deportation and the activities of the

IWW and Mexican Communist Party. He also took advantage of his trip to the United States to provide information on radicals in Mexico to the Justice Department. On July 18, the day of his alleged deportation, he turned up in J. Edgar Hoover's office accompanied by E. C. Davison, the general secretary-treasurer of the Machinists' Union. Davison confirmed that Haberman, contrary to reports regarding his alleged communist activities, was working with AFL leaders to defeat radicalism in Mexico.[44]

In the meeting with Hoover, Haberman complained that his activities had been deliberately misrepresented by Americans in Mexico to discredit him. He distanced himself from communist "fanatics" and informed Hoover that Moscow had provided Frank Seaman (a pseudonym of Charles Francis Phillips) and Sen Katayama with ample funds. He attacked Gale and suggested that U.S. intelligence keep an eye on J. H. Retinger, who, according to Haberman, was well funded and believed to have been a German agent during the war.[45]

When Hoover asked if the purpose of Lincoln Steffens's recent visit to Mexico City was to negotiate a secret treaty between Obregón and the Soviet Union, Haberman denied it, saying that Steffens was a "perfectly harmless type" who was there simply to study conditions. He warned Hoover that American journalist Katharine Anne Porter, who was also close to many Mexican radicals, was getting inside information from the military attaché at the U.S. embassy in Mexico City—an individual "stated to be addicted to strong drink and to give many parties in which the fair sex participate." Haberman explained that Obregón had tolerated radicals until the waving of the red flag in the Chamber of Deputies and the discovery of an alleged communist plot to assassinate PAFL leaders made him lose patience with them. According to Haberman, CROM leaders had pressed Obregón to deport the foreign radicals.[46]

Haberman may have exaggerated his influence on Obregón's decision to order the expulsions, but he probably did play a role in the deportations. His CGT rivals certainly thought so. Protesting that the demonstrations in the Chamber of Deputies were actually carried out by CROM supporters, an IWW committee complained that Haberman was among those who orchestrated the disruptions.[47] Although Haberman wrote at the time of Gale's expulsion in early April 1921 that "some of us tried hard to get the order rescinded,"[48] when asked at a Socialist Party meeting in New York on August 29 if he approved of the deportation, he said, "Theoretically I do not, but practically, I do." He complained that Gale had provided information on him to the Justice Department.[49]

It is difficult to pinpoint exactly when and how Haberman became the "mutual friend" of Gompers and Calles. His contacts with the left wing of the AFL may have laid the foundation for this friendship. A member of the IAM, he also knew Fred Mooney, Mother Jones, and James Lord of the United Mineworkers.[50] Gompers probably developed a clearer view of his activities during conferences with Calles and Obregón in Mexico City in January 1921. U.S. officials may have at least flirted with a suggestion from Gale that "friendly relations with Haberman might be established to good advantage by proper parties and would be the most effective tactics to use in dealing with him."[51]

We do not yet have direct evidence that U.S. officials approached the "proper parties" about working with Haberman, but this may have been done through the AFL. When Haberman telegraphed AFL headquarters that he would be in Washington on July 26, 1921, Gompers quickly arranged for the PAFL executive committee to meet with him. Although PAFL officials had already scheduled a meeting at that time, Gompers encouraged Haberman to believe that a special meeting had been called just to accommodate him. Gompers obviously hoped to flatter him and lay the basis for a future collaborative relationship.[52]

Haberman's discussions with AFL leaders revealed the contours of the Mexican government's strategy to gain U.S. recognition and promote economic development. Fundamental agreement on the issue of continued foreign investment in Mexico made it ideologically comfortable for him and AFL officials to endorse Obregón's efforts to attract foreign capital. Haberman had communicated a soothing, reassuring message to American investors shortly before Obregón's presidential inauguration. While in New York during the late fall of 1920—to see the Third International's representative, according to military intelligence—he publicly praised the dawning of a new reform era in Mexico but assured foreign investors that the new climate did not threaten their interests. "I want to tell Americans who have capital to invest or who are thinking of transferring their activities to other countries," he said, "that Mexico is in a better state today than she had been for years."[53]

Calles used Haberman's trip to the United States in July 1921 to reassure AFL leaders that the Mexican government would repeal Article 27 through the Supreme Court, but not through a special treaty as proposed by U.S. officials. Haberman briefed AFL leaders on the Mexican government's proposal to buy American goods only from firms approved by the AFL. He also told Socialist Party audiences in the United States about the arrangements to create an industrial bureau with an advisory board to determine which firms were acceptable to the AFL. As a publicist for the Mexican government, he stressed that foreign investors would find exciting opportunities to make money in Mexico.[54]

In an attempt to promote friendlier relations between the peoples and the governments of Mexico, Haberman proposed that AFL leaders send instructors to teach scientific and applied mining in Mexican trade schools. Gompers approved of the proposal and assured Haberman that he would discuss the matter with officials of the UMW and the United Mine, Mill and Smelter Workers of America. These discussions lend credence to Haberman's assertion to the Justice Department that he was on a two-month leave of absence—paid for by the Mexican government—to gather information needed to open a technical school in Mexico.[55]

Haberman's denials of incriminating allegations in the Bureau of Investigation's files and his efforts to disassociate himself from communists in Mexico did not dispel Hoover's skepticism about his activities. "In brief," Hoover noted, "Haberman would lead one to believe that he has been made the butt, as well as the target, of all forces antagonistic to his interests and that they have been deliberately engaged in a campaign of vilification against him."[56] About a month after Haberman's visit with Hoover, however, the Justice Department dropped the case against him for having allegedly evaded the draft.[57]

Haberman's return to Mexico City in the late fall of 1921 prompted criticism from both the left and the right. While radicals stepped up their attacks on him as a secret agent of Gompers, the Mexico City newspaper *Omega* criticized Calles for having persuaded Obregón to allow the "Bolshevik agitator" to return after deporting him earlier. Soon, however, Carrillo Puerto, now the socialist governor of Yucatán, appointed Haberman as an agent for the Comisión Exportadora de Yucatán (Yucatecan Export Commission), which had replaced the Comisión Reguladora del Mercado de Hénequen (Regulatory Commission for the Henequen Market) as the state henequen marketing body.[58]

The American consul in Progreso, Yucatán, was alarmed by Haberman's new appointment, but he pointed out that Carrillo Puerto and his radical colleagues had become more conservative by the summer of 1922. "Perhaps they have lost their way in the jungle of socialistic uncertainty and confusion," the consul observed, "and perhaps they are pausing to provide for their own future financial independence."[59]

The AFL also kept an eye on political developments in Yucatán, where the PSY convened a labor conference in August 1921 to consider, among other issues, an invitation to join the Third International. According to Karl Schmitt, Carrillo Puerto planned to accept the invitation, but Calles dispatched a delegation of CROM leaders who applied enough pressure to convince the conference delegates to reject Moscow's overtures. The conference also received a telegram from J. W. Kelly, an AFL organizer who had accompanied E. C. Davison to CROM's convention earlier that summer and who was working with Haberman to cement ties between the CROM and the AFL. Kelly urged the conference to decline Moscow's invitation. Since Haberman was conferring with PAFL leaders and Machinists' officials in the United States at the time, it is possible that he told Kelly about the conference in Izamal and may have suggested that the telegram be sent.[60]

Before returning to Mexico in late 1921, Haberman met with Harry Weinberger, a New York civil-liberties attorney who had pressed the Justice Department to dismiss its case against Haberman for alleged wartime evasion of the draft. Weinberger's list of clients included several Mexican anarchists jailed in the United States, and he utilized his friendship with Haberman on their behalf. Often meeting at the liberal Civic Club in New York City, he and Haberman devised a strategy to secure CROM and AFL resolutions calling for the release of these prisoners and to persuade the Mexican government to underwrite the campaign to win political amnesty for the imprisoned anarchists.

This strategy, which tapped Haberman's connections with top

Mexican officials and PAFL leaders, was only partially successful. Obregón and later Calles wrote letters to the governor of Texas requesting pardons for Weinberger's clients, but they apparently never provided money for the legal efforts to free them. Ricardo Flores Magón died in prison at Fort Leavenworth in November 1922, but the AFL joined the CROM to pass a resolution in 1924 that urged the United States to pardon Abraham Cisneros, Jesús M. Rangel, Jesús Gonzales, Leonardo M. Vásquez, Pedro Perales, and Charles Cline. The release of these prisoners in 1926 owed much to the combined efforts of the CROM and the AFL.[61]

Frustrated at times over Haberman's lack of attentiveness to the efforts on behalf of the jailed Mexican anarchists, Weinberger lost contact with him between June and December 1922.[62] After Haberman addressed the Socialist Party's national convention in Cleveland in April, he went to New York to negotiate marketing arrangements for Yucatecan henequen planters.[63] Upon returning to Mexico City, he discovered that his nephew, Basilio Iliesco, whom he had invited to live with him and given a job in the Department of Education, had thrown the Haberman home into disarray. Mrs. Haberman had run away from Mexico City with their four-year-old son and Iliesco, with whom she had become romantically involved. Feeling betrayed, Haberman informed U.S. immigration officials that his nephew had filed a false affidavit when he entered the United States, claiming Mexican rather than Romanian citizenship. On a leave of absence from the Education Ministry, Haberman went to Los Angeles to try to recover his son.[64]

Haberman's personal affairs, frequent travels, and numerous political activities undoubtedly partially accounted for his failure to devote as much attention to Weinberger's political clients as his partner would have liked. Perhaps more compelling political and ideological considerations, however, limited his commitment to Ricardo Flores Magón and other anarchists imprisoned in the United States. It may have been politically popular in Mexico to protest civil rights violations of Mexicans in the United States, but CROM leaders and Mexican officials did not demonstrate equal concern for left-wing elements at home. Given Haberman's participation in joint efforts by the CROM and the Mexican government to crush the CGT, one might justifiably question the depth of his commitment to civil rights.

Although Haberman opposed the violent overthrow of capitalism, he did not reject the use of violence against communists and anarchists. During a two-hour conversation in late 1922 with Louis DeNette, an agent from the Bureau of Investigation, he attacked the anarchosyndicalist CGT for fomenting strikes and complained that industry managers needed a more centralized, forceful strategy to combat the union's syndicalist tactics. He told DeNette that CGT workers were becoming more militant because of the tendency of many employers to grant some of their demands.

Suggesting that the U.S. government observe the fate of the next strike in Mexico City, Haberman explained that Mexican officials had adopted a plan, "yet a well-guarded secret in Mexican Governmental circles," which he had authored to combat the CGT. According to this plan, the government would encourage managers in plants that employed CGT members to encourage a general strike and then fire all of the strikers. Federal troops would guard the plants as CROM-affiliated strikebreakers replaced CGT workers. Haberman told DeNette that harsh measures, "even the use of machine guns," would be adopted to send a "salutary warning" to CGT unions. He admitted that the scheme was "sanguinary," but he emphasized that "in no other way can the lesson be conveyed to the Communists that they must respect property and cease their Bolshevik propaganda."[65]

Although Haberman possibly exaggerated when he claimed to be the author of this plan to weaken the CGT, the statements that he made to a skeptical DeNette accurately described his activities and ideology. Haberman admitted that he was working to promote U.S. recognition of Obregón, and he acknowledged his affiliation with the Socialist Party. He also emphasized his genuine desire to improve the conditions of workers, but he insisted to DeNette that "such betterment can never be brought about by the bomb of the 'red' anarchist nor by bringing a country to ruin, such as has been done in Russia."[66] His candid assessment of his activities certainly contained more substance than many intelligence reports that linked him to the IWW and the Communist Party.

Haberman's analysis of Obregón, Calles, and de la Huerta also proved infinitely more accurate than that provided by many intelligence reports. "General Calles, like most of the advanced thinkers of today," he told DeNette, "is in favor of bettering the condition of the workers, knowing that society is built on the fruits of labor." He added, however, that Calles opposed bolshevism and was "working with might and main to eradicate all such tendencies in Mexico." Emphasizing that Calles enjoyed the full support of Obregón and de la Huerta in this campaign, Haberman added that the Sonoran Triangle understood that "an economic condition cannot be changed instantly, and that red banners and bombs cannot satisfy hunger or provide work." He stressed that Obregón, Calles, and de la Huerta planned to "educate their countrymen to habits of industry and thrift . . . to give the fullest protection to capital, while insuring that labor receives its just recompense."[67]

Haberman assured DeNette that the deportations of Gale and other foreign radicals had diminished the threat of communism. U.S. intelligence reports contained allegations that Haberman had contacts with Soviet representatives, but, in reality, he was becoming increasingly anti-Soviet.[68] At the Socialist Party's convention in New York City on May 21, 1923, he denounced Communists as "just as impudent and just as big liars in one place as another."[69]

When Bertram Wolfe, an American Communist who soon became influential in the PCM, attended a CROM-sponsored May Day demonstration earlier that month in Mexico City, he found Haberman somewhat testy over the Soviet Union. "So many flags and signs, and not one that mentions Russia," commented Wolfe. Visibly upset, Haberman snapped back in anger, "We're through with Russia. . . . We'll fight that ____ country and those ____ Communists. We're through with Russia."[70]

By this time, Calles had proposed that a renewed public relations offensive be launched in the United States in coordination with AFL leaders, and Obregón had agreed to enter discussions with the U.S. government to resolve differences that blocked the establishment of diplomatic relations. Calles recognized Haberman's utility as a liaison between the CROM and the AFL, but Obregón apparently decided after gaining U.S. diplomatic recognition that Haberman had outlived his usefulness in Mexican politics. On September 5, 1923, Claude Dawson, the American consul general in Mexico City, reported Haberman's dismissal from the Department of Education because of his role in promoting a student strike at the Preparatory School. Since the dismissal of Haberman and his chief aide, Fred Leighton, came shortly after the

Bucareli Conferences, Dawson concluded that Obregón intended to crack down on radicals to placate the United States.[71]

Reportedly just one jump ahead of deportation, Haberman fled Mexico City, much to the amusement of his left-wing critics. An editorial in *The Liberator* described his forced departure as "amusing to those who know Haberman to be a fawning professional anti-Bolshevik job hunter in the labor movement who served until recently as a press-agent of Obregon."[72] One of his critics caustically pointed out the irony of Haberman's fate:

> Obregon's staunchest aids in the drive against "the Reds" were the so-called labor leaders drawing government pay checks. Now, however, these gentlemen are finding that they have undermined the very foundation of their incomes! Secure in the knowledge that he no longer needs them, the President calmly betrays the men who betrayed the Mexican proletariat to him, by kicking them out bag and baggage, amid the relieved applause of all the big capitalists. The final housecleaning of labor fakers began . . . with the dismissal of the understrapper, Roberto Haberman, who was forced to flee the capital to escape deportation.[73]

Consul Dawson relayed information obtained from the *Chicago Tribune*'s correspondent in Mexico City that Haberman had become a naturalized Mexican citizen and that the Mexican government was interested in punishing him for his role in the student strike at the Preparatory School. Praising the newspaper representative for providing important information on Haberman and other radicals for several months, Dawson suggested that the State Department locate Haberman and deport him from the United States if he had become a Mexican citizen. Following an investigation, however, the State Department learned that Haberman had not been naturalized as a Mexican citizen.[74]

Reports of Haberman's banishment from the inner councils of Mexican politics again proved premature, for Dawson noted on November 9, 1923, that he had turned up in Mexico City, "much to the surprise of the public knowing his antecedents."[75] Dawson cited an editorial in *Excelsior* which denounced Haberman as a Bolshevik and observed that he had returned to Mexico after his alleged expulsion "by occult and extraordinary means." The editorial noted that Haberman was working with Calles.[76]

Haberman's close ties to Calles and his contacts with AFL leaders gave him a charmed political life in Mexico. As de la Huerta's

rift with Obregón and Calles widened during the electoral campaign in the fall of 1923, Calles sought to solidify AFL support for
his candidacy. He blocked Haberman's deportation and sent him
instead to confer with Gompers about the upcoming election.
Gompers had called a special meeting of the PAFL's executive committee and CROM representatives to mobilize support for Calles
and discuss the IFTU's efforts to strengthen its influence in Mexico.
It was Haberman who suggested that the next PAFL convention
be held in Mexico City to coincide with the inauguration of Calles
on December 1, 1924. Confident that the election of Calles was a
foregone conclusion, he worked with Chester Wright to prepare a
resolution to that effect which was approved by the PAFL executive committee and CROM representatives at the meetings on
October 25–27, 1923.[77]

The Bureau of Investigation reported Haberman's contacts with
Gompers during these meetings and noted his press statements
predicting the election of Calles. Agent DeNette again questioned
Haberman's earlier assertion that Calles was anticommunist. His
report suggests that the bureau may also have been concerned
about Gompers's activities, for DeNette noted the length of time
Gompers stayed in El Paso and his planned date of return to
Washington. He informed the bureau that the AFL and the CROM
planned to meet jointly at the AFL's annual convention. The
bureau also observed that Haberman accompanied Gompers to
Juárez, where both gave speeches promoting Calles's candidacy.[78]

Shortly after the outbreak of the de la Huerta Rebellion in December 1923, Haberman left Mexico for the United States. The
Bureau of Investigation reported that he may have been on his way
to Europe to obtain "foreign money" which he had allegedly offered Calles to persuade him from withdrawing as a presidential
candidate. Arriving in San Antonio on December 17, Haberman
went to New Orleans, where he and J. W. Kelly, an AFL organizer
described by the bureau as a "radical," held conferences in the
office of the consul general of Mexico. Leaving New Orleans, they
went not to Europe, but to Washington for meetings with Gompers
to coordinate a strategy to defeat the *delahuertistas*.[79]

Haberman delivered a letter from Morones to Gompers requesting help to prevent de la Huerta's agents from procuring military
supplies in the United States. Asking AFL workers along the bor-

der to watch for smuggled weapons and supplies destined for the *delahuertistas,* Gompers offered an analysis of the rebel movement: "The avowed purpose of the rebel de la Huerta, tool of reaction, is to crush the labor movement, to enforce compulsory labor by denying the right of workmen to leave their work, to give back the public land to great concessionaires, to set Mexico back a decade or more into darkness."[80] Sinclair Snow's suggestion that this statement was Haberman's handiwork is probably correct. Haberman, perhaps worried that de la Huerta's popularity among independent labor unions and elements of the CGT might attract the support of progressive forces in the United States, may have drafted the statement in order to dramatize the significance of this rebellion for organized labor. He undoubtedly recognized that his task would be easier if he were to describe the "avowed" purpose of the *delahuertistas* as reactionary.[81]

The coordinated AFL-CROM effort to defeat the *delahuertistas* strengthened Haberman's role in promoting AFL support for Calles and closer labor relations. As a CROM delegate working directly under Calles, he attended the convention of the Conference for Progressive Political Action in July 1924 and endorsed the presidential nomination of Robert LaFollette. He gave speeches in the United States to promote the LaFollette ticket and touted what he described as a "Monroe Doctrine of Labor" to combat "the exploitation of human and natural resources by Wall Street capitalists."[82] Stressing the CROM's anticommunist orientation, he described the mutual benefits that had already accrued to the CROM and the AFL as a result of their friendship. He pointed out that Mexico, with a single exception, had bought only union-made goods from the United States. To underscore that Mexico was faithfully honoring its international financial obligations, he noted that the government had imposed austerity on its employees to service the foreign debt.[83]

The de la Huerta Rebellion and assassination of Carrillo Puerto shook Haberman's faith in a peaceful transition to socialism and convinced the PCM's Bertram Wolfe that the coalition against the *delahuertistas* represented the correct revolutionary strategy. Encouraged by the Mexican government's official mourning over the deaths of Lenin and Carrillo Puerto, Wolfe detected a more pro-Soviet shift in Haberman's philosophy during a conversation on

February 9, 1924. "I always believed," Haberman told Wolfe at a gathering to mourn the passing of the two revolutionary figures, "that we might show the world that a proletarian revolution could be made peacefully. . . . But this counter-revolution . . . has convinced me that we'll have to borrow a leaf from the book of Russian history and use some dictatorship on these fellows."[84]

Despite his statements to Wolfe, Haberman did not move to the left. Wolfe looked favorably upon the flocking of official labor and peasant organizations to anti-*delahuertista* forces in Mexico as an indication of a growing revolutionary worker-peasant alliance. Although he and Haberman supported the Obregón-Calles forces, they were at odds over politics in the United States, where the Communist Party was trying to build a coalition of workers and farmers by extending its influence in the Farmer-Labor Party (FLP) movement. State Department reports that Haberman planned to attend the FLP convention in St. Paul, Minnesota, on June 17, 1924, proved false. Haberman distanced himself publicly from the FLP and made clear that he would support the progressive base within the AFL, which had discarded its policy of "nonpartisanship" to back LaFollette. Haberman's close ties to AFL officials put him in a position to work for even closer AFL-CROM relations after the defeat of the *delahuertistas* and election of Calles, who used him to promote a noninterventionist U.S. policy toward Mexico. Haberman assured the American public that Calles would protect foreign capital and provide compensation to landowners whose properties might be affected by government land reform policies.[85]

Haberman acted as an interpreter in meetings during the summer of 1924 between Gompers and Calles, who told the AFL executive council at a luncheon in his honor that his election represented the "expressed will of the working classes." Gompers praised Calles for being "One Hundred Per Cent." Calles invited the executive council to attend his inauguration on December 1. "You can have the absolute assurance," he asserted, "that I will never be a traitor."[86]

Haberman attended an executive council meeting on October 20 to brief AFL officials on the arrangements for their trip to Mexico City. AFL delegates would be the CROM's guests, and members of the executive council would be official guests of the government.[87] Haberman also addressed the AFL convention in November to express gratitude for American labor's support. He told the delegates that they would be the special guests of honor at the inauguration of "Brother and Comrade" Calles, "the first chief executive of a nation on this continent elected by organized labor, and only by organized labor."[88]

Haberman again acted as an interpreter at the joint CROM-AFL session in Juárez on November 18, 1924. He read a telegram from Morones which expressed regrets that he could not attend the conferences. Haberman assured the AFL delegates that Morones, who had been shot during a meeting of the Chamber of Deputies, was on the road to full recovery after the attempt on his life by "representatives of the capitalists."[89]

The AFL and the CROM attached much importance to their efforts on behalf of Calles. Gompers asked Haberman to see that Jack McFarland, a representative of the Fox Film Production Company, was assigned an interpreter and guide while in Mexico to film the inauguration of Calles. McFarland intended to highlight labor's contributions to Calles's election.[90]

Caught up in the pomp and ceremony, Haberman reportedly overstepped his authority, however, in lavishing attention on the AFL delegates to the inauguration. When the AFL convention ended and Gompers was about to leave for Mexico City, Haberman pressed the commanding officer of the Juárez garrison to provide Gompers with an escort of a hundred men. The officer initially refused, saying that he had no authority, but acquiesced when Haberman told him that he had Obregón's blanket authority. When the party reached Chihuahua, however, the officer telegraphed the War Department, which referred the message to Obregón. Indignant that a foreigner could move Mexican troops without authorization, Obregón directed the officer to return to his post at Juárez and signed an order for Haberman's expulsion. "If I should permit that damned gringo to move a hundred troops this time," he said, "he might move a thousand next time."[91]

Haberman's close ties to Calles saved him from deportation. When Calles interceded on Haberman's behalf, Obregón revoked the expulsion order on condition that Haberman apply immediately for Mexican citizenship. Haberman complied, and the government expedited his application. He reportedly became a naturalized Mexican citizen during the first week of December 1924.[92]

Haberman continued to play a role in the Calles administration and the post-Gompers PAFL, convinced that Mexico now more closely resembled a genuine "Labor Government" than did Britain or the Soviet Union.[93] When Gompers told convention delegates in November 1924 that the AFL would stand "shoulder to shoulder" with the CROM, a jubilant Haberman responded with feisty words of praise for the AFL's role in the struggle against capitalism, "the common enemy." "The capitalism of the United States," he told the AFL audience, "is the imperialism of Mexico. You have been our greatest help, and . . . we want you to understand Mexico, so that as Brother Gompers said, we will keep on fighting our common enemy shoulder to shoulder."[94]

Such rhetoric did not tell the whole story. The CROM's promise to protect the AFL's flank from the threat of communism also underscored the "shoulder to shoulder" commitment against radical unionism. It should be noted again that Gompers had returned from his trip to Mexico City in January 1921 convinced that the greatest threat to the Mexican labor movement was bolshevism, not American capitalism or imperialism.

Haberman played an important role in wedding the CROM to the AFL. Prior to the Bucareli Conferences, the Mexican government relied on a strategy to win U.S. recognition by courting the AFL and other progressive groups. Haberman's contacts and journalistic skills made him very useful to this campaign. The constant threat of U.S. intervention encouraged Obregón and Calles to use the CROM to promote noninterventionist forces in the United States. Haberman also took advantage of his numerous trips to the United States to promote support for the Mexican government among Socialist Party audiences. As a trade-union socialist, he helped to strengthen the SPA's support for AFL policies in Mexico. The significant role which he played in promoting the PAFL as a counterweight to interventionist pressures enhanced his staying power in Mexican politics.

As a journalist, Haberman interpreted Mexican events for American audiences and circulated among American writers in Mexico City who produced sympathetic accounts of the Revolution. He had frequent contacts with Carleton Beals, Frank Tannenbaum, and Ernest Gruening—three of the best-known American writers who called for a more progressive U.S. policy toward Mexico in the 1920s. State Department officials worried that his influence on American journalists would enhance the Mexican government's campaign to win popular support in the United States.[95]

J. Edgar Hoover concluded that Haberman was much more radical than he acknowledged. Although Hoover contended that what undermined Haberman's radicalism was "his seeming inability to cooperate personally with active communist and other radical leaders,"[96] it is clear that more than simply personality differences prevented Haberman from working with many other radicals in Mexico. His willingness to spy for the U.S. Justice Department may have reflected a degree of personal opportunism, but it also flowed from sharp ideological disagreements with Communists and anarchosyndicalists. Haberman was as committed to the defeat of rival left-wing forces in Mexico as he was to defending the Revolution against reactionary elements and U.S. intervention. While left-wing critics denounced him as an instrument of U.S. imperialism and the AFL, right-wing forces complained that he was trying to implant bolshevism and that he had duped AFL leaders.[97]

Mexico in the 1920s was a fertile breeding ground for corruption and political opportunism. The official relationship between the CROM and the Mexican government enabled Morones and other labor bosses to acquire immense personal wealth. Evidence suggests that Haberman also may have dipped into union funds and the public treasury to enrich himself. Although one must view U.S. intelligence reports on Haberman with skepticism—since his intelligence file contains many inaccurate representations and unsubstantiated allegations—these reports cannot simply be ignored.

The Bureau of Investigation's Gus T. Jones reported in the spring of 1926 that Haberman was involved in a scheme to defraud the Mexican government. Haberman and other unidentified Mexicans purchased roadbuilding equipment for the government through a San Antonio company which Jones described as "nothing more than a junk shop." They overbilled the Mexican government and pocketed a profit of ten thousand dollars. Jones noted that CROM leaders were in a good position to profit from Mexico's ambitious highway-building campaign. This campaign came under the supervision of Morones, whom Calles appointed as Minister of Industry, Commerce, and Labor. "Of course we are making no investigation," Jones added, "as we are not interested in any grafting from the Mexican Government on the part of these individuals."[98]

In the rough-and-tumble arena of Mexican politics, Haberman carved out a career that lasted until his retirement in 1954—no minor accomplishment, particularly for a foreign radical.[99] Such longevity required tactical flexibility and numerous compromises. Obregón and Calles, especially the latter, recognized the useful role that Haberman could play in the campaign to defeat communist and anarchosyndicalist forces and court AFL leaders. Haberman's opportunism and commitment to a peaceful transition to socialism made his brand of radicalism more acceptable to the Sonoran politicians who promoted clientelist relationships with organized labor and the peasantry in order to "institutionalize" the Mexican Revolution. Receiving a government paycheck encouraged Haberman to set aside reservations about Morones and join the CROM's campaign to win friends abroad and coopt, isolate, and defeat its left-wing rivals at home.

To a certain extent, Haberman's activities were an expression of the AFL's progressive wing. The strengthening of his role as an intermediary between the CROM and the AFL paralleled the growing involvement of IAM officials in Mexico. He undoubtedly provided the IAM with much information on the social policies of Obregón and Calles, who gained the support of American labor leaders for their efforts to achieve broader social reforms. The AFL convention passed a resolution in 1922 that was introduced by several IAM members urging U.S. recognition of Obregón. Singling out the Mexican government's ambitious budgetary commitment to education, the resolution praised Obregón's support for progressive social welfare and humanitarian legislation.[100] Haberman's activities reflected an effort to garner inter-American labor support for this broader campaign to reform Mexican society.[101]

The discussions that Haberman and E. C. Davison had with J. Edgar Hoover on July 18, 1921, revealed the limits of the IAM's progressive policies in Mexico. One of Haberman's responsibilities to the AFL was to spy on radicals in the Mexican labor movement. By collaborating with the Justice Department, AFL leaders hoped to convince Hoover that the anticommunist, reformist thrust of their policies in Mexico did not threaten U.S. interests.

The mobilization of CROM-AFL resources to crush the de la Huerta Rebellion strengthened Haberman's commitment to future PAFL relations. His expanded role in the Calles administration continued to irritate U.S. officials, who kept him under surveillance and tried to find evidence of legal violations in case they chose to prosecute him.[102] PAFL officials later publicly defended him against charges that he and Morones were Bolsheviks, pointing out that they had been important allies in the struggle to keep bolshevism out of the Western Hemisphere.[103]

7

The AFL and U.S. Hegemony
in Latin America

Revolutionary nationalist movements in Latin America since World War II have faced a sophisticated array of U.S. policy initiatives designed to limit the sweep of reformist forces. Organized labor has served as an instrument of U.S. policy in Latin America and elsewhere, cooperating with the State Department, Central Intelligence Agency, and corporate leaders in tripartite structures such as the American Institute for Free Labor Development to promote pro-American, capitalist-oriented trade unions. Its foreign policy, as Hobart A. Spalding, Jr., has noted, operates on the assumption that "what is good for the U.S. government abroad (and therefore for U.S. capitalism) is almost always good for U.S. labor, and therefore for labor everywhere."[1]

This collaboration reflects a consensus in policymaking circles that organized labor can play an important role in socializing Latin American workers to anticommunism and accomplish strategic geopolitical objectives. Although the activities of the AFL (and later the AFL-CIO), working in tandem with government officials and representatives of the private sector, accelerated in Latin America after 1945, corporatist tendencies in the Latin American policies of the United States germinated during the Mexican Revolution and the First World War.

Numerous studies have shed light on the AFL-CIO's role as an agent of foreign policy in Latin America in the post–1945 era, but the question of how a labor-capital-government consensus on Latin America evolved as a result of efforts to contain the Mexican Revolution is not as clear. Studies generally note that Gompers received government funding for the PAFL in an attempt to ensure Mexico's support for the Allies in the First World War, but they do not explain adequately how the AFL's activities in Mexico be-

fore and after the war shaped and were shaped by evolving corporatist arrangements in U.S. foreign policy. By probing the areas
of conflict and consensus among AFL leaders, corporate representatives, and U.S. officials over the Mexican Revolution, we get a
clearer view of the origins of a tripartite consensus on how best to
confront revolutionary nationalism. This sheds light on the wider
implications of labor's Pan-American ideology for future revolutionary nationalist movements in Latin America.[2]

Gompers criticized private-sector interests that urged intervention in Mexico, but even before the Revolution erupted, some who
recognized that the expansion of American economic interests in
Latin America required improved relations developed a budding
interest in the AFL's regional image. Among those was John Barrett, former diplomat and Director of the International Bureau of
the American Republics (later the Pan American Union). Barrett
told Gompers that Latin American representatives were very interested in his views on labor-capital relations and that he had sent
them copies of Gompers's speeches on the subject. No formal
cooperation between Gompers and Barrett emerged at this time,
but the latter's cultivation of friendly relations with the AFL indicated a nascent recognition that labor could perhaps play a role in
shaping a more progressive approach to Latin America. This new
approach would strengthen American trade and investment and
secure geopolitical interests without formal imperialism.[3]

The AFL's growing involvement in Mexico coincided with the
Wilson administration's drive to promote the economic integration of Latin America through a more coordinated policy of trade
and investment. Secretary of the Treasury William G. McAdoo regarded the government-sponsored Pan American Financial Congress, which met in May 1915, as a springboard to capture much
of the European trade with Latin America that the First World War
disrupted. President Wilson believed that American capital and
trade could liberate Latin Americans from what he viewed as economic exploitation by European financiers. John Barrett, the director of the Pan American Union, emphasized to him that greater
Pan-American cooperation could effectively promote American
economic interests.[4] As Robert Seidel points out, Barrett's blueprint for the economic integration of Latin America was an effort

"to impel foreign progress and development as an adjunct to the perceived export needs of the American economy."[5]

Santiago Iglesias and John Murray convinced Gompers that the Pan American Financial Conference and International High Commission, which was created at the opening session, meant the increased exploitation of Latin American workers. Gompers lobbied for labor representation on the committees set up to foster closer inter-American economic relationships. He urged McAdoo that summer to appoint someone "representing human interest" to these commissions. Hoping to put labor's concerns on the agenda of the second Pan American Financial Conference, which was to convene in 1917, he found McAdoo unwilling to endorse his call for a tripartite approach to the economic integration of Latin America.[6]

An exchange of letters between Gompers and McAdoo in the summer of 1915 revealed differences over the campaign to promote American economic expansion in Latin America. Unwilling to incorporate labor into the Pan-American financial deliberations undertaken by government officials, financial experts, and commercial interests, McAdoo told Gompers that he had no authority to make any appointments to the conference. To defend the government-spearheaded effort to encourage greater trade and investment in Latin America, he explained to Gompers that "we have reached the point in our economic development when it is essential to the happiness and welfare of our people that we shall secure a share of the world's markets, because we produce more than we can consume at home."[7]

Although Gompers endorsed economic expansion abroad, he did not accept McAdoo's theory that a saturated domestic market necessitated foreign outlets for American goods and capital. "There are many people in our country," he reminded McAdoo, "who are in need of the actual necessities of life. Have we really more than we *can* consume, or is it simply that many of our people are not able to obtain sufficient to enable them to share in the consumption of the products of our country?"[8]

Despite McAdoo's unwillingness to concede formal labor representation on the High Commission, the AFL's growing contacts with Mexican labor leaders and Constitutionalist representatives soon proved very useful to U.S. officials, with whom Gompers joined discussions in the summer of 1916 to find a peaceful resolution to the diplomatic crisis provoked by the Pershing Expedition. The State Department involved the AFL and conceded a greater role for the Labor Department in the efforts to resolve the crisis. Under the leadership of Secretary William B. Wilson and Assistant Secretary Louis F. Post, the Labor Department became an important bridge between AFL leaders and the White House as the Wilson administration began to use labor as an instrument of policy in Mexico.[9]

President Wilson refused to grant labor representation on the Mexican-American Joint Commission, which met first on September 6, 1916, to adjust diplomatic differences between the two countries. However, the growing frustration of the American commissioners over Carranza's refusal to discuss internal economic and political issues prior to the removal of U.S. troops prompted Franklin Lane to summon Gompers to Atlantic City, the site of the conferences. Using Gompers to lobby the Mexican commissioners for a less rigid bargaining position, Lane informally included labor in the efforts to adjust diplomatic differences and safeguard the long-range strategic interests of the United States. Although this meant listening to AFL criticisms of the interventionist activities of Harrison Gray Otis, William Randolph Hearst, and Harry Chandler, the American commissioners did not feel that the ad hoc integration of labor into these discussions threatened their objectives in any way.[10]

As the specter of U.S. involvement in the European war loomed larger and Gompers joined the advisory commission to the Council of National Defense, resolving the Mexican "problem" became a matter of even greater importance. Gompers's opposition to old-style colonialism and his denunciations of jingoistic corporate interests did not preclude the strengthening of collaborationist strategies to contain revolutionary nationalism. His attempt to persuade Carranza's negotiators to accept U.S. proposals reflected a conviction that the United States should continue to play a role in defining the parameters of economic and political change in Mexico.

Despite periodic attacks on specific interventionist forces, Gompers acknowledged the right of the U.S. government to intervene in Mexico under certain conditions to ensure the kind of stable political climate necessary to safeguard foreign capital. His foreign policy objectives even took precedence over efforts to reverse Carranza's repressive labor policies in late 1916. These tendencies within the AFL leadership made it easier for U.S. officials and private sector representatives to promote tripartite initiatives in Mexico after the United States entered the First World War.[11]

Gompers's growing involvement in Mexico and his activities on the Council of National Defense encouraged him to ask Secretary McAdoo again for labor representation on the high commission of the Pan American Union. He stressed that the AFL's objectives included fostering better relations between the governments of Latin American countries and the United States. He also argued that granting the AFL a role in shaping policies toward Latin America would strengthen the broader strategic relationship, which had become even more important because of the international situation.[12]

U.S. entry into World War I postponed the scheduled meeting of the second Pan American Financial Conference in 1917. Wartime concerns also encouraged U.S. policymakers to postpone resolving the diplomatic problems raised by Article 27 of the Mexican Constitution until after the war. The de jure recognition of Carranza in September 1917, following verbal assurances from Carranza to Ambassador Henry Fletcher that Article 27 would not jeopardize foreign holdings in Mexico, upset lobbyists for the oil, landholding, and mining interests. Using their friendships with several important State Department officials, Judge Delbert Haff, Frederic Kellogg, Harold Walker, Chandler Anderson, and Frederick Watriss urged that Carranza be given an ultimatum to repudiate Article 27 or face possible U.S. military action. Anderson even tried unsuccessfully to line up J. P. Morgan and Company and other bankers for a tougher approach to Carranza by suggesting that American bankers threaten to withdraw their support for the Liberty Loan program until Carranza eliminated Article 27.[13]

Not all capitalists who had investments in Mexico endorsed the hard-line tactics of oil and mining lobbyists. Gould Harrold, a member of the Mexican Property Owners Non-Intervention League and owner of a big sugar plantation in Sonora, came to AFL headquarters to explain his organization's activities to counter the interventionist efforts of oil and mining interests. His ideas pleased

Gompers, who complied with a request from Judge Douglas to get Harrold an interview with the president. Refused access to the White House earlier, Harrold went with Gompers to a meeting of the advisory commission of the Council of National Defense. Gompers prevailed upon Secretary of War Baker to arrange an interview for Harrold with President Wilson, who expressed support for the initiatives proposed by Harrold's organization. Although Harrold carried with him to Mexico a letter from Gompers, these efforts lacked an official sanction. Until the formation of the Pan American Federation of Labor, labor-capital collaboration to promote a less confrontationalist policy toward Mexico would continue along more private, informal lines.[14]

Judge Douglas searched for ways to graft this kind of cooperation onto U.S. policy toward his client in Mexico City. Although his contractual relationship with Carranza may have necessarily put him at odds with U.S. officials on certain issues, the Wilson administration had shown a willingness to use him at times as an unofficial channel to exert American influence. President Wilson had gained confidence over the years that Douglas, too, sought to preserve the strategic relationship between Mexico and the United States.[15]

Oil and mining lobbyists complained to the State Department about Douglas's activities, but he claimed to have the support of some important American corporate interests. A Bureau of Investigation agent noted that A. E. L. Leckie, an attorney who accompanied Douglas to Mexico City in the fall of 1917, represented numerous business concerns and was on friendly terms with William Mitchell, the managing director of the London-Mexican Banking Company in Mexico City. Optimistic about business opportunities, Leckie intended to open a branch office in Mexico City and use his friendly contacts with members of Carranza's administration to represent large firms doing business in Mexico. The Bureau of Investigation's agent believed that Leckie would "act as an eye for Mr. Douglas . . . and . . . also undoubtedly recommend . . . from time to time matters which if Mr. Douglas can get Carranza to accept will be of great benefit to the United States."[16]

According to the Bureau of Investigation's report, Douglas believed that "American corporations should receive a more liberal policy regarding their treatment from the Mexican Government" and that Carranza "should put the bars down and invite and make it possible for the safe investment of American capital in Mexico to help in developing her resources and creating new industries." He hoped to convince Carranza that breaking diplomatic relations with Germany "would result in Mexico receiving from the United States practically everything Mexico . . . may ask for . . . and likewise secure . . . that which she needed most, which was financial support through American bankers." The report concluded that Douglas also intended to discourage Carranza from supporting revolutionary movements in Central America.[17]

Douglas played an important role in establishing the PAFL. Following consultations with his client in Mexico City in the spring of 1918, he suggested to Gompers that an AFL committee proceed to Mexico to lay the groundwork for the PAFL with members of a national labor organization that was about to emerge from an upcoming May convention in Saltillo. When President Wilson sought more flexible options to undermine Carranza's economic nationalism that spring, he told the State Department to approach the New York banking community about opening loan negotiations with Carranza. President Wilson used Gompers as a liaison between Douglas, the White House, and the bankers.[18]

Gompers, who was trying to persuade President Wilson at the time to fund the PAFL, participated in discussions of a plan to use informal financial diplomacy to further U.S. wartime and postwar objectives in Mexico. The project recommended that the U.S. government act as the "moral guarantor" of a loan to Carranza from private sources. The loan would then be used to refund Mexico's national debt, strengthen its credit, and underwrite economic reconstruction. Endorsed also as a way to combat German economic influence after the war, the plan called for the creation of a joint commission to oversee Mexico's finances. Finally, it addressed concerns about Article 27 and the sanctity of foreign capital by stressing that "the conditions under which the loan would be made would involve the settlement of all major questions of economic and diplomatic character pending between the United States and Mexico, and would, of course, be subject to the approval of the United States government."[19]

A parallel initiative from the private sector to use the AFL in financial diplomacy tapped the Department of Labor as a channel to the White House. A key figure in this initiative was John R. Phillips, president of the Los Angeles-based San Lorenzo Sugar Company, which had interests in Mexico. The Labor Department's E. H. Greenwood acted as an intermediary between Phillips, Gompers, and President Wilson. The basic components of Phillips's proposal to open unofficial negotiations with Carranza included a settlement of the debt issue, the development of a sounder financial structure, granting of a loan to stabilize the Mexican government, and settlement of the Article 27 problem in a less dogmatic way. Phillips emphasized that the loan would be contingent upon Carranza's agreement to alter the constitution "to eliminate the portion which might seem to be inconsistent with most friendly relations with her sister nations or which might impose undue hardships upon alien residents and property owners."[20]

Greenwood and Phillips wanted the State Department cut out of the discussions, and President Wilson apparently agreed. Greenwood provided Gompers with the memorandum that the White House requested from Phillips, and stressed that the proposal should be discussed only with President Wilson. "Official participation in the usual routine matter," he said, "will not facilitate the affair."[21]

After failing initially to convince President Wilson to fund the first Pan-American labor conference, Gompers secured government money after winning approval for such arrangements from Secretary Wilson, George Creel, who headed the Committee on Public Information, and Felix Frankfurter, a member of the War Industries Board and liaison with labor. President Wilson listened to the recommendations of capitalists like Phillips and Lewis Warfield, both of whom had extensive interests in Mexico and endorsed a role for the AFL in foreign policy initiatives to contain the Mexican Revolution.[22]

Analyses of AFL collaboration with the Wilson administration to set up the PAFL generally stress the strategic objective of wooing Mexico away from its pro-German wartime neutrality. Such analyses neglect underlying economic considerations. Wartime concerns certainly figured heavily in the equation, but also important was the issue of how to preserve the fundamental economic relationship between the United States and Mexico. It is no coincidence that while trying to secure government funds for the joint labor conference during July and early August 1918, Gompers was also heavily involved in discussions with U.S. officials and representatives of the private sector to undermine Article 27 through financial diplomacy.

Gompers gave out conflicting signals about the motives behind the creation of the PAFL. AFL socialists Iglesias and Murray had urged him in 1915 to construct a regional labor federation to protect workers from the Wilson administration's drive to promote economic expansion in Latin America. When Gompers publicized the AFL's desire to establish solidarity with Latin American workers at that time, he captured much of this internationalist spirit by emphasizing that inter-American labor contacts could "help in the establishment of a broad international movement of the whole world, and that international parliament of man for which philosophers have dreamed and poets have sung, and which it is the mission of the workers to establish."[23]

To view the PAFL as simply a one-dimensional product of this "internationalism" does not tell the whole story. It is misleading to suggest that AFL wartime cooperation to create the PAFL as an instrument of Wilsonian policy was an aberration that temporarily sidetracked the earlier idealistic desire of Gompers for Pan-American labor solidarity. This leads to an uncritical examination of the AFL's prewar conception of a regional labor federation. Collaborationist tendencies had shaped the AFL's evolving ideology of Pan-Americanism well before 1918. Gompers's preliminary efforts to promote support for a regional labor federation among Latin American workers may also have been influenced by the IWW's growing interest in forming a regional organization. Although an IWW-led regional labor congress never materialized, Covington Hall, an IWW poet and editor, had called for the projected organization in June 1915.[24]

Still, it is a bit misleading to describe the PAFL as merely a creation of the government designed to enhance the Allied war effort. In a departure from his earlier lofty appeal for hemispheric labor solidarity, Gompers candidly acknowledged in early 1917 that the dream of creating a regional labor organization "was not a matter of premeditation grown out of years of desire of the workers of this hemisphere to form a Pan American Federation and a closer alliance of all Pan-American countries but had its origin in the development of the past two and a half years as manifested in the European conflict."[25] William Whittaker, who stresses the "long evolution of inter-American trade unionism," is partially correct when he describes as "incongruous" this statement that the PAFL was the exclusive product of the European war.[26] Whittaker idealizes Gompers's motives, however. Although Murray and Iglesias were more concerned about Latin American workers when they recommended the formation of the PAFL in 1915, Gompers had already begun to view a regional labor organization in the larger context of strategic international issues.

This certainly does not mean that Gompers had no interest in the living conditions of Latin American workers; it suggests, nevertheless, that in his view the PAFL movement had additional strategic implications, especially considering the revolutionary conditions in Mexico and the international crisis. Although the PAFL embodied the socialist vision of internationalism endorsed by Murray and Iglesias, it also represented the ideological expression of corporate liberalism, perhaps on both sides of the border. According to Judge Douglas, Carranza supported the formalization of ties between American and Mexican workers. The Mexican ambassador in Washington publicly endorsed the AFL's initiative, and Obregón facilitated the initial moves to create the PAFL.[27]

Corporatist-minded Mexican politicians may have had the AFL in mind when they promoted the labor convention that resulted in the birth of the CROM in May 1918. They may have concluded that a dependent labor organization, besides serving an important function in domestic affairs, could cultivate the support of noninterventionist forces in the United States and help ease the mounting tensions between Carranza and the U.S. government that spring by establishing friendly relations with the AFL. Alberto J. Pani, Carranza's Secretary of Industry, Commerce and Labor, who was interested in promoting the growth of business and labor organizations to regulate class conflict, promote economic development, and consolidate Carranza's government, also had a sophisticated grasp of international and financial issues. As a negotiator on the American-Mexican Joint Commission in late 1916, he had held informal discussions with Gompers, who emphasized the AFL's earlier efforts against U.S. intervention and radicalism in Mexico. These discussions perhaps reinforced Pani's conviction that a nonradical labor organization under government control could play a valuable role as a mediator of both domestic and international conflicts.[28]

William English Walling, a prowar Socialist and close associate of Gompers, wrote a book on Mexico that suggested the influence of the PAFL upon the birth and growth of the CROM. Although Walling oversimplified the issue, he correctly called attention to the symbiotic relationship between the CROM and the AFL. He emphasized that one of the chief purposes in founding the CROM was to create "a labor organization which should be sufficiently similar to the American Federation of Labor to form an effective union with it in the Pan-American Federation, then in process of formation."[29]

A broader vision of the PAFL guided those in Washington who wanted to integrate labor into a framework to stabilize the Mexican Revolution. The initiatives in financial diplomacy that involved Gompers emphasized the importance of ensuring U.S. hegemony over Mexico's postwar economy. Mexican economic nationalism posed an obstacle, but a less confrontational policy that employed more subtle corporatist mechanisms might be more effective and less costly than military intervention to get rid of Article 27.

Fearing that the Revolution might radicalize along lines similar to the Russian case, Lewis Warfield pressed President Wilson for a greater AFL role in Mexico. He lobbied the White House for a "departure from the customary diplomatic forms in negotiations."[30] Also worried about postwar social conflict in the United States, John R. Phillips endorsed a key role for AFL leaders in working out more harmonious relationships with employers at home and shaping foreign policy initiatives. Adding a labor twist to core-periphery relations, he argued, "Just as we need Mexico's foodstuffs and natural products, so are the laboring classes in Mexico in need of the guidance of constructive labor leadership from the United States."[31]

The end of World War I and the dismantling of formal structures to regulate class conflict did not dampen AFL enthusiasm for the PAFL. AFL leaders believed that a reconstructed world order should include higher wages and a basic respect for labor's rights, that if the world could not be made "safe for labor," then bolshevism loomed on the horizon as an unacceptable alternative. The growing penetration of capital into less developed areas also underscored that the fate of American workers was becoming inextricably linked to the fortunes of their counterparts in areas such as Latin America. The task, then, was to promote improved living standards for Latin American workers within a hemispheric structure that recognized the United States as the dominant power and the AFL as the leading force of a Pan-American labor movement.[32]

To accomplish this task within the framework of Wilsonian internationalism, or what historian Thomas McCormick calls "global corporatism," proved difficult in Mexico. Mexican delegates to the joint labor conference in November 1918 were not eager to embrace AFL efforts to win their approval of Wilsonian postwar objectives. Article 27 of the Mexican Constitution was a particularly sensitive issue, as evidenced by the storm of opposition aroused at the conference when the AFL introduced a resolution that opposed economic nationalism. To complicate matters further, the Mexican delegates irritated AFL leaders by pointing out how racial discrimination hurt Mexican workers in the United States and by reminding them that their efforts to make the world "safe for labor" did not include Wobblies jailed during the war. Mexican labor leaders warned that they did not intend to convert their organization into an appendage of the AFL and instrument of U.S. foreign policy.[33]

AFL leaders believed that the extension of business unionism into Mexico would benefit Mexican workers economically and undermine radical syndicalist influences. By getting Mexican workers and employers to adopt a contractual approach through collective bargaining, they hoped to stabilize labor relations and enlarge Mexico's economic pie. The report filed by Lord, Iglesias, and Murray following their trip to Mexico in May 1918 suggested that employers in the mining industry welcomed the substitution of business unionism for the syndicalist tactics which, they claimed, were damaging the entire industry. These employers expressed a willingness to pay higher wages if Mexican labor cooperated to build a more stable collective-bargaining system.[34]

AFL leaders viewed their efforts to promote business unionism in Mexico within a broader geopolitical framework. By socializing Latin American labor movements to "pure and simple unionism," they believed that they could undercut future nationalist revolutions in the region. Matthew Woll hailed the AFL's approach as the antidote for the virus of political instability which plagued Latin America:

> The leaders of our trade union movement foresaw the absolute necessity of organizing the workers of South America along trade union lines for the purpose of protecting their interests and advancing their economic conditions. In all parts of Central and South America the attention of the workers was purposely misguided and kept at fever heat over politics by the privileged few, the exploiters of labor, the predatory rich. Just so long as they were kept in this frame of mind they paid no attention to the only real movement—a trade union movement that would have protected their working and living conditions. They kept on shouting politics but worked for 70 cents a day.
>
> After all the question is predominantly economic. Back of the cause of unrest is the economic condition of the masses. There is just as much unrest and discontent in the republics in Europe as there is under constitutional monarchies. . . . It is a subject of general comment that the frequency of political revolutions in many of the South American republics accomplish nothing insofar as the economic well-being of the industrial workers is concerned. The thing that will bring practicable results there, here, and elsewhere, is fair wages, shorter hours and reasonable working conditions. This can be accomplished through and only through the trade unions.[35]

A Navy Department report prepared by Capt. Louis C. Richardson on March 11, 1919, contained little with which AFL leaders would have disagreed. Richardson, who had been on duty in Tampico since June 1917, was one of those who recognized that a stable postwar Mexico required an improved economic structure and a more rational U.S. policy. He praised the cooperation of local Mexican officials to prevent wartime disruptions in oil production and shipments: "The only reason we have not had strikes at Tampico since I assumed command . . . is that the Governor put the leaders in jail when they attempted to strike." In his view, the key problem facing the United States was the question of how to steer the legitimate demands of Mexican workers for better wages and living conditions into nonradical channels. He reported that the IWW and "unscrupulous politicians" had previously manipulated these popular demands for social change.[36]

Richardson complained about the oil companies' activities in Tampico. Emphasizing that the oil firms opposed every tax increase no matter how small, he defended Mexico's right to generate sufficient tax revenues from its natural resources to promote economic development and educate its people. He anticipated labor strife unless wages in the region rose enough to meet workers' basic needs. He conceded, however, that the oil firms would not accept any wage increase "unless compelled to."[37]

Urging the U.S. government to underwrite a loan to induce Carranza to revoke Mexico's "confiscatory laws" and agree to other American economic demands, Richardson warned that military intervention would require setting up a protectorate and undermine U.S. influence in Latin America. This would have far-reaching implications for domestic political economy, he explained, because Latin American markets for U.S. manufactured goods would probably be lost. "If we do not have a profitable outlet for our surplus," he said, "it will mean reduction of wages and unemployment for our workmen. This will tend to cause labor unrest, strikes, and the spread of I.W.W. and Bolshevism."[38]

Oil diplomacy threatened to destroy the infrastructure of global corporatism that had been created during the war to deal with Mexico. AFL leaders warned that the antilabor, interventionist orientation of the big oil firms drove Mexican workers to radicalism and intensified nationalist resentments. They stressed that the jingoistic demands of the "organized exploiters of the oil, mineral, timber and land values in Mexico" increased Latin American hostility toward the U.S. government.[39]

Efforts to extend global corporatism into the postwar handling of Mexico continued but lost considerable vitality as the AFL came under sharp attack from conservative domestic forces that resented labor's wartime gains. Wilson's Department of Labor continued to express interest in the PAFL as an organization that could help to shape a more progressive world order and cultivate support for the preeminent role of the United States in Latin America. Secretary Wilson delivered the keynote speech to the PAFL conference in November 1918, upholding AFL-style unionism as the model for Latin American labor movements. The Labor Department's E. H. Greenwood, who became a deputy secretary-general at the opening meeting of the International Labor Organization (ILO) in Washington in 1919, attended the PAFL convention in Mexico City in January 1921 as a representative of the Geneva-based ILO.[40]

Wartime cooperation nurtured a more favorable view of the AFL's efforts to secure representation on the International High

Commission of the Pan American Union. Secretary of the Treasury Carter Glass assigned Gompers to the Guatemalan Group Committee at the second Pan American Financial Congress in 1920, but Gompers was unable to accomplish much except to deliver a speech in which he touted the AFL's opposition to radicalism and urged the committee to consider the material conditions of workers. Approaching Princeton professor of economics Edwin Walter Kemmerer with a resolution to place the topic of working-class living standards on the next meeting's agenda, he found Kemmerer willing at first to offer a motion to appoint a committee to consider his proposal. Kemmerer, who had been hired by the Guatemalan delegation as a consultant on monetary and financial matters following a State Department recommendation, withdrew his motion, however, to avoid putting pressure on the Guatemalan representatives, who lacked their government's authorization to act upon the AFL resolution.[41]

Gompers then appealed unsuccessfully to the High Commission of the Pan American Union, whose new director-general was Leo S. Rowe, a political scientist, educator, and former Treasury and State Department official who had helped to construct a legal code for Puerto Rico between 1900 and 1902.[42] Perhaps taking his cue from the refusal of Dana Munro, a State Department financial specialist on Central America and secretary of the Guatemalan committee, to consider the AFL's proposal,[43] Rowe rejected the appeal. He told Gompers that while "undoubtedly sound in purpose and practical in every sense of the word," the resolution could not be discussed because the financial conferences were not authorized to deal with the "labor question." He hinted, however, that future conferences might address the AFL's concerns.[44]

Gompers continued his campaign for greater cooperation between the PAFL and the Pan American Union in 1923. A meeting with Rowe on February 1 did not produce any tangible results, but Gompers noted Rowe's considerable knowledge about the material conditions of Latin American workers. Rowe praised the AFL's role in establishing better relations between the governments of Latin American countries and the United States, and he agreed that Latin American workers should organize for higher wages. He promised to discuss with officers of the Pan American Union the possibility of having Gompers address a meeting.[45]

During conferences with Gompers and other AFL leaders in November, Rowe displayed more enthusiasm for a greater PAFL role in conjunction with the Pan American Union. In a meeting with Gompers, Mathew Woll, Chester Wright, and Canuto Vargas, Rowe discussed the Pan American Union's recent appointment of a committee to study matters related to organized labor in the region. Gompers complained about the absence of delegates from Mexico and the United States on the committee, composed of representatives from the Dominican Republic, Venezuela, Panama, Bolivia, and Nicaragua. Rowe shared his concern that the exclusion of delegates from the United States and Mexico would diminish the committee's effectiveness. He also agreed that the PAFL would be a much more appropriate instrument to conduct such a study. When asked by Woll, however, if the committee would grant PAFL representation, Rowe expressed doubts. He urged AFL leaders to consult Secretary of State Hughes about the possibility of presenting their views to the Pan American Union.[46]

Rowe's deference to the State Department did not encourage AFL leaders, who were skeptical about getting a favorable response from Hughes. They chose to solicit first the opinion of the Mexican chargé d'affaires in Washington. Manuel Téllez told Wright and Vargas that he supported their efforts to link the PAFL to the Pan American Union, but he added that the labor committee appointed by the Pan American Union constituted little more than a "perfunctory" gesture. Gompers discussed the issue with Hughes at a social gathering, but apparently nothing was done to facilitate the PAFL's proposal to strengthen its connections with the Pan American Union. The desire expressed at the 1924 PAFL congress in Mexico City to secure official labor representation on the Pan American Union went unfulfilled.[47]

The conferences between Rowe and AFL leaders suggest that the major stumbling block to an institutionalized corporatist policy on Latin America was the State Department's refusal to incorporate labor. Secretary of the Treasury Glass took the initial step in 1920 by appointing Gompers to the Guatemala committee, but Munro's reluctance to endorse an AFL resolution to enlarge the scope of future conferences encouraged Kemmerer to withdraw his earlier offer to sponsor the resolution. The inauguration of a Republican administration did little to enhance AFL efforts to put labor's concerns on the agenda of the Pan American Union. Although tentative and lukewarm at best, the support which Gompers received from Rowe and financial experts like Kemmerer surpassed the level of State Department enthusiasm for tripartite initiatives in Latin America.

AFL leaders hoped that their Mexican track record would make U.S. officials more amenable to their efforts to promote a national policymaking consensus on Latin America. The heightened interest that Rowe expressed in conferences with AFL leaders in November 1923 and his suggestion that they approach Hughes probably stemmed, at least in part, from the change in U.S. policy toward Mexico after the Bucareli Conferences. By this time, official recognition of Obregón had brought the United States into line with the AFL's earlier endorsement of the Mexican government. The fact that a bitter campaign to determine Obregón's successor was underway undoubtedly stimulated awareness that a broader policy might benefit efforts to stabilize Mexico.

The consultation of AFL leaders with the Mexican chargé d'affaires about linking the PAFL to the Pan American Union was an attempt to capitalize on the AFL's relationship with the CROM and the Mexican Government to enhance labor's position at home and in Latin America. AFL leaders hoped that U.S. officials and Pan American Union representatives would grant them a role in future economic and geopolitical initiatives in Latin America.

Coinciding with these efforts to win a spot in the Pan American Union was an attempt by AFL leaders to define more clearly their version of Pan-Americanism. The Mexican Revolution provided an important laboratory for the incubation of this ideology. In trying to shape a Mexican labor movement that had "cut its teeth" on anarchosyndicalism and revolutionary nationalism, AFL leaders had concerns that extended beyond the narrower interests of labor. If their objectives in Mexico were simply to reduce immigration and combat the use of Mexicans as strikebreakers in the United States, or if their sole interest in Mexico and Latin America was to strengthen the bargaining power of workers in the region, then it is unlikely that even the most halting steps toward tripartite initiatives would have been taken. It is important, therefore, to examine the broader implications of labor's Pan-Americanism to determine the areas of conflict and consensus among labor, capital, and government and their effect on U.S. policy toward the Mexican Revolution.

Mexican opposition to U.S. pressures spawned tendencies that were antagonistic to the brand of Pan-Americanism espoused by the U.S. government. Isidro Fabela, former secretary of foreign relations under Carranza, publicly warned in June 1921 that U.S. imperialism threatened all Latin American countries. He stressed that U.S. domination of Mexico would have serious regional implications and urged a greater spirit of *panhispanismo*—the union of Hispanic countries in a closer network of business, political, and cultural contacts. Expressing concern that the United States might again intervene militarily in Mexico, he emphasized that such action would jeopardize Spanish interests and called on Spain to play a leading role in the proposed union of Hispanic nations.[48]

The State Department monitored Spain's efforts to cultivate closer cultural and commercial contacts with Latin America. Spain mounted a commercial offensive in 1923 to make its products more competitive in the area. Government subsidies launched Spanish steamers carrying a full line of samples to Mexico in February 1924 to promote Spanish goods and study the particular trade needs of Latin American countries. The State Department noted that this effort convinced many Mexicans that a stronger future commercial and cultural relationship with Spain should be developed.[49]

Lewis Warfield, an American investor in Mexico who had urged President Wilson in July 1918 to include the AFL in a more enlightened approach to Carranza, worried that bullying tactics would only undermine U.S. influence and encourage these *panhispanista* tendencies. He told Wilson that the growing commercial relationship between Argentina and Mexico was a product of Mexican unhappiness over U.S. interference. Warfield acknowledged that the word of the United States "should be fiat on this hemisphere," but he recommended a less bellicose policy and warned that fears of U.S. territorial expansion in Mexico and Central America were widespread among intellectuals in these countries. His vision of Pan-Americanism included more progressive economic policies and a role for the AFL in initiatives to ease fears of U.S. imperialism.[50]

The National Civic Federation apparently made at least tentative

efforts to encourage a closer relationship between the Pan American Union and the PAFL in order to safeguard long-range U.S. influence in Latin America. Gompers's meeting with Rowe on February 1, 1923, followed a conference with Franklin D. Roosevelt,
a member of the NCF's executive committee, on economic conditions in Puerto Rico and the Virgin Islands.[51] Just two weeks earlier
the NCF's Committee on Foreign Relations had brought Rowe and
Gompers together to address a meeting. Gompers praised the Pan
American Union as the equivalent of a League of Nations for Latin
America, described the PAFL as "supplementary" to the Pan
American Union, and emphasized the AFL's broader political objectives in Latin America. "The purpose of that Pan-American
movement," he said, "is not only for the promotion of the rights
and the interests of the working people of the several republics—of
all the republics on this hemisphere, but also to aid . . . in the
movement for amity and good relations between the governments
of the Pan-American Republics."[52]

AFL leaders linked their call for participation in the Pan American Union to the preservation of U.S. influence in Latin America.
Disturbed by the development of forces that were denouncing the
"imperialistic tendencies" of the United States, they condemned
those who advocated a "Spanish-American" movement as an alternative to U.S.-led Pan-Americanism, and they attacked Spain's
new cultural and commercial offensive in Latin America. They
warned U.S. officials that the strategic relationship with Latin
America was too important to be entrusted exclusively to commercial interests. To combat the *panhispanista* movement, they offered
the AFL as the "one agency that can 'rehabilitate' the colossus of
the North in the minds of the peoples of the Latin-American
Republics."[53]

The era of the First World War had bred increased labor militancy, social revolution, heightened fears of radicalism, growing
demands for self-determination in colonial areas, and concern over
the inability of the advanced capitalist nations to prevent economic
rivalries from exploding into world conflict. The continued instability of European politics in the early 1920s reinforced Gompers's
view of Latin America's strategic importance. "If civilization is
challenged," he told the NCF's Committee on Foreign Relations,

"if the Republics of Pan-America are threatened, it is necessary first in the meantime to endeavor to bring about the unity and solidarity and the peace of the countries and the peoples of the whole world; but if that fails, the last stand of civilization may have to be fought out upon this hemisphere."[54]

These remarks, which came shortly after the French invasion of Germany's Ruhr district, indicated Gompers's pessimism about the European situation. Although he expressed sympathy for the French action, he admitted apprehension over future developments unless the matter could be resolved "honorably and fairly for France and the allied countries." To the applause of the NCF audience, he said that this incident probably could have been avoided had the United States joined the League of Nations. He also said that he agreed with his wife, who told him that if the incident led to another world war, "it would practically mean the decimation of the white race."[55]

European instability impressed upon Gompers the importance of Pan-American institutions should conditions deteriorate enough to make the Western Hemisphere a battleground for "the last stand of civilization." He appealed to the NCF audience for a cooperative approach to Latin America. In a reference perhaps to the Japanese, or perhaps to anticolonial movements, he made clear that the "white race" could ill afford to react passively to an assault upon the foundations of its civilization. Although Gompers denied harboring prejudice toward other nationalities and races, he noted the "great rising tide of color" throughout the world and emphasized "the common duty of every man and every woman to be willing to do anything and everything to maintain the civilization which has been the accomplishment and the result of a historic development of thousands and thousands of years."[56]

This appeal to the NCF's Committee on Foreign Relations for a cooperative Pan-American policy on cultural and racial grounds should not obscure the AFL's fundamental stress on the economic basis of such collaboration. Despite sharp disagreements with U.S. officials and capitalists who had interests in Mexico, American labor leaders made clear they would not repudiate the right of the U.S. government to intervene to protect those investments. This did not mean that the AFL would give unqualified support every time investors called for intervention. It does suggest, however, the limits of its "anti-interventionism"; specifically, it raises the question of how one can reconcile the vigorous anti-interventionist statements of AFL leaders on several occasions with their endorsement of President Wilson's two direct interventions in Mexico. It also raises the question of why AFL leaders refused to challenge the right of American capitalists to call on the military for protection of investments abroad.

To get to the heart of the matter, we must first review the AFL's theoretical position on the prerogatives of foreign capital in Mexico. Consistent with President Wilson's views, Gompers had acknowledged in 1913 that the Mexican situation might require U.S. intervention to provide the kind of stable environment for foreign interests that would eliminate the threat of intervention by European nations on behalf of their capitalists. His efforts to persuade Carranza's negotiators in late 1916 to accommodate American concerns about the status of foreign capital in Mexico, and his wartime involvement in financial diplomacy to undermine Article 27, indicated a refusal to accept nationalist alterations in the international legal and political framework in which capital operated. He sought to reform rather than repudiate that framework. The AFL's endorsement of Obregón stemmed partly from confidence that he would bend enough on Article 27 to make U.S. intervention unnecessary. Contacts with Robert Haberman, CROM leaders, and Mexican officials in the early 1920s convinced AFL leaders that the Mexican government would dilute economic nationalism sufficiently without overtly compromising Mexico's national political sovereignty.

Perhaps the greatest challenge to the AFL's support in principle of the right of American capitalists in Mexico to call upon the U.S. government for protection came during the postwar interventionist campaign highlighted by Senator Albert Fall's investigation of conditions in Mexico. Under attack from open-shop forces domestically, AFL leaders denounced the shrill voices that urged intervention and even the establishment of an American protectorate in Mexico. "Ordinarily we concede to Americans the right to invest in Mexico or in any other country," reported Matthew Woll to the 1920 AFL convention, "and under ordinary circumstances Americans who do not [sic] so invest are entitled to the protection of their government." He warned, however, that the predatory prac- tices of many capitalists in Mexico strained this support:

> It is an accepted principle that the people of one country who emi- grate from it to another are bound by the laws of the country to which they emigrate, and this principle applies equally to those who acquire titles and grants as well as those who engage in business. When there is added to such a condition the fact that much of the land to which certain adventurers obtained possession corruptly and in collusion with the previous governments of Mexico unfaith- ful to their people, they are not justified in having other nations of which they are citizens protect them in those corrupt practices and holdings.
>
> And where American capitalists engage in intrigue and in delib- erate defiance of the law of a foreign land in which they invest, we deny that they have any just claim upon the government of the United States for its protection.[57]

Aimed specifically at the big oil interests, this message reflected AFL unhappiness over the broader postwar drift away from global corporatism. The Wilsonian framework provided the AFL a chance to remake the postwar order along more progressive lines, and Gompers viewed the League of Nations as an important interna- tional instrument for curbing the predatory actions of capitalists in "Third World" areas. A world without a League of Nations would be one in which financiers dictated international relations.

Gompers's growing dissatisfaction with the Republican opposi- tion to the League prompted him to criticize Secretary of State Hughes publicly. In an article in the *American Federationist*, Gom- pers attacked international financiers for pursuing investment strategies that had a detrimental impact upon domestic economic development and international affairs. "They seek to export capital regardless of the results on the exporting nations," he wrote, "re- gardless of the fact that such capital may be much more needed at home. . . . Insofar as they regard themselves as pure and simple businessmen, the international bankers do not hold themselves re- sponsible for the political results of what they do, for the entan- glement of our government to protect their rights in politically backward countries."[58]

Despite their denunciation of international bankers, AFL leaders blocked efforts from within to repudiate the use of American troops to protect financiers' investments abroad. Amid expressions of labor solidarity and anti-interventionist rhetoric at the 1924 AFL convention following CROM-AFL efforts against the de la Huerta Rebellion, a challenge came from the floor to push the AFL's Latin American policies further to the left. Andrew Furuseth and Paul Scharrenberg, of the International Seamen's Union, introduced a resolution that denied bankers the right to use the U.S. army or navy to collect debts owed private American citizens. The Committee on Resolutions refused to recommend approval of the resolution.[59]

The committee's opposition to the resolution produced a heated exchange between Furuseth and Matthew Woll, secretary of the Resolutions Committee. Woll explained why the resolution could not be endorsed: "With the constant growth of international social intercourse between the peoples of all civilized nations, with the rapid extension of international finance, industrialism and commercialism, the restrictions proposed for the end sought by the resolution, confined as it is to our nation alone, would tend to isolate our people and nation from participation in the world's developments and thereby strengthen rather than weaken the causes for war." Although Woll refused to recommend approval of the resolution, he urged "the pressing forward upon the wage earners and the peoples of all other nations the substitution of processes to maintain national honor, safeguard international intercourse and obligations by methods and processes of a peaceful order and that makes unnecessary the appeal to war with all its hideousness and brutality."[60]

Furuseth strenuously objected. "It is all very well to speak of the progress and development of humanitarianism," he replied, "but there is no one who has an understanding of international affairs but knows that the loans made by international bankers are the forerunners of international wars." Stressing that unequal international relationships put countries like those in Latin America at a distinct disadvantage, he continued:

> If the loans are made by and through the real consent of the people there might be some justification for the position taken by the committee, but we all know that that is not so. We know that loans are made under conditions that will inevitably provoke war and conflict, and that the people in whose name the loans are made have no more to say about it, no more control over it, than we have over the course

of the sun or moon. All they can do is to bleed and pay—pay with their sweat, if they may, with their blood, if they must. It is an utter disregard for public morality, it is an utter disregard for the highest duties of man, and it is so unnatural, so dishonorable in its essence that it ought not to be condoned, far less be excused in a body such as this.

The banker . . . takes the chances, because he knows that if he is the citizen of a great nation there is always the remedy of seizing the custom houses of the weaker party, and collecting the money by sheer force. If that is excusable, then highwaymen's work is excusable also.[61]

The last word belonged to Woll. After Furuseth declared that he would vote against the committee's report, Woll expressed support for the resolution's goal of world peace, but he warned that its proposed solution would damage U.S. economic interests. "Our own people are engaged and are seeking foreign markets," Woll emphasized, "in order that the productive activities of our people might find greater returns, both for ourselves and to advance civilization in other nations." Furuseth's resolution "would tend to make it impossible, undesirable, for our own people to venture into the world's markets or the world's development and would seem to be giving the opportunity to all other nations to capture and control these world developments."[62]

Gompers's public attack on the "League of Financiers" in early 1924 expressed concern over American capital's global expansion without proper regard for domestic needs, but wartime corporatist experiences had weakened this opposition somewhat. Lewis Warfield had told President Wilson that the war had chipped away at the reluctance of AFL leaders to endorse a more dynamic role for American capital in Mexico. Nurtured by more progressive American investment practices and accompanied by AFL-style unions, an improvement in Mexico's economic conditions would diminish the number of jobless Mexicans seeking to emigrate to the United States. It would also expand Mexico's purchasing capacity and increase orders from American industries. Warfield reported that AFL leaders recognized that labor stood to profit from this more integrated approach to Mexican economic development.[63]

Fearful that the exodus of capital would damage American workers, yet unwilling to deny American capitalists access to the instruments of the State for protection abroad, AFL leaders hoped

that what Charles Maier has called "productionism" would provide a larger slice of the hemispheric economic pie to "respectable"
labor unions. Productionism includes the notion that countries
should endorse an international division of labor as the best way
to create a bigger economic pie and determine political relationships in the world arena. As Thomas McCormick writes, "The
interdependence of comparative advantage is to replace the dangerous and destabilizing competition of militarism, formal imperialism, and economic autarchy."[64]

Although AFL leaders pressed for a less militaristic approach to
Mexico, they did not repudiate the core-periphery relationship that
defined Mexico's position in the world capitalist economy as a producer of foodstuffs and raw materials for the advanced industrialized nations. They did not want to promote industrialization
in Mexico that would compete with American industry and workers in world markets. The willingness of AFL leaders to endorse a
greater role for American capital in Mexico stemmed in part from
the fact that Mexico's industrial productive capacity was confined
to light industry that served domestic markets and did not consti-
tute a competitive threat to American industries in international
markets.[65]

The open-shop atmosphere of the early 1920s weakened organized labor and diminished the willingness of U.S. officials to
include the AFL in foreign policy matters. State Department officials complained about the AFL's activities in Mexico. These officials warned against the concerted power of organized labor, no
matter what its philosophical orientation, and worried that radical
forces in the CROM and the Mexican government were duping
AFL officials.[66]

By 1924, the aid that the U.S. government had provided the
Mexican government to crush the de la Huerta Rebellion had vin-
dicated, if only temporarily, the AFL's policies. Favorable reports
from private-sector interests in Mexico that praised the AFL's conservative influence upon the Revolution reached State Department
officials. When president-elect Calles came to the United States as
an official guest of the government in the fall of 1924, AFL leaders
hailed the fact that they were included by the State Department
in delegations appointed to welcome him. "Never before," wrote
Chester M. Wright, "has a visiting head of a foreign nation been

received by representatives of the American government and the American labor movement."[67]

Wright was wrong if he regarded the glittery symbolism of this event as an indication that the State Department had experienced a change of heart and decided to allow the AFL to share the stage in Mexico. In fact, the State Department initially objected to the AFL's presence on the welcoming committee. The pomp and ceremony that accompanied the delegation to greet Calles could not hide deeper festering antagonisms over the AFL's Mexican policies. To be sure, American export interests arranged a dinner for the Mexican president-elect, and the Ford Motor Company would soon conclude arrangements to open an assembly plant in Mexico City, but the conflicts between AFL leaders and the Coolidge administration surfaced shortly after Calles assumed the presidency. The U.S. ambassador in Mexico City complained about the close relationship between Calles and AFL leaders, and he worried that organized labor and radicalism would jeopardize foreign capital in Mexico. To Ambassador James R. Sheffield, a nonradical union was just as bad as a radical one. For the next several years, AFL leaders found themselves defending the Calles government against U.S. accusations that it was Bolshevik, that it persecuted the Catholic church, and that it intended to confiscate foreign holdings.[68]

Although Republican officials in the early 1920s refused to grant the AFL a role in shaping their Mexican policies, AFL leaders continued to emphasize the antiradical basis of their collaborationist appeal. They stressed the patriotic character of their involvement in foreign relations and the broader regional implications of their activities in Mexico. To those who might question committing AFL resources to Latin America at a time when organized labor needed its resources against powerful open-shop forces at home, the executive council stressed that "every condition of labor, political and economic, in Latin America is of concern to us and has a bearing on our own domestic problems." The price of neglect, warned the council, would be too high to pay:

> The organized labor movements of Latin America will somewhere find affiliation with an international movement. If they cannot find it with the Pan-American Federation of Labor, supported by the American Federation of Labor, they will seek and find it elsewhere

and we shall have in all Latin America the threat of European domination. . . . The result of the domination of European radical and revolutionary philosophies among the labor movements of Latin America can only be imagined, but that it would be disastrous must be conceded.[69]

Santiago Iglesias emphasized publicly that the origins of the PAFL lay in the AFL's desire to prevent the rise of a revolutionary labor movement "at its backdoor."[70] In 1924, Gompers proudly pointed to the success of the AFL's efforts. "There has been a consistent and rapid development of trade unionism throughout Latin America," he noted, "and an equally rapid departure from the teachings of the European anarchist and syndicalist authorities who were in previous times so readily accepted."[71]

AFL leaders argued that their response to the Mexican Revolution benefitted labor and the broader strategic interests of the U.S. government, but they denied that their policies served private economic interests. "Our labor movement," Gompers wrote in his autobiography, "has never been associated with any effort to secure economic concessions or struggle for world-markets; hence, we are not handicapped by having to explain or defend our motives."[72] More than a bit deceptive, this statement contradicted, for example, Woll's economic rationale for defeating the anti-interventionist resolution introduced by the Seamen's Union at the 1924 convention.

Willing, however, to acknowledge that their activities promoted U.S. hegemony, and hoping to build on the arrangements that produced the PAFL, AFL leaders set out to erect an ideological force field around Latin America to prevent the intrusion of "alien" radical philosophies. Although in fundamental agreement with officials over the importance of U.S. hegemony in Latin America, they fought to redefine the nature of that hegemony. AFL leaders called for greater concern for the material conditions and organizational prerogatives of workers, increased respect for the political integrity of Latin American nations, and less emphasis on military intervention. They thus encouraged a debate over the national image projected by the United States in Latin America and criticized commercial interests for promoting shortsighted policies that sullied the reputation of the United States. Their search for a kind of consensual hegemony often put them at odds with U.S. officials and commercial interests and sometimes invited criticism from repressive governments in Latin America that opposed organized labor and complained about AFL meddling in the affairs of state.[73]

The "return to normalcy" did not diminish the enthusiasm of AFL leaders for the basic features of Wilsonian internationalism. However, important divisions within the business community and the Republican Party in the 1920s hampered the formation of a political coalition that promoted labor's integration into a tripartite approach to domestic and foreign policy. AFL leaders' pleas for an integrated policy toward Mexico were still falling on deaf ears when Gompers died in December 1924.[74]

The continuity of the AFL's post-Wilson response to the Mexican Revolution demonstrated an underlying endorsement of the "politics of productivity," which Charles Maier has described as the "American organizing idea" for rebuilding the international economic order after 1945.[75] As William Appleman Williams, Charles Maier, Thomas McCormick, and other historians have noted, tendencies toward building this kind of integrated world system appeared during the Wilsonian era.[76] Productionism's emphasis on greater labor-capital cooperation to improve output and efficiency at home and promote economic expansion abroad to dispose of surplus goods appealed to AFL leaders. By deemphasizing conflict between the United States and Latin America and discouraging reliance on military intervention, the "politics of Pan American productivity" represented a satisfactory solution to AFL leaders as they tried to increase labor's bargaining power at home and promote business unionism and their vision of the United States in Latin America. Not until the triumph of a new political coalition with a more integrated approach to domestic political economy and foreign policy would AFL leaders be incorporated more fully into this kind of framework.[77]

8

Legacy

The AFL's response to the Mexican Revolution was neither an idealistic attempt simply to promote the well-being of Mexican workers nor merely an effort to execute U.S. policy. Rather, it was the product of an interplay between progressive forces within the AFL, especially trade-union socialists, and the tendencies toward corporatism which became more pronounced during Woodrow Wilson's presidency. Gompers skillfully directed this interplay, using AFL socialists as point men in Mexico while blocking attempts to commit the AFL to a forthright anti-imperialist position. Sympathetic with the struggle of Mexican workers against domestic and foreign reactionary forces, AFL leaders often sharply criticized the interventionist activities of powerful financial interests. They refused, however, to repudiate the right of investors to call on American troops to protect their holdings in Mexico. Although Gompers in general favored a less confrontational approach to successive revolutionary governments in Mexico and often defended those governments against U.S. attempts to dictate Mexico's internal policies, he quietly endorsed the military interventions undertaken by President Wilson.

From the AFL's perspective, the Mexican Revolution was a popular social upheaval that produced a fundamental change in the nature of the Mexican state. To a much greater extent than Díaz, the Sonorans who recast and reinstitutionalized the postrevolutionary state in the 1920s recognized the need for a sophisticated response to the social conflicts that plagued Mexican society. They knew how to accommodate the demands of peasants and workers while limiting the scope of change by defeating more radical elements. The AFL's response to the Revolution both encouraged and limited the expression of these popular forces.

A complex set of domestic and external forces contributed to the growth of a captive labor movement in postrevolutionary Mexico.

The AFL helped to strengthen domestic forces in Mexico that regarded unions as clienteles of the state. Although the AFL publicly downplayed the Mexican government's manipulation of the CROM, Gompers preferred no other arrangement after late 1916, when Carranza's nationalism and a growing preoccupation with strategic concerns convinced Gompers that the Mexican people were simply not ready for a liberal, democratic order.

After Carranza's ouster, AFL leaders welcomed the arrival in Mexico City of an administration that had the labor movement firmly in tow. The official relationship between Obregón and the CROM contradicted Chester Wright's assurances to the AFL's rank and file that Obregón had "no desire to coddle the labor movement or to make it an instrument or annex of the government." In an attempt to qualify his statement, Wright added that "perhaps it would be more nearly accurate to say that there is no conscious or expressed desire in that direction."[1]

The Sonoran wing of the Mexican Revolution, so popular with AFL leaders, promoted policies in the 1920s that laid the basis for institutionalizing corporatist controls over the labor movement in the 1930s. These corporatist controls have limited the expression of workers' demands, although they certainly have not been able to repress rank and file militancy or convert labor unions into completely passive instruments of the state. By endorsing the official relationship between the CROM and the Mexican government in the 1920s in order to defeat more radical alternatives, AFL leaders encouraged the corporatist origins of the modern Mexican state.[2]

Gompers's efforts to steer the Mexican Revolution in a direction acceptable to the AFL constituted more than simply a form of cultural imperialism. They generally conformed to the behavior of a "labor aristocracy." According to V. I. Lenin, imperialism created larger economic pies in the advanced industrialized nations and thus enabled monopoly capitalists to offer a larger slice to skilled workers. Labor aristocrats received what amounted to a bribe in the form of higher wages and recognition of their organizations. In return, they supported the activities of corporations abroad and opposed revolutionary movements at home and abroad.[3]

The economistic philosophy that underlay Gompers's policies at home also shaped the AFL's activities in Mexico. American skilled workers reaped bread and butter benefits from the core-periphery relationship between the United States and Mexico. AFL leaders endorsed reforms in Mexico provided they did not threaten to pull Mexico out of the geopolitical orbit of the United States.

This does not mean that AFL leaders gave corporations a blank check in Mexico. They were especially critical of American investors in the extractive industries. The interventionist demands of the oil companies after World War I and the antilabor atmosphere in the United States prompted the AFL to sharpen its attacks on these interests. Furthermore, the open-shop atmosphere of the 1920s encouraged American capitalists to become more stingy with their bribe to AFL leaders. The weakened state of organized labor in the 1920s enabled capitalists and U.S. officials to use repression rather than collaboration as a response to class conflict.

Although Gompers attacked international financiers for viewing themselves as "pure and simple" businessmen and failing to take responsibility for the often detrimental impact of their activities upon international affairs, he ignored the political implications of extending "pure and simple" unionism abroad. AFL leaders defended Mexico's political integrity in the 1920s and promoted the consolidation of the postrevolutionary state, but they contributed to the deepening of Mexico's economic dependence on the United States.[4]

Although AFL leaders were not afflicted with what Robert Freeman Smith has called the "article 27 syndrome,"[5] they opposed Mexican economic nationalism. They favored a more flexible policy on Article 27, but their position later hardened when President Lázaro Cárdenas expropriated the oil industry in 1938. While the Congress of Industrial Organizations, the AFL's new domestic rival in the 1930s, took a more progressive view of the reformist regime of Cárdenas, AFL leaders criticized the oil expropriation and what they regarded as Mexico's drift toward communism.[6]

The AFL's response to the Mexican Revolution later made possible the growth of tripartite structures designed to maintain U.S. hegemony in Latin America. Gompers had consistently sought a consensus of big business, labor, and government, continuing to appeal to the Pan American Union and the National Civic Federation until he died in December 1924. Only tentative progress toward forging a consensus was made at that time, and the PAFL collapsed in the late 1920s. Nevertheless, American officials and capitalists who sought to preserve the long-range strategic and economic relationship with Mexico through financial diplomacy and less confrontational means had a favorable view of the AFL's policies in Mexico. This would have greater significance after World War II, when international bankers, multinational corporations, and U.S. officials conceded a more aggressive role for organized labor in foreign policy.

On the other hand, Gompers's activities narrowed the distance between the AFL and the Socialist Party (SPA) over policies in Latin America. His efforts to preserve peace during the Pershing Crisis and his frequent denunciations of interventionist forces impressed the SPA. In August 1925, Morris Hillquit, leader of the orthodox Marxist "Center" of the SPA, praised the AFL's Latin American policies at an International Socialist Congress in France. Although Hillquit acknowledged inconsistencies in the AFL's opposition to war, he smoothed over the limitations of the AFL as a force for world peace when he concluded that AFL leaders had "consistently opposed the imperialist policy of the government." Hillquit cited the AFL's efforts to prevent war against Mexico, and he praised the AFL for creating a regional labor organization. "American workers," he said, "have thus succeeded in the task in which their government has signally failed; i.e., gaining the confidence of the South American people. The Pan American Federation of Labor is a potent factor for the preservation of peace on the American continent."[7]

Gompers's policies in Mexico contained contradictions that would later create problems for organized labor. By encouraging a dependent labor movement in Mexico that was friendly to the United States and receptive to foreign capital, AFL leaders helped to preserve Mexico as a low-wage haven for American firms. The implications of this became apparent in 1925 when Calles granted concessions to the Ford Motor Company to open a plant in Mexico. Calles assured Ford officials that they could expect no trouble from labor unions.[8]

The kind of tripartite cooperation that Gompers so persistently sought reached its fullest expression after World War II. Corporate and government funds have helped to underwrite organized labor's activities in Latin America during the Cold War. These activities have included supporting the overthrow of elected governments in several Latin American nations that U.S. officials viewed as threats to American economic and strategic interests.[9]

Cracks have recently appeared in the foundation of American labor's support for U.S. intervention in Latin America. In a world system of core-periphery relationships, as Thomas McCormick points out, the "partial modernization" of areas outside the core is necessary to enable the advanced industrialized nations to sell their surplus. As a result, capital investments have shifted from primary commodity production to certain manufacturing operations.[10] This trend in recent years has strained organized labor's willingness to endorse U.S. policies in the region. Corporate quests for higher rates of profit abroad, Latin America's debt crisis, and "runaway shops" have helped to erode America's manufacturing base and produce a hemorrhage of American jobs. Coupled with the antilabor policies of Ronald Reagan's administrations, these developments created a crisis for organized labor in the 1980s.

This explains the growth of considerable opposition within the AFL-CIO to continued support for U.S. policies in Central America. For example, the formation of the National Labor Committee in Support of Democracy and Human Rights in El Salvador in 1981 challenged the interventionist attitudes of the AFL-CIO bureaucracy. Also, a majority of unions in the AFL-CIO condemned the attempts by President Reagan to overthrow the Sandinista government in Nicaragua.[11]

A militant spirit of internationalism has accompanied this growing internal opposition to labor's support for interventionism. Kenneth Blaylock, president of the American Federation of Government Employees, captured this spirit in a speech to the AFL-CIO convention in October 1985. "Now I don't know about the rest of you people here," he said, "but when I look at Iran, I look at Vietnam, I look at Nicaragua, I look at El Salvador, Guatemala, I would like for one time for my government to be on the side of the people, not on the side of rich dictators living behind high walls."[12]

Despite this militant challenge, the AFL-CIO, through the American Institute for Free Labor Development and its Department of International Affairs, continues to act as an instrument of U.S. policy in Latin America. Not even the pronounced antilabor policies of President Reagan could deter AFL-CIO president Lane Kirkland from serving on the Kissinger Commission, whose report recommended American military intervention and substantial economic aid to Central America. The leadership of the AFL-CIO clings to its conviction that a healthy labor movement requires collaboration at home and abroad, even when it results in the overthrow of democratically elected governments and the establishment of anti-labor regimes in Latin America. We have not yet seen evidence that those who control the AFL-CIO's foreign policy apparatus are ready to repudiate their longstanding commitment to U.S. economic and military hegemony in the region.

Notes

INTRODUCTION

1. In recent years, numerous scholars of the Mexican Revolution have challenged the mythology that the Partido Revolucionario Institucional, Mexico's ruling party, has encouraged to support its legitimacy. They stress the limited gains made by peasants and urban workers and the Revolution's failure to achieve fundamental economic and social change. For a discussion of this revisionist literature, see David C. Bailey, "Revisionism and the Recent Historiography of the Mexican Revolution," *Hispanic American Historical Review* 58 (February 1978): 62–79. On the ideology of the Mexican Revolution, see especially Arnaldo Córdova, *La ideología de la Revolución Mexicana: La formación del nuevo régimen* (México: Ediciones Era, 1973); Adolfo Gilly, Arnaldo Córdova, Armando Bartra, Manuel Aguilar Mora, and Enrique Semo, *Interpretaciones de la revolución mexicana* (México: Editorial Nueva Imagen, 1979); Ramón Eduardo Ruiz, *The Great Rebellion: Mexico, 1905–1924* (New York: W. W. Norton & Company, 1980); G. M. Joseph, *Revolution From Without: Yucatán, Mexico, and the United States, 1880–1924* (Cambridge: Cambridge University Press, 1982). More recently, however, works have appeared that challenge the more cynical interpretation of the Revolution. See, for example, John Tutino, *From Insurrection to Revolution in Mexico: Social Bases of Agrarian Violence* (Princeton, N.J.: Princeton University Press, 1987), and Alan Knight, *The Mexican Revolution*, 2 vols. (Cambridge: Cambridge University Press, 1986). Knight especially argues that the Revolution was a popular social movement that produced significant change. John Mason Hart, *Revolutionary Mexico: The Coming and Process of the Mexican Revolution* (Berkeley, Los Angeles, London: University of California Press, 1987), acknowledges that although peasants and workers were defeated in their autonomous demands for social justice, the Revolution did produce important social, economic, and political changes. Hart points especially to the successful efforts of the Mexican State to diminish foreign ownership and control of Mexico's land and natural resources.

2. For Gompers's account of his life and contributions to the labor movement, see Samuel Gompers, *Seventy Years of Life and Labor: An Autobiography*, 2 vols. (New York: Augustus M. Kelley, 1967).

3. On the Marxian origins of Gompers's early radical thought, see especially Stuart Bruce Kaufman, *Samuel Gompers and the Origins of the*

American Federation of Labor, 1848–1896 (Westport, Conn.: Greenwood Press, 1973). See also Stuart B. Kaufman, ed., *The Samuel Gompers Papers, Volume 1; The Making of a Union Leader, 1850–86* (Urbana: University of Illinois Press, 1986).

4. On organized labor's contributions to Progressive Era movements, see Philip S. Foner, *History of the Labor Movement in the United States*, Volume V; *The AFL in the Progressive Era, 1910–1915* (New York: International Publishers, 1980).

5. An excellent study of the reaction of American radicals to the Mexican Revolution is Diana K. Christopulos, "American Radicals and the Mexican Revolution, 1900–1925" (Ph.D. diss., State University of New York at Binghamton, 1980).

6. Quoted in *New York Times*, 16 October 1925.

7. For a view of this current of reform, which flowed from the top down, see especially Martin J. Sklar, "Woodrow Wilson and the Political Economy of the Modern United States Liberalism," *Studies on the Left* 1 (Fall 1960): 17–48; Gabriel Kolko, *The Triumph of Conservatism: A Reinterpretation of American History, 1900–1916* (New York: Free Press, 1963); James Weinstein, *The Corporate Ideal in the Liberal State: 1900–1918* (Boston: Beacon Press, 1968); R. Jeffrey Lustig, *Corporate Liberalism: The Origins of Modern American Political Theory, 1890–1920* (Berkeley, Los Angeles, London: University of California Press, 1982). See Alan L. Seltzer, "Woodrow Wilson As 'Corporate-Liberal': Toward a Reconsideration of Left Revisionist Historiography," *Western Political Quarterly* 30 (June 1977): 183–212, for criticisms of this view. Leo Panitch, "The Development of Corporatism in Liberal Democracies," *Comparative Political Studies* 10 (April 1977): 61–90, is a useful discussion of the tendencies toward corporatism in bourgeois democratic nations.

Attacking Weinstein for minimizing workers' resistance to collaborationist schemes, many labor historians have pointed out the NCF's limited influence in promoting the AFL as a legitimate part of American industrial society. See, for example, Philip S. Foner, *History of the Labor Movement in the United States*, Volume III; *The Policies and Practices of the American Federation of Labor, 1900–1909* (New York: International Publishers, fourth printing, 1981), 61–110; David Montgomery, *Workers' Control in America: Studies in the History of Work, Technology, and Labor Struggles* (Cambridge: Cambridge University Press, first paperback edition, 1980), 48–90.

8. Weinstein, *The Corporate Ideal*, xv, views "Progressive Era" liberalism as "the product, consciously created, of the leaders of the giant corporations and financial institutions that emerged astride American society in the last years of the nineteenth century and the early years of the twentieth." According to his interpretation, large corporate interests accepted the need to promote cooperation, social responsibility, and the interests of the community in order to rationalize the economy and foster economic expansion. Their ideology of social control, according to Weinstein, in-

cluded concessions to conservative labor unions and an expanded role for the state in regulating corporate activity. I will use the term "corporate liberal" throughout this study to refer to members of the progressive wing of the capitalist class, intellectuals, and politicians who were willing to make a place for the AFL in domestic and international political economy in order to undermine radicalism and ensure the long-range stability of American industrial society.

9. On the fate of labor and radicalism during the war, see Philip S. Foner, *History of the Labor Movement in the United States,* Volume VII, *Labor and World War I, 1914–1918* (New York: International Publishers, 1987).

10. Thomas J. McCormick, "Drift or Mastery?: A Corporatist Synthesis for American Diplomatic History," *Reviews in American History* 10 (December 1982): 318–330. For divergent reactions to McCormick's suggestions, see John Lewis Gaddis, "The Corporatist Synthesis: A Skeptical View," *Diplomatic History* 10 (Fall 1986): 357–362; Michael J. Hogan, "Corporatism: A Positive Appraisal," *Diplomatic History* 10 (Fall 1986): 363–372.

11. McCormick, 326.

12. Ibid., 327; Charles Maier, "The Politics of Productivity: Foundations of American International Economic Policy after World War II," *International Organization* 31 (Autumn 1977): 607–633; Charles Maier, "The Two Postwar Eras and the Conditions for Stability in Twentieth-Century Western Europe," *American Historical Review* 86 (April 1981): 327–352. For a good discussion of labor and corporatism, see Leo Panitch, "Trade Unions and the Capitalist State," *New Left Review* 125 (January-February 1981): 21–43. Also useful is Robert W. Cox, "Labor and Hegemony," *International Organization* 31 (Summer 1977): 385–424.

13. Philip Taft, *The A.F. of L. in the Time of Gompers* (New York: Harper & Brothers, 1957), 320–333. See also Lewis L. Lorwin, *Labor and Internationalism* (New York: The Macmillan Company, 1929), 275–301.

14. William G. Whittaker, "American Labor Looks South: The Gompers Era, 1894–1924" (Ph.D. diss.: Georgetown University, 1965), 857–858. Other works by Whittaker include "Samuel Gompers, Anti-Imperialist," *Pacific Historical Review* 38 (November 1969): 429–445, and "Samuel Gompers, Labor, and the Mexican-American Crisis of 1916: The Carrizal Incident," *Labor History* 17 (Fall 1976): 551–567.

15. Sinclair Snow, *The Pan-American Federation of Labor* (Durham, N.C.: Duke University Press, 1964), 51. See also Charles William Toth, "The Pan-American Federation of Labor" (M.A. thesis, University of Illinois, 1947).

16. Jack Scott, *Yankee Unions, Go Home! How the AFL Helped the U.S. Build an Empire in Latin America* (Vancouver: New Star Books, 1978). For the flavor of these critical studies, see also Henry W. Berger, "Union Diplomacy: American Labor's Foreign Policy in Latin America, 1932–1955" (Ph.D. diss., University of Wisconsin, 1966); Idem, "Unions and Empire: Organized Labor and American Corporations Abroad," *Peace and Change*

3 (Spring 1976): 34–48; Simeon Larson, "U.S. Intervention in Nicaragua: The Reaction of Organized Labor, 1920–1927," *New Labor Review* 6 (Spring 1984): 61–82; Hobart A. Spalding, Jr., *Organized Labor in Latin America: Historical Case Studies of Urban Workers in Dependent Societies* (New York: Harper Torchbooks, 1977), Chapter Six; Idem, "U.S. and Latin American Labor: The Dynamics of Imperialist Control," in June Nash, Juan Corradi, and Hobart A. Spalding, Jr., eds., *Ideology & Social Change in Latin America* (New York: Gordon and Breach, 1977); Ronald Radosh, *American Labor and United States Foreign Policy* (New York: Random House, 1969), Chapters Eleven, Twelve, and Thirteen; Susanne Bodenheimer, "U.S. Labor's Conservative Role in Latin America," *The Progressive* 31 (November 1967): 26–30; Donald R. Torrence, "American Imperialism and Latin American Labor 1959–1970: A Study of the Role of the Organización Regional Interamericana de los Trabajadores in the Latin American Policy of the United States" (Ph.D. diss., Northern Illinois University, 1975).

17. Radosh, *American Labor and United States Foreign Policy.*

18. Harvey Levenstein, *Labor Organizations in the United States and Mexico: A History of Their Relations* (Westport, Conn.: Greenwood Publishing Company, 1971).

19. Philip S. Foner, *U.S. Labor Movement and Latin America: A History of Workers' Response to Intervention,* Vol. I; *1846–1919* (South Hadley, Mass.: Bergin & Garvey Publishers, Inc., 1988).

20. Roger D. Hansen, *The Politics of Mexican Development* (Baltimore: Johns Hopkins University Press, 1971), 17.

21. On these nationalist resentments, see Ruiz, *The Great Rebellion,* Chapter Seven. Hart, *Revolutionary Mexico,* also emphasizes that Mexico's status as an appendage of foreign capital produced nationalist resentments which shaped the ideological character of the Revolution. For a recent view that downplays economic nationalism as a force in the Revolution, see Knight, *The Mexican Revolution.*

22. An excellent survey of social conditions under Díaz is Moisés González Navarro, *El porfiriato: la vida social,* in Daniel Cosío Villegas, ed., *Historia moderna de México,* 9 vols. (México: El Colegio de México, 1955–1973), 4. On the conditions of rural workers, see Friedrich Katz, "Labor Conditions on Haciendas in Porfirian Mexico: Some Trends and Tendencies," *Hispanic American Historical Review* 54 (February 1974): 1–47.

23. Eric R. Wolf, *Peasant Wars of the Twentieth Century* (New York: Harper Torchbooks, 1973), 26.

24. Hart, *Revolutionary Mexico,* Chapter Ten, provides an excellent analysis of how workers and peasants who fought in the Revolution were incorporated into the postrevolutionary state as subordinate groups.

25. On U.S. efforts to pressure successive Revolutionary governments, see especially Robert Freeman Smith, *The United States and Revolutionary Nationalism in Mexico, 1916–1932* (Chicago: University of Chicago Press, 1972).

26. Gregg Andrews, "Robert Haberman, Socialist Ideology, and the Politics of National Reconstruction in Mexico, 1920–25," *Mexican Studies/Estudios Mexicanos* 6 (Summer 1990): 189–211.

27. On his use of racist arguments to oppose the annexation of these areas, see, for example, Samuel Gompers, "Future Foreign Policy of the United States," a speech delivered in Saratoga, New York, August 20, 1898, *American Federation of Labor Records: The Samuel Gompers Era* (Microfilm edition, 1979), Reel 110 (hereafter cited as *AFL Records*, followed by reel number).

For discussions of Gompers's views on imperialism and the Spanish-American War, see Berger, "Unions and Empire," 35–37; Whittaker, "Samuel Gompers, Anti-Imperialist," 429–445; Horace B. Davis, "American Labor and Imperialism Prior to World War I," *Science and Society* 27 (Winter 1963): 70–76; Ronald Radosh and Horace B. Davis, "American Labor and the Anti-Imperialist Movement: A Discussion," *Science and Society* 28 (Winter 1964): 91–104; John C. Appel, "The Relationship of American Labor to United States Imperialism, 1895–1905" (Ph.D. diss., University of Wisconsin, 1950); Idem, "American Labor and the Annexation of Hawaii: A Study in Logic and Economic Interest," *Pacific Historical Review* 23 (February 1954): 1–18; Delber Lee McKee, "The American Federation of Labor and American Foreign Policy, 1886–1912" (Ph.D. diss., Stanford University, 1952); Idem, "Samuel Gompers, the A.F. of L., and Imperialism, 1895–1900," *The Historian* 21 (February 1959): 187–199; Philip S. Foner, *History of the Labor Movement in the United States*, Volume II, *From the Founding of the A.F. of L. to the Emergence of American Imperialism* (New York: International Publishers, Third printing, 1980), 418–439.

28. "Future Foreign Policy of the United States," August 20, 1898, *AFL Records*, Reel 110. On Easley's role in convening the conference, see Marguerite Green, *The National Civic Federation and the American Labor Movement, 1900–1925* (Washington, D.C.: Catholic University of America Press, 1956), 6–7.

29. "Unions and Empire," 36–37.

30. *Labor and Foreign Policy: Gompers, the AFL, and the First World War, 1914–1918* (Rutherford, N.J.: Fairleigh Dickinson University Press, 1975), 34–37.

1: IN SEARCH OF REFORM AND STABILITY

1. Gompers, *Seventy Years of Life and Labor*, II: 303.

2. James D. Cockcroft, *Intellectual Precursors of the Mexican Revolution, 1900–1913* (Austin: University of Texas Press, 1968), 97–98, 114–127; Juan Gómez-Quiñones, *Sembradores: Ricardo Flores Magón y el Partido Liberal Mexicano: A Eulogy and a Critique* (Los Angeles: Aztlán Publications, 1973), 16–18, 23–26. On the surveillance and systematic harassment of PLM members in the United States, see William Dirk Raat, "The Diplomacy of

Suppression: *Los revoltosos*, Mexico, and the United States, 1906–1911," *Hispanic American Historical Review* 56 (November 1976): 529–550; and idem, *Revoltosos: Mexico's Rebels in the United States, 1903–1923* (College Station: Texas A & M University Press, 1981).

3. A copy of the PLM's manifesto is in Cockcroft, *Intellectual Precursors*, 239–245.

4. For a recent study of the American radical community's response to the PLM before 1910 and its critique of the Díaz dictatorship, see Christopulos, "American Radicals and the Mexican Revolution," Chapter Three.

5. Grace H. Stimson, *The Rise of the Labor Movement in Los Angeles* (Berkeley and Los Angeles: University of California Press, 1955), 321–322; American Federation of Labor, *Report of Proceedings of the Twenty-Eighth Annual Convention* (Washington, D.C.: The Law Reporter Printing Company, 1908), 153 (hereafter cited as AFL, *Proceedings*).

6. Mother Jones to Gottlieb Hoehn, June 17, 1909; Ricardo Flores Magón, Antonio I. Villarreal, and Librado Rivera to Mother Jones, November 31, 1909; Mother Jones to William Howard Taft, December 2, 1909; Mother Jones to Ricardo Flores Magón, November 4, 1911; in Edward M. Steel, ed., *The Correspondence of Mother Jones* (Pittsburgh: University of Pittsburgh Press, 1985), 69–70, 72–74, 101.

7. Snow, *The Pan-American Federation of Labor*, 6–7, 11; John Murray, "The Private Prison of Díaz," *International Socialist Review* 9 (April 1909): 737–752; Raat, *Revoltosos*, 49–53, 167; Stimson, *Rise of the Labor Movement in Los Angeles*, 226–227, 321–322; Christopulos, "American Radicals and the Mexican Revolution," 92–95.

8. Gompers, *Seventy Years of Life and Labor*, II, 308–309; Philip S. Foner, ed., *Mother Jones Speaks: Collected Writings and Speeches* (New York: Monad Press, 1983), 369–374; *New York Times*, May 22, June 11, 12, 1910. Raat, *Revoltosos*, 48–49, credits Gompers for having influenced Congress to initiate these hearings.

9. Conference with John Murray and Chester Wright, November 16, 1916. *AFL Records*, Reel 119.

10. Executive Council Minutes, January 17, 1911, *AFL Records*, Reel 3; Whittaker, "American Labor Looks South," 468–469; Berger, "Union Diplomacy," 17–18; Bernard Mandel, *Samuel Gompers: A Biography* (Yellow Springs, Ohio: Antioch Press, 1963), 336; Raat, *Revoltosos*, 43–46.

11. "Porfirian Labor Politics: Working Class Organizations in Mexico City and Porfirio Díaz, 1876–1902," *The Americas* 37 (January 1981): 258.

12. Marjorie Ruth Clark, *Organized Labor in Mexico* (Chapel Hill: University of North Carolina Press, 1934), 11–15. Walker, "Porfirian Labor Politics," 277–286, links the development of a more repressive labor policy to a sluggish economy after 1900, which made it difficult to grant labor concessions without alienating the capitalist sector. Ruiz, *The Great Rebellion*, Chapter Eight, discusses the depressed economic conditions on the eve of the Revolution.

13. Clark, *Organized Labor*, 11; Charles C. Cumberland, *Mexican Revolution: Genesis under Madero* (Austin: University of Texas Press, 1974), 16–17. Historians disagree over how much the PLM influenced labor unrest during the final years of the *porfiriato* and the degree to which European anarchist, socialist, and syndicalist concepts shaped the ideologial roots of workers' protests. Cockcroft, *Intellectual Precursors*, argues that the PLM was a major force behind the labor unrest. Supporting Cockcroft's thesis is Salvador Hernández, "Tiempos libertarios. El magonismo en México: Cananea, Río Blanco y Baja California," in Ciro F. S. Cardoso, Francisco G. Hermosillo, and Salvador Hernández, *La clase obrera en la historia de México*, Vol. III; *De la dictadura porfirista a los tiempos libertarios* (México: Siglo Veintiuno Editores, 1980). See also David LaFrance, *The Mexican Revolution in Puebla, 1908–1913: The Maderista Movement and the Failure of Liberal Reform* (Wilmington, Del.: Scholarly Resources, 1989). John M. Hart, *Anarchism and the Mexican Working Class, 1860–1931* (Austin: University of Texas Press, 1978), also stresses the radical ideological origins of the Mexican labor movement. For a revisionist view challenging the thesis that the PLM played a major role in fomenting porfirian labor unrest, and denying that European socialist and anarchist ideas were the primary ideological catalyst of workers' protests, see Rodney D. Anderson, *Outcasts in Their Own Land: Mexican Industrial Workers, 1906–1911* (DeKalb: Northern Illinois University Press, 1976).

14. Richard Ulric Miller, "American Railroad Unions and the National Railways of Mexico: An Exercise in Nineteenth-Century Proletarian Manifest Destiny," *Labor History* 15 (Spring 1974): 239–260; Lorena M. Parlee, "The Impact of United States Railroad Unions on Organized Labor and Government Policy in Mexico (1880–1911)," *Hispanic American Historical Review* 64 (August 1984): 443–475; Ramón Eduardo Ruiz, *Labor and the Ambivalent Revolutionaries: Mexico, 1911–1923* (Baltimore: Johns Hopkins University Press, 1976), 20–21.

15. Parlee, "The Impact of United States Railroad Unions," 472–475, argues that the Díaz government's efforts to become the majority shareholder in the National Railways encouraged a more sympathetic response to the demands of Mexican railroad workers and thus served to retard the development of a more radical consciousness by diverting militancy into nationalist channels.

16. Cockcroft, *Intellectual Precursors*, Chapters Seven, Eight; Raat, *Revoltosos*, 58–59.

17. Gompers, *Seventy Years of Life and Labor*, II, 310.

18. Quoted in Mandel, *Samuel Gompers*, 337. The standard account in English of the *magonista* invasion of Baja California is Lowell Blaisdell, *Desert Revolution, Baja California, 1911* (Madison: University of Wisconsin Press, 1962).

19. Mandel, *Samuel Gompers*, 337, attributes Mitchell's willingness to protest against possible U.S. intervention to the influx of cheap Mexican labor under Díaz, which heavily affected American miners.

20. *New York Call*, March 24, April 11, April 13, 1911. See also Christopulos, "American Radicals and the Mexican Revolution," 157–159, for the flavor of similar labor protests.

21. Christopulos, "American Radicals and the Mexican Revolution," 154–159.

22. Ibid., 147–151; Blaisdell, *Desert Revolution*, 95–97; Raat, *Revoltosos*, 60–61.

23. Eugene V. Debs, "The Crisis in Mexico," *International Socialist Review* 12 (July 1911): 23.

24. John Murray to Samuel Gompers, June 8, 1916, *AFL Records*, Reel 80; Mother Jones to Ricardo Flores Magón, November 4, 1911, in Steel, ed., *The Correspondence of Mother Jones*, 100. The quote is in Pan-American Federation of Labor, *Report of the Proceedings of the Third Congress*, 1921, 74 (hereafter cited as PAFL, *Proceedings*).

25. Mother Jones to Mr. Calero, Secretary of Justice in the Republic of Mexico, October 25, 1911, in Steel, ed., *The Correspondence of Mother Jones*, 97–100.

26. Ibid., 98–99.

27. Ibid., 99–100.

28. Jones to Flores Magón, November 4, 1911, in ibid., 100–101. Flores Magón did indeed again fall into the "clutches of the law" by the end of 1911 and died in Fort Leavenworth prison in 1923.

29. For an account of the Casa written by one of its founders, see Rosendo Salazar, *La Casa del Obrero Mundial* (México: Costa-Amic, 1962). See also John M. Hart, "The Urban Working Class and the Mexican Revolution: The Case of the Casa del Obrero Mundial," *Hispanic American Historical Review* 58 (February 1978): 1–20.

30. *Labor Organizations*, 11.

31. Snow, *Pan-American Federation*, 4–5; AFL, *Proceedings*, 1912, 234–235, 256–257.

32. Cumberland, *Mexican Revolution: Genesis under Madero*, Chapter Twelve; Ruiz, *Great Rebellion*, Chapter Nine; Benjamin Keen and Mark Wasserman, *A Short History of Latin America*, 3rd ed. (Boston: Houghton Mifflin Company, 1988), 276–279.

33. Friedrich Katz, *The Secret War in Mexico: Europe, the United States, and the Mexican Revolution* (Chicago: University of Chicago Press, 1981), 46–49; Keen and Wasserman, *Short History*, 278–279; Ruiz, *Great Rebellion*, 388–390; P. Edward Haley, *Revolution and Intervention: The Diplomacy of Taft and Wilson with Mexico, 1910–1917* (Cambridge, Mass.: MIT Press, 1970), Chapters One, Two.

34. Miller, "American Railroad Unions and the National Railways of Mexico," 255–258.

35. Cumberland, *Mexican Revolution*, Chapter Eleven; Haley, *Revolution and Intervention*, Chapter Three; Conference with John Murray and Chester Wright, November 16, 1916, *AFL Records*, Reel 119.

36. Robert Lansing, "Present Nature and Extent of the Monroe Doctrine, and Its Need of Restatement," June 11, 1914, enclosed in Lansing to the Secretary of State, June 16, 1914, 710.11/1861/2, *Foreign Relations of the United States: The Lansing Papers* (Washington, D.C.: U.S. Government Printing Office, 1940), II, 463–465. For a discussion of how Mexico fit into Wilson's economic and political thought regarding underdeveloped nations, see Smith, *The United States and Revolutionary Nationalism in Mexico*, 23–34. Other works that have contributed to my understanding of Woodrow Wilson's reaction to the Mexican Revolution include N. Gordon Levin, Jr., *Woodrow Wilson and World Politics: America's Response to War and Revolution* (London: Oxford University Press, 1968); Lloyd C. Gardner, *Safe for Democracy: The Anglo-American Response to Revolution, 1913–1923* (New York: Oxford University Press, 1984); idem, "Woodrow Wilson and the Mexican Revolution," in Arthur S. Link, ed., *Woodrow Wilson and a Revolutionary World, 1913–1921* (Chapel Hill: University of North Carolina Press, 1982); Katz, *Secret War*; Mark T. Gilderhus, *Diplomacy and Revolution: U.S.-Mexican Relations Under Wilson and Carranza* (Tucson: University of Arizona Press, 1977); idem, *Pan American Visions: Woodrow Wilson in the Western Hemisphere, 1913–1921* (Tucson: University of Arizona Press, 1986); idem, "Wilson, Carranza, and the Monroe Doctrine: A Question in Regional Organization," *Diplomatic History* 7 (Spring 1983): 103–115; Frederick S. Calhoun, *Power and Principle: Armed Intervention in Wilsonian Foreign Policy* (Kent, Ohio: Kent State University Press, 1986); Haley, *Revolution and Intervention*; Arthur S. Link, *Woodrow Wilson: Revolution, War, and Peace* (Arlington Heights, Ill.: Harlan Davidson, Inc., 1979); Kendrick A. Clements, "Woodrow Wilson's Mexican Policy, 1913–15," *Diplomatic History* 4 (Spring 1980): 113–136; and idem, *Woodrow Wilson: World Statesman* (Boston: Twayne, 1987).

37. Quoted in Ray Stannard Baker, *Woodrow Wilson: Life and Letters,* Vol. IV; *President, 1913–1914* (Garden City, N.Y.: Doubleday, Doran & Company, Inc., 1931), 280.

38. Ibid., 292.

39. AFL, *Proceedings*, 1913, 364.

40. Transcript of discussion of President Gompers on Resolution No. 163, Seattle Convention of the AFL, November 21, 1913, *AFL Records*, Reel 111.

41. Ibid.

42. Ibid.

43. Cumberland, *Mexican Revolution*, 221–228; Clark, *Organized Labor*, 20–25; Ruiz, *Labor and the Ambivalent Revolutionaries*, 26–41; Carr, *El movimiento obrero y la política en México*, 45–56. An important work that challenges the traditional portrayal of Huerta as simply a reactionary and emphasizes many of his efforts to push domestic social reforms is Michael C. Meyer, *Huerta: A Political Portrait* (Lincoln: University of Nebraska Press, 1972).

44. Robert E. Quirk's *An Affair of Honor: Woodrow Wilson and the Occupation of Veracruz* (Lexington: University Press of Kentucky, 1962) provides detailed coverage of the Tampico incident and the American occupation of Veracruz. Hart, *Revolutionary Mexico,* Chapter Nine, shows that American military officers in Veracruz secretly stockpiled weapons and ammunition which were turned over to *carrancista* officers when the American occupation ended.

45. Jean Meyer, "Los obreros en la Revolución Mexicana: Los 'Batallones Rojos'," *Historia Mexicana* 21 (July-September, 1971): 7. See Haley, *Revolution and Intervention,* Chapters Six and Seven, for a good discussion of the Wilson administration's endorsement of the Constitutionalists and Carranza's refusal to welcome the U.S. invasion or outside attempts to mold the post-Huerta government.

46. Haley, *Revolution and Intervention,* 146–147; William Jennings Bryan to American Commissioners, May 20, 1914, and L. J. Canova to Secretary of State Bryan, July 10, 1914, United States Department of State, *Records Relating to Internal Affairs of Mexico, 1910–1929* (Washington, D.C.: National Archives Microfilm Publication, Microcopy 274, 1959), File numbers 812.00/23452b, 812.00/27406, Reels 70, 82 (hereafter cited as *RDS,* followed by file and reel number).

47. Gompers, *Seventy Years of Life and Labor,* II, 311.

48. In *Seventy Years of Life and Labor,* II, 322–333, Gompers maintains that the First World War forced him to abandon pacifism, but C. Roland Marchand, *The American Peace Movement and Social Reform, 1898–1918* (Princeton: Princeton University Press, 1972), 275–287, points out that his evolution away from pacifism began considerably earlier. Larson, *Labor and Foreign Policy,* 65, notes that John Frey, editor of the *Moulder's Journal,* claimed that Gompers privately told him as early as 1911 or 1912 that the European situation was weakening his commitment to pacifism.

49. *New York Times,* April 20, 1914. Max Kasimirsky, a general organizer for the United Hebrew Trades, announced plans to link the upcoming May Day demonstration to opposition to war with Mexico. *New York Times,* April 24, 1914. For an analysis of the American left's response to the occupation of Veracruz, see Christopulos, "American Radicals and the Mexican Revolution," 234–241.

50. *New York Times,* April 21, 1914.

51. On international rivalries and the fall of Huerta, see Katz, *The Secret War in Mexico,* Chapters Five and Six.

52. Executive Council Minutes, July 18, 1914, *AFL Records,* Reel 4.

53. Gompers to Zuberan [*sic*], July 25, 1914, *AFL Records,* Reel 77.

54. AFL, *Proceedings,* 1914, 364.

55. Meyer, "Los obreros en la Revolución Mexicana," 9–10; Clark, *Organized Labor,* 26–35; Ruiz, *Labor and the Ambivalent Revolutionaries,* 47–51.

56. Meyer, "Los obreros en la Revolución Mexicana," 10–17; Clark, *Organized Labor,* 28–29; Levenstein, *Labor Organizations,* 19–21; Ruiz, *Labor and the Ambivalent Revolutionaries,* 49–53.

57. Carr, *El movimiento obrero y la política en México*, 67–68.

58. In *La Casa del Obrero Mundial*, 164–165, Rosendo Salazar, one of the Casa leaders with whom Murray spent a great deal of time on this trip, claims that Murray was investigating the Casa-Carranza pact on behalf of Gompers. Citing an interview with Salazar, Levenstein, *Labor Organizations*, 22–23, maintains that Murray conferred with Gompers before going to Mexico. However, Snow, *The Pan-American Federation of Labor*, 8–11, contends that Murray was not introduced to Gompers until the summer of 1915.

59. Snow, *The Pan-American Federation of Labor*, 9–12; AFL, *Proceedings*, 1915, 56–59, 187–188.

60. Snow, *The Pan-American Federation of Labor*, 9–10, 17–19; AFL, *Proceedings*, 1915, 56–59, 187–188, 291.

61. Gompers to McAdoo, June 23, 1915; McAdoo to Gompers, June 29, 1915; Gompers to McAdoo, July 2, 1915; *AFL Records*, Reel 79. Chapter 7 will explore in greater detail the AFL's efforts to win representation on the International High Commission of the Pan American Union.

62. *Labor and Foreign Policy*, 57. See also 51–53, 56.

63. Easley to Gompers, June 24, 1915, *AFL Records*, Reel 79.

64. *U.S. Labor Movement and Latin America*, 147.

65. Woodrow Wilson to Secretary of State, July 2, 1915, *RDS*, 812.00/15409–1/2, Reel 46.

66. Revolutionary Committee of the World's Workers of Mexico to Gompers, June 10, 1915; Gompers to Woodrow Wilson, June 14, 1915; J. P. Tumulty to Gompers, June 16, 1915; Gompers to Rafael Quintero, secretary, La Casa del Obrero Mundial, June 18, 1915; *AFL Records*, Reel 79.

67. Gompers to Woodrow Wilson, August 9, 1915; Woodrow Wilson to Gompers, August 11, 1915; both enclosed in Gompers to Carranza, March 8, 1916, *AFL Records*, Reel 80.

68. Martínez to Woodrow Wilson, August 12, 1915, *AFL Records*, Reel 79.

69. Gompers to Martínez, August 23, 1915, *AFL Records*, Reel 79.

70. Ibid.

71. Gompers to Woodrow Wilson, September 22, 1915, *AFL Records*, Reel 79.

72. T. V. Shannon to the President, September 28, 1915; Gompers to Robert Lansing, October 20, 1915; Alvey A. Adee to Gompers, October 26, 1915; *RDS*, 812.00/16345, 812.00/16555, Reel 49. Gompers to Edmund E. Martínez, December 30, 1915, *AFL Records*, Reel 79.

73. Gompers to Martínez, December 30, 1915, *AFL Records*, Reel 79.

2. LABOR DIPLOMACY AND THE PERSHING EXPEDITION

1. Smith, *The United States and Revolutionary Nationalism in Mexico*, 44–47; Douglas W. Richmond, *Venustiano Carranza's Nationalist Struggle, 1893–1920* (Lincoln: University of Nebraska Press, 1983), 197.

2. Kelley to Duffy, April 20, 1916, *AFL Records*, Reel 80.

3. Duffy to Kelley, April 14, 1916, *AFL Records*, Reel 80. See also Duffy to Kelley, April 5, 1916, *AFL Records*, Reel 80.

4. Memorandum, March 14, 1916, *AFL Records*, Reel 80; Conference with Secretary of State Lansing re: Mexican-American Relations, April 5, 1916, *AFL Records*, Reel 119.

5. Gompers to Carranza, March 8, 1916, *AFL Records*, Reel 80.

6. Kelley to Duffy, April 10, 1916, *AFL Records*, Reel 80.

7. Duffy to Gompers, May 2, April 14, 1916, *AFL Records*, Reel 80.

8. Gompers to Carranza, March 8, 1916, *AFL Records*, Reel 80.

9. Conference with Secretary of State Lansing, April 5, 1916, *AFL Records*, Reel 119.

10. Memorandum on conference with John Murray and John I. Nolan, May 10, 1916, *AFL Records*, Reel 119. Gompers also wrote to Attorney General Thomas Gregory suggesting that he meet with Murray. Vouching for Murray's trustworthiness, he enclosed a copy of a letter from Murray providing information on the counterrevolutionary activities of Los Angeles publisher Otis and his son-in-law Harry Chandler, who had large landed interests in Baja California. Murray claimed to have seen copies of plans devised by these men to finance military operations into Mexico. Gompers to Gregory, May 19, 1916; Murray to Gregory, May 19, 1916; *AFL Records*, Reel 23.

11. Florence C. Thorne, memorandum on conference with John Murray and John I. Nolan, May 10, 1916, *AFL Records*, Reel 119.

12. Ibid.

13. Ibid.

14. Ruiz, *Labor and the Ambivalent Revolutionaries*, 54–55; Hart, *Anarchism and the Mexican Working Class*, 150–151.

15. Thorne, memorandum on conference with Murray and Nolan, May 10, 1916, *AFL Records*, Reel 119.

16. Gompers to Secretary, Casa del Obrero Mundial, May 23, 1916, *AFL Records*, Reel 80.

17. Gompers to Carranza, May 23, 1916; Gompers to R. Lee Guard, May 25, 1916; *AFL Records*, Reel 80; R. Lee Guard to Secretary of State Robert Lansing, May 25, 1916; Guard to Woodrow Wilson, May 25, 1916; *RDS*, 812.504/54, Reel 162.

18. Gompers to Murray, May 26, 1916, *AFL Records*, Reel 80.

19. Duffy to Gompers, May 26, 1916, *AFL Records*, Reel 80.

20. Florence C. Thorne to Gompers, June 16, 1916, *AFL Records*, Reel 23.

21. Duffy to Gompers, May 26, 1916, *AFL Records*, Reel 80.

22. Ibid.

23. Murray to Gompers, June 8, 1916, *AFL Records*, Reel 80.

24. Gompers to Martínez, May 27, 1916; Martínez to Gompers, June 8, 1916; *AFL Records*, Reel 80.

25. Casa Obrero Mundial and Confederación de Sindicatos to A.F. of L., June 11, 1916; Gompers to Casa, June 12, 1916; *AFL Records*, Reel 80;

Guard to Gompers, June 16, 1916, *AFL Records,* Reel 23. Gompers sent the telegram on June 21, 1916 to the Confederación de Sindicatos in Veracruz, Governor Salvador Alvarado in Yucatán, the Casa del Obrero Mundial in Mexico City, and Dr. Atl in Mexico City; *AFL Records,* Reel 80.

26. Murray to Gompers, June 8, 1916; Gompers to William B. Wilson, June 10, 1916; Gompers to Florence C. Thorne, June 12, 1916; Thorne to Gompers, June 16, 1916; all in *AFL Records,* Reel 80.

27. Quoted in Richmond, *Carranza's Nationalist Struggle,* 196.

28. Woodrow Wilson to Secretary of State, June 18, 1916, *RDS,* 812.00/18516–1/2.

29. Thorne to Gompers, June 12, 1916, *AFL Records,* Reel 23.

30. Thorne, memorandum, June 16, 1916, *AFL Records,* Reel 80.

31. Ibid.

32. For a good discussion of these activities, see Christopulos, "American Radicals and the Mexican Revolution, 314–331.

33. Thorne to Gompers, June 16, 1916, *AFL Records,* Reel 23.

34. Thorne, memorandum, June 21, 1916, *AFL Records,* Reel 119.

35. For an account of Gompers's efforts to secure the release of the American prisoners and prevent war between the U.S. and Mexico, see Whittaker, "Gompers, Labor, and the Mexican-American Crisis of 1916," 551–567.

36. Thorne, memorandum, June 16, 1916, *AFL Records,* Reel 80.

37. Thorne, memorandum, June 22, 1916, *AFL Records,* Reel 80.

38. Thorne, memorandum, June 23, 1916, *AFL Records,* Reel 80.

39. Ibid.

40. Thorne, memorandum, June 22, 1916, *AFL Records,* Reel 80.

41. Thorne, memorandum, June 23, 1916, *AFL Records,* Reel 80.

42. Thorne, memorandum, June 24, 1916, *AFL Records,* Reel 80.

43. Thorne, memorandum, June 26, 1916, *AFL Records,* Reel 80.

44. Ibid.

45. Executive Council Minutes, June 26, 1916, *AFL Records,* Reel 5.

46. Thorne, memoranda, June 26, 27, 1916, *AFL Records,* Reel 80.

47. Thorne, memorandum, June 27, 1916, *AFL Records,* Reel 80.

48. Gompers to Charles Perry Taylor, June 28, 1916, *AFL Records,* Reel 80.

49. Haley, *Revolution and Intervention,* 219; Marchand, *The American Peace Movement,* 243; Christopulos, "American Radicals and the Mexican Revolution," 321–322.

50. Secretary of State to President Wilson, July 3, 1916, 812.00/17714–1/2, *The Lansing Papers,* II, 561.

51. Thorne, memorandum, June 28, 1916, *AFL Records,* Reel 80.

52. Thorne, memorandum, June 30, 1916, *AFL Records,* Reel 80.

53. "United States—Mexico—Labor—Their Relations," *American Federationist* 23 (August 1916): 633–652.

54. *Labor Organizations,* 41.

55. "Gompers, Labor, and the Mexican-American Crisis of 1916," 551–567.

56. *U.S. Labor Movement and Latin America*, 170.

57. See Haley, *Revolution and Intervention*, 219–223, for a discussion of the Wilson administration's decision to resolve the crisis by establishing a joint commission. Christopulos, "American Radicals and the Mexican Revolution," Chapter Seven, assesses the influence of radicals, labor, and peace groups upon President Wilson's ultimate rejection of war with Mexico.

58. Richmond, *Carranza's Nationalist Struggle*, 191; David Starr Jordan, *The Days of a Man: Being Memories of a Naturalist, Teacher and Minor Prophet of Democracy* (Yonkers-on-Hudson, N.Y.: World Book Company, 1922), II, 691.

59. Gilderhus, *Diplomacy and Revolution*, 45.

60. "Gompers, Labor, and the Mexican-American Crisis of 1916," 553.

61. Executive Council Minutes, July 1, 1916, *AFL Records*, Reel 5.

62. Quoted in Clark, *Organized Labor in Mexico*, 280.

63. "Gompers, Labor, and the Mexican-American Crisis of 1916," 564–565.

64. Wright to Gompers, July 9, 1916, *AFL Records*, Reel 81.

65. Christopulos, "American Radicals and the Mexican Revolution," 326–331.

66. Gompers, *Seventy Years of Life and Labor*, II, 308.

67. Duffy to Gompers, July 13, 1916, *AFL Records*, Reel 81.

68. On Ferguson's relationship with Gompers and his endorsement of labor-capital cooperation to increase U.S. trade, see Radosh, "Development of the Corporate Ideology of American Labor Leaders," 36–39.

69. Thorne, memorandum, June 30, 1916, *AFL Records*, Reel 80.

70. Ibid.

71. Thorne, memorandum, July 1, 1916, *AFL Records*, Reel 81.

72. *New York Call*, July 5, 1916.

73. Thorne to Gompers, June 16, 1916, *AFL Records*, Reel 23; Gompers to Woodrow Wilson, July 17, 1916, *AFL Records*, Reel 81. A copy of the telegram to Carranza is enclosed in Gompers to Woodrow Wilson, July 27, 1916, *RDS*, 812.00/18842, Reel 55.

74. *Labor Organizations*, 49.

75. *New York Call*, July 5, 1916; Thorne, memorandum, July 7, 1916, *AFL Records*, Reel 81. Loveira and Pages intended to leave for New York on July 7 and then proceed to South America. Morones was to go to Cuba on July 8, and García was to return to Mexico.

76. Thorne, memorandum, July 7, 1916, *AFL Records*, Reel 81.

77. Gompers to Alvarado, July 18, 1916; Gompers to the Workers of All American Countries, July 6, 1916; Gompers to Members of the Confederación de Sindicatos Obreros, July 18, 1916; *AFL Records*, Reel 81. The quote is from Gompers to M. Áviles, August 21, 1916, *AFL Records*, Reel 81.

78. Thorne, memorandum, July 31, 1916, *AFL Records*, Reel 81; Levenstein, *Labor Organizations*, 51–52.

79. Thorne, memorandum, July 31, 1916; Gompers to Duffy, July 30, 1916; *AFL Records*, Reel 81.

80. Thorne, memorandum, July 31, 1916, *AFL Records*, Reel 81.

81. Ibid.; Ravola to Gompers, October 17, 1916, enclosed in Secretary of War to Secretary of State, November 17, 1916, *RDS*, 812.504/72, Reel 162; Linda Hall, *Álvaro Obregón: Power and Revolution in Mexico, 1911–1920* (College Station: Texas A & M University Press, 1981), 196–198.

82. Thorne, memorandum, July 31, 1916, *AFL Records*, Reel 81.

83. Gompers to Flood, July 31, 1916, *AFL Records*, Reel 23.

84. Gompers to Thomas A. French, August 3, 1916; Gompers to George W. P. Hunt, July 12, 1916; *AFL Records*, Reel 81.

85. Hart, *Anarchism and the Mexican Working Class*, 151–157; Clark, *Organized Labor in Mexico*, 40–43; Ruiz, *Labor and the Ambivalent Revolutionaries*, 55; Carr, *El movimiento obrero y la política en México*, 74–77.

86. Haley, *Revolution and Intervention*, 227–247; Richmond, *Carranza's Nationalist Struggle*, 198. The quote is from Anne Wintermute Lane and Louise Herrick Hall, eds., *The Letters of Franklin K. Lane* (Boston: Houghton Mifflin Company, 1922), 225.

87. Gompers to Franklin Lane, October 5, 1916, *AFL Records*, Reel 23; Memorandum, October 12, 1916, *AFL Records*, Reel 81; Conference attended by Gompers, John Murray, and Chester Wright, November 16, 1916, *AFL Records*, Reel 119.

88. Memorandum, October 12, 1916, *AFL Records*, Reel 81; Gompers, *Seventy Years of Life and Labor*, II, 317.

89. Memorandum, October 12, 1916, *AFL Records*, Reel 81.

90. Ibid.

91. AFL, *Proceedings*, 1916, 64.

92. Conference attended by Gompers, Murray, and Wright, November 16, 1916, *AFL Records*, Reel 119.

93. Ibid.

94. Ibid.

95. Ibid.

96. Murray, memorandum, November 21, 1916, *AFL Records*, Reel 81.

97. Gompers to Lane, November 15, 1916, *AFL Records*, Reel 23; Haley, *Revolution and Intervention*, 243–244.

3. CARRANZA'S NATIONALISM, WORLD WAR, AND THE
PAN AMERICAN FEDERATION OF LABOR, 1917–1920

1. Arthur S. Link, *Wilson: Campaigns for Progressivism and Peace, 1916–1917* (Princeton, N.J.: Princeton University Press, 1965), 336–339; Smith, *The United States and Revolutionary Nationalism in Mexico*, 93–96.

2. Gompers to William G. McAdoo, February 5, 1917, *AFL Records*, Reel 82.

3. Ibid.

4. Memorandum, February 3, 1917, *AFL Records*, Reel 82. For more on Harrold's organization, see Hart, *Revolutionary Mexico*, 282.

5. Ibid.; Memoranda, February 14, 16, 1917, *AFL Records*, Reel 82.

6. Gompers to Carranza, February 16, 1917, *AFL Records*, Reel 82.

7. At a Council of National Defense meeting on March 31, 1917, the State Department's Frank Polk showed Gompers a cable from the American ambassador in Russia which said that it might be useful if Gompers were to send a message to Petrograd. Fearing a deepening of the revolution following the overthrow of the czar, the State Department believed that a constructive cable of support from Gompers to Petrograd workers might help to undermine socialist influences on the Russian political situation. Gompers complied with the request. See Ambassador Francis to Secretary of State, March 23, 1917, *AFL Records*, Reel 82; Gompers, Memorandum, April 1, 1917, *AFL Records*, Reel 83.

8. Pan-American Federation of Labor Conference Committee, Manifesto to the Workers of Latin America, February 9, 1917, *AFL Records*, Reel 82.

9. Snow, *The Pan-American Federation of Labor*, 31–32; Memorandum, July 18, 1917, *AFL Records*, Reel 120.

10. For a sampling of the responses by various Latin American unions to a questionnaire sent out by the PAFL Conference Committee, see Snow, *The Pan-American Federation of Labor*, 33–34.

11. Press Statement Regarding Pan-American Labor Conference Committee, August 20, 1917, *AFL Records*, Reel 112.

12. Gompers to Alvarado, July 27, 1917, *AFL Records*, Reel 86.

13. Levenstein, *Labor Organizations*, 58.

14. Ibid., 58–59; Clark, *Organized Labor in Mexico*, 58–59.

15. Snow, *The Pan-American Federation of Labor*, 32–35.

16. An American firm, Inselin and Company, agreed in June 1917, to mint Mexican gold coins for Carranza, but the U.S. Treasury repudiated the agreement. See Katz, *The Secret War in Mexico*, 517.

17. Gompers to Woodrow Wilson, July 16, 1917, *AFL Records*, Reel 23; Meeting on Mexico with Col. Edmundo Martínez, July 18, 1917, *AFL Records*, Reel 120; Gompers, memorandum, July 18, 1917, *AFL Records*, Reel 86; Gompers to Martínez, August 13, 1917, *AFL Records*, Reel 23.

18. Gompers to Woodrow Wilson, August 13, 1917, *AFL Records*, Reel 23.

19. Memorandum, July 18, 1917, *AFL Records*, Reel 86.

20. Smith, *The United States and Revolutionary Nationalism in Mexico*, 97–116; Katz, *The Secret War in Mexico*, 516–517.

21. Confidential memorandum, enclosed in Delbert J. Haff to Robert Lansing, May 5, 1917, *RDS*, 812.00/21233, Reel 61.

22. A copy of this report is enclosed in A. Bruce Bielaski, Chief, Bureau of Investigation, to Leland Harrison, October 11, 1917, *RDS*, 812.00/21377, Reel 61.

23. Memorandum, February 16, 1917, *AFL Records*, Reel 82.

24. Report enclosed in Bielaski to Harrison, October 11, 1917, *RDS,* 812.00/21377, Reel 61. Bonillas's pro-American sympathies prompted critics to dub him "Meester" Bonillas during his campaign for the presidency in 1920. See Cumberland, *Mexican Revolution: The Constitutionalist Years,* 406.

25. Report enclosed in Bielaski to Harrison, October 11, 1917, *RDS,* 812.00/21377, Reel 61.

26. Secretary of War to Secretary of State, June 2, 1917, *RDS,* 812.00/21121, Reel 61; Press statement regarding Pan-American Labor Conference Committee, August 20, 1917, *AFL Records,* Reel 112; Gompers, memorandum, December 19, 1917, *AFL Records,* Reel 120.

27. Richmond, *Carranza's Nationalist Struggle,* 198–199; Smith, *The United States and Revolutionary Nationalism in Mexico,* 117–119; Katz, *The Secret War in Mexico,* 499–500; Gardner, *Safe for Democracy,* 211.

28. Charles A. Douglas to Gompers, March 28, 1918, *AFL Records,* Reel 93.

29. Katz, *The Secret War in Mexico,* 497–498. See also John Womack, Jr., "The Mexican Economy during the Revolution, 1910–1920: Historiography and Analysis," *Marxist Perspectives* 4 (Winter 1978): 80–123.

30. Smith, *The United States and Revolutionary Nationalism in Mexico,* 117–119.

31. Henry Bruére and Thomas R. Lill, Memorandum for President Wilson in Reference to Mexico, August 15, 1918, *AFL Records,* Reel 97; Gompers, memorandum, July 18, 1918, *AFL Records,* Reel 96; Confidential memorandum to Charles A. Douglas, July 30, 1918, *AFL Records,* Reel 96; Douglas to Gompers, August 27, 1918, *AFL Records,* Reel 97.

32. Bruére and Lill, Memorandum, August 15, 1918, *AFL Records,* Reel 97.

33. Snow, *The Pan-American Federation of Labor,* 35–36.

34. Gompers to Santiago Iglesias, April 6, 1918, *AFL Records,* Reel 22.

35. Gompers to President Wilson, April 16, 1918, *AFL Records,* Reel 94.

36. Gompers to J. P. Tumulty, April 24, 1918; Tumulty to Gompers, April 25, 1918; *AFL Records,* Reel 94; Woodrow Wilson to Gompers, May 7, 1918, *AFL Records,* Reel 95.

37. *Labor Organizations,* 65.

38. Rosendo Salazar and José G. Escobedo, *Las pugnas de la gleba, 1907–1922* (México: Comisión Nacional Editorial, 1972), 227–238; Clark, *Organized Labor in Mexico,* 59–61; Carr, *El movimiento obrero y la política en México,* 88–94.

39. Carr, *El movimiento obrero y la política en México,* 88–89, argues that although no evidence has been uncovered to prove that Espinosa Mireles was acting under orders from Carranza, it is possible that Carranza wanted to capitalize on labor's budding nationalism by promoting a "semiofficial" labor organization. Rosendo Salazar and José Escobedo, principals in the labor movement at that time, challenged the accusation that the Coahuilan governor was trying to coopt the labor movement and advance

his personal political career. They believed that he had genuine prolabor sympathies. See Salazar and Escobedo, *Las pugnas de la gleba*, 231–232. Carranza's recent biographer claims that although Carranza supported and financed the labor congress, the convention was probably the work of Espinosa Mireles. See Richmond, *Carranza's Nationalist Struggle*, 134. Jorge Basurto, *El proletariado industrial en México (1850–1930)* (México: Universidad Nacional Autónoma de México, 1975), 190–191, argues that the efforts to institutionalize and incorporate the labor movement into the state were probably initiated by General Obregón.

40. Henry Fletcher to Secretary of State, May 23, 1917; Lansing to Secretary of War, June 4, 1917; *RDS*, 812.00/20962, Reel 60; Frank L. Polk, Counselor, to Secretary of War, September 17, October 30, 1917, *RDS*, 812.00/21265, Reel 61; A. Bruce Bielaski to Leland Harrison, Office of the Counselor, October 17, 1917, *RDS*, 812.00/21445, Reel 62; Hall, *Álvaro Obregón*, 185–189.

41. Myron Parker to Secretary of State, October 3, 1919, *RDS*, 812.00/23117, Reel 68; Smith, *The United States and Revolutionary Nationalism in Mexico*, 120; Hall, *Álvaro Obregón*, 190; Gompers, *Seventy Years of Life and Labor*, II, 319; Snow, *The Pan-American Federation of Labor*, 36.

42. Gompers and Murray to Luis Morones, May 10, 1918, *AFL Records*, Reel 22; AFL, *Proceedings*, 1918, 248–249.

43. Conference with Lord, Murray, Iglesias, and Florence Thorne, May 8, 1918, *AFL Records*, Reel 120.

44. Gompers to Lansing, May 10, 1918, *AFL Records*, Reel 95; Leon J. Canova, Memorandum to Mr. Auchincloss, May 21, 1918, *RDS*, 812.504/158, Reel 162.

45. AFL, *Proceedings*, 1918, 250. Using a manuscript in the papers of Santiago Iglesias, Sinclair Snow claims that Carranza said very little to the AFL delegates about the aim of their mission. The author of this manuscript, according to Snow, was probably John Murray. See *The Pan-American Federation of Labor*, 9.

46. AFL, *Proceedings*, 1918, 250–251; Unidentified, undated statement regarding Pan American unity, *AFL Records*, Reel 113.

47. Salazar and Escobedo, *Las pugnas de la gleba*, 249–250.

48. AFL, *Proceedings*, 1918, 252.

49. Carr, *El movimiento obrero y la política en México*, 94–95. Camile Nick Buford, "A Biography of Luis N. Morones, Mexican Labor and Political Leader" (Ph.D. diss.: Louisiana State University, 1971), 20, stresses that the view in Mexico that Morones played a key role in securing the withdrawal of Pershing's forces enhanced his national reputation at CROM's founding convention in Saltillo.

50. AFL, *Proceedings*, 1918, 251–252.

51. Ibid., 252.

52. For details of the covert funding, see Larson, *Labor and Foreign Policy*, 150–151; Snow, *The Pan-American Federation of Labor*, 41–46; Levenstein, *Labor Organizations*, 71–75.

53. Memorandum, July 17, 1918; E. H. Greenwood to Gompers, July 7, 1918; E. H. Greenwood to Woodrow Wilson, July 31, 1918; *AFL Records,* Reel 96. Phillips also urged a less abrasive policy toward Carranza when Pershing's forces were in Mexico. See J. R. Phillips to Franklin K. Lane, January 20, 1917, *RDS,* 812.00/20434, Reel 58.

54. E. H. Greenwood to Woodrow Wilson, August 1, 1918, *AFL Records,* Reel 97.

55. J. R. Phillips to E. H. Greenwood, July 26, 1918, *AFL Records,* Reel 96.

56. Ibid.

57. Lewis Warfield to Woodrow Wilson, July 2, 1918, *Woodrow Wilson Papers* (Washington, D.C.: Presidential Papers Microfilm, The Library of Congress, 1958), Reel 216 (hereafter cited as *Wilson Papers,* followed by microfilm reel number).

58. Ibid.

59. Memorandum, June 27, 1918, enclosed in ibid. Also in the same file is a letter from Warfield to President Wilson, July 18, 1917. Warfield stood to profit personally from a more liberal investment policy in Mexico. He urged financing of a proposal to develop in conjunction with the Carranza government a Mexican merchant marine. The materials for the hulls of these vessels were to come from his timber and iron ore interests on Mexico's Pacific Coast.

60. "Latin America: Laboratory of American Foreign Policy in the Nineteen-Twenties," *Inter-American Economic Affairs* 11 (Autumn 1957): 8.

61. Woodrow Wilson to Gompers, July 24, 1918, *Wilson Papers,* Reel 156; AFL, *Proceedings,* 1919, 87; Gompers, Speech at the Jargis Plaza, Laredo, Texas, November 13, 1918, *AFL Records,* Reel 113; Snow, *The Pan-American Federation of Labor,* 51–59; Levenstein, *Labor Organizations,* 78–89.

62. Levenstein, *Labor Organizations,* 79–86; Snow, *The Pan-American Federation of Labor,* 54–55. The quote is in AFL, *Proceedings,* 1919, 88.

63. Levenstein, *Labor Organizations,* 86–89; Snow, *The Pan-American Federation of Labor,* 56–57. See also Gompers, Speech to the Executive Council Meeting of the American Alliance for Labor and Democracy in New York City, November 30, December 1, 1918, *AFL Records,* Reel 113.

64. Carr, *El movimiento obrero y la política en México,* 94–96; Philip Taft, *Defending Freedom: American Labor and Foreign Affairs* (Los Angeles: Nash Publishing, 1973), 38; AFL, *Proceedings,* 1919, 87.

65. Joseph G. Rayback, *A History of American Labor,* expanded and updated ed. (New York: The Free Press, 1966), 273–275; Philip S. Foner, *History of the Labor Movement in the United States,* Volume VII; *Labor and World War I, 1914–1918* (New York: International Publishers, 1987), 338–345.

66. Levenstein, *Labor Organizations,* 91. The quote is in Gompers, Press release, August 30, 1919, *AFL Records,* Reel 114. Larson, *Labor and Foreign Policy,* 17, criticizes Gompers for not taking advantage of the AFL's relatively strong position during the war to set forth labor's agenda for postwar reconstruction.

67. Samuel Gompers, "Labor's Menace in Mexico," *American Federationist* 26 (May 1919): 404.

68. *Labor Organizations*, 91.

69. Statement read for Gompers before the convention of the Associated Advertising Clubs of the World, New Orleans, September 22, 1919, *AFL Records*, Reel 114.

70. Murray to Gompers, February 21, 1919, *AFL Records*, Reel 100.

71. Gompers to Ygnacio Bonillas, September 4, 1919; Gompers to Lansing, September 4, 1919; *AFL Records*, Reel 102; Snow, *The Pan-American Federation of Labor*, 63–64.

72. AFL, *Proceedings*, 1919, 294.

73. Ibid., 296.

74. Executive Council meeting, November 19, 1920, *AFL Records*, Reel 121.

75. Secretary of State Lansing and Under Secretary Henry P. Fletcher were among those whose appetite for intervention in Mexico grew after the war. For a look at the interplay between them, Senator Fall, and the Senate Foreign Relations Committee involving efforts to force a diplomatic break with Carranza, see Henry P. Fletcher, memorandum, December 9, 1919, *RDS*, 812.00/23263–1/2, Reel 69. E. L. Doheny headed a delegation of the Organization of Oil Producers in Mexico to the Paris peace negotiations. For a discussion of his activities there, see Katz, *The Secret War in Mexico*, 529–530.

76. Murray to Gompers, February 21, 1919, *AFL Records*, Reel 100; AFL, *Proceedings*, 1919, 360, 414; Executive Council Minutes, August 28, 1919, *AFL Records*, Reel 6. See also Gompers, Press interview, July 10, 1919, *AFL Records*, Reel 114; Walter G. Matthewson, Acting Secretary-Treasurer, California State Federation of Labor, to Woodrow Wilson, October 24, 1919, *RDS*, 812.00/23184.

77. War Department Weekly Report No. 349, General Conditions Along the Mexican Border, December 20, 1919, enclosed in Secretary of War to Secretary of State, December 27, 1919, *RDS*, 812.00/23297, Reel 69.

78. Clark, *Organized Labor in Mexico*, 71–73; Carr, *El movimiento obrero y la política en México*, 108–110.

79. John Murray, "Labor's Call Across the Border," *The Survey* 42 (April 5, 1919): 46–47; Gompers, "Labor's Menace in Mexico," 404; AFL, *Proceedings*, 1920, 124; Gompers to General A. Obregón, May 5, 1920, *AFL Records*, Reel 104.

80. See Carr, *El movimiento obrero y la política en México*, 108–121, 127–130, for a good discussion of the social and political philosophies of the Sonoran revolutionaries and the CROM's decision to line up with them politically. See also idem, "Las peculiaridades del nortemexicano, 1880–1927: Ensayo de interpretación," *Historia Mexicana* 3 (January-March 1972): 320–346.

81. James Lord, "Labor in Mexico," in George H. Blakeslee, ed., *Mexico*

and the Caribbean: Clark University Addresses (New York: G. E. Stechert and Company, 1920), 104.

82. AFL, *Proceedings*, 1921, 88–89.

4. AFL-CROM RELATIONS AND MEXICAN
RECONSTRUCTION, 1920–1923

1. On the assassination of Zapata, see Womack, *Zapata and the Mexican Revolution*, 322–330.

2. *The Great Rebellion*, 400.

3. Obregón to Gompers, April 20, 1920, *AFL Records*, Reel 103; Division of Mexican Affairs, Memorandum of Visit of Colonel Myron M. Parker, May 4, 1920, *RDS*, 812.00/23837, Reel 71; C. M. Johnston, memorandum, Division of Mexican Affairs, May 24, 1920, and Myron M. Parker to Bainbridge Colby, May 24, 1920, *RDS*, 812.00/24169, Reel 71; R. Lee Guard, memoranda, May 24, 25, 1920, *AFL Records*, Reel 104. See also Buford, "A Biography of Luis N. Morones," 40.

4. Basurto, *El proletariado industrial en México*, 220.

5. Francis Dyer to Secretary of State, October 1, 1920, *RDS*, 812.504/238, Reel 163; Matthew E. Hanna to Secretary of State, September 29, 1920, *RDS*, 812.504/236, Reel 163.

6. Cornelius Ferris, Jr., American Consul in Charge, Mexico City, to Secretary of State, September 22, 1920, *RDS*, 812.504/237, Reel 163; Hanna to Secretary of State, November 3, 1920, *RDS*, 812.00/24772, Reel 73. The quote is in Johnston to Davis, August 18, 1920, *RDS*, 812.00/24478, Reel 73.

7. AFL, *Proceedings*, 1920, 125–126.

8. Ibid., 473–474.

9. Wilson to Colby, November 5, 1920, enclosed in Hanna to Beck, October 3, 1923, *RDS*, 812.00/26464, Reel 80.

10. George Summerlin to Secretary of State, September 7, 1920, *RDS*, 812.00/24636, Reel 73; Morones to Gompers, December 1, 1920, *AFL Records*, Reel 104.

11. Press statement, December 22, 1922 [*sic*], *AFL Records*, Reel 115; PAFL, *Proceedings*, 1921, 133–134.

12. PAFL, *Proceedings*, 1921, 133–134. Conference, PAFL Executive Committee, and Roberto Haberman, July 26, 1921, *AFL Records*, Reel 121.

13. Chapter Six will provide an in-depth look at the activities of Haberman and his links to the AFL.

14. Whittaker, "American Labor Looks South," 665–667; PAFL, *Proceedings*, 1921, 4–6; AFL, *Proceedings*, 1921, 83. A Justice Department report claimed that Morones and Haberman were on a secret mission to buy ammunition for the Mexican government. A copy of this report is included in a State Department memorandum, March 10, 1926, enclosed in Alexander Kirk to J. Edgar Hoover, March 13, 1926, United States Department of Justice, *Bureau of Investigation*, File number 25–230–63 (hereafter cited

as *DJBI,* followed by file no.). The *New York Times,* January 10, 1921, attributed the detention of CROM leaders to Haberman's alleged connections with the Third International.

15. PAFL, *Proceedings,* 1921, 3; Summerlin to Secretary of State, October 14, 1919, *RDS,* 812.00/23170, Reel 69; Christopulos, "American Radicals and the Mexican Revolution," 412–413, 416.

16. PAFL, *Proceedings,* 1921, 68, 74–76.

17. Philip S. Foner, ed., *Mother Jones Speaks: Collected Writings and Speeches* (New York: Monad Press, 1983), 321–322.

18. In ibid., 649–650. See also Mother Jones to John H. Walker, May 27, 1921, in ibid., 652.

19. "Pan-American Labor Congress at Mexico City," *American Federationist* 28 (March 1921): 195.

20. Press interview, April 13, 1921, *AFL Records,* Reel 115.

21. Gompers to William English Walling, May 17, 1921, *AFL Records,* Reel 105.

22. Salazar and Escobedo, *Las pugnas de la gleba,* 308–312; Hart, *Anarchism and the Mexican Working Class,* 159–161; Karl M. Schmitt, *Communism in Mexico: A Study in Political Frustration* (Austin: University of Texas Press, 1965), 9–10; Paco Ignacio Taibo II, "El breve matrimonio rojo; comunistas y anarcosindicalistas en la CGT en 1921," *Historias* 7 (Octubre-Diciembre 1984): 45–71.

23. Hart, *Revolutionary Mexico,* 340; Ruiz, *Labor and the Ambivalent Revolutionaries,* 98–99; Hart, *Anarchism and the Mexican Working Class,* 159–162.

24. Hart, *Revolutionary Mexico,* 340; Ruiz, *The Great Rebellion,* 297.

25. Ruiz, *Labor and the Ambivalent Revolutionaries,* 98; Carr, *El movimiento obrero y la política en México,* 132–134. Although the secret pact that the CROM and Obregón signed in 1919 provided for the creation of a Department of Labor to be headed by someone sympathetic to workers and called for the CROM to designate the new secretary of agriculture, Obregón failed to keep his promises regarding these high-level appointments. As a result, tensions existed between Morones and Obregón throughout the latter's presidency.

26. On Obregón's response to labor-capital conflicts, see especially Ruiz, *Labor and the Ambivalent Revolutionaries,* 81–109.

27. Ibid., 134–144; Clark, *Organized Labor in Mexico,* 98–100; Salazar and Escobedo, *Las pugnas de la gleba,* 316–318; A. B. Wolvin to L. C. Southard, March 19, 1921, enclosed in Wolvin to George B. Christian, Jr., Secretary to the President, March 19, 1921, *RDS,* 812.00/24928, Reel 74.

28. Ruiz, *The Great Rebellion,* 388.

29. On those business interests that advocated recognition of Obregón, see Smith, *The U.S. and Revolutionary Nationalism in Mexico,* 197–202; Hart, *Revolutionary Mexico,* 342–344; and Randall George Hansis, "Álvaro Obregón, the Mexican Revolution, and the Politics of Consolidation, 1920–1924" (Ph.D. diss., University of New Mexico, 1971), 179–182.

30. Mark Perlman, *The Machinists: A New Study in American Trade Union-ism* (Cambridge: Harvard University Press, 1961), 67.

31. Conference, PAFL Executive Committee, and Roberto Haberman, July 26, 1921, *AFL Records*, Reel 121.

32. Ibid.

33. Meeting of the PAFL Executive Committee, August 1, 1921, *AFL Records*, Reel 121.

34. Ibid.

35. Ibid.

36. Ibid. Perlman, *The Machinists*, 67, finds no evidence to suggest that the agreement between the AFL and the Mexican government on the purchase of union-made goods ever amounted to much. However, Haberman claimed that the Obregón administration consistently bought goods from American union firms with only one exception. Because of liberal credit terms granted by Samuel Vauclain, president of Baldwin Locomotive, de la Huerta signed a contract to buy locomotives and other materials from the Philadelphia nonunion firm. The only union firm interested in the contract demanded a large cash payment that the Mexican government could not make. See Agent Manuel Sorola, report, July 2, 1924, enclosed in J. E. Hoover to Arthur Bliss Lane, July 16, 1924, *DJBI*, 25–230–52. For details of the agreement with Baldwin Locomotive, see Summerlin to Secretary of State, August 12, 1921, *RDS*, 812.00/25150, Reel 75.

37. On the Republican Party's approach to labor in the 1920s, see Robert H. Zieger, *Republicans and Labor, 1919–1929* (Lexington: University Press of Kentucky, 1969).

38. Memorandum, July 27, 1921, *AFL Records*, Reel 121. On Gompers's appointment to the advisory committee of the American delegation to the Washington Conference, see Gompers to Warren G. Harding, July 19, 1921, and Charles E. Hughes to Gompers, November 3, 1921, *AFL Records*, Reel 105.

39. J. Edgar Hoover, Memorandum of Interview with E. C. Davison, General Secretary-Treasurer, International Association of Machinists, and Robert Haberman, August 2, 1921, *DJBI*, 25–230.

40. Memorandum, July 27, 1921, *AFL Records*, Reel 121. On Daugherty's anti-union views, see Zieger, *Republicans and Labor*, 13.

41. Among those deported were Linn Gale, Frank Seaman, Sebastián San Vicente, Natalia Michaelova, M. Paley, José Rubio, Fort Meyer, and José Allen. The latter was actually a Mexican who was working as a spy for U.S. military intelligence. See Christopulos, "American Radicals and the Mexican Revolution," 424–435, and Hart, *Anarchism and the Mexican Working Class*, 160, for a discussion of these deportations.

42. A copy of a letter from Miller to the Military Intelligence Division is enclosed in Matthew C. Hanna, Charge d'Affaires, to Secretary of State, May 21, 1921, *RDS*, 812.00/25020, Reel 75.

43. Hughes to Hoover, May 28, 1921, *RDS*, 812.00/25010, Reel 75.

Rice's letter is enclosed in Herbert Hoover to Secretary of State, May 27, 1921, ibid.

44. A copy of the Mexican consul's speech, "Mexico Is America's Market," is enclosed in Z. L. Cobb to Secretary of State, March 10, 1922, *RDS*, 812.00/25456–1/2, Reel 77.

45. Ibid.

46. Cobb's address, "The President Alone Can Break This Deadlock," is also enclosed in ibid.

47. Claude Dawson, American consul at Tampico, to Secretary of State, June 8, 1921, *RDS*, 812.00/25016, Reel 75. A clipping of the article in *The Mexican Post*, June 12, 1921, is enclosed in Summerlin to Secretary of State, June 17, 1921, *RDS*, 812.00/25057, Reel 75.

48. Hansis, "Álvaro Obregón, the Mexican Revolution, and the Politics of Consolidation," 173.

49. Dawson to Secretary of State, June 30, 1921, *RDS*, 812.00/25062, Reel 75.

50. Gompers to Hughes, July 7, 1921, *RDS*, 812.00/25080, Reel 75.

51. Hughes to Gompers, July 8, 1921, *RDS*, 812.00/25080, Reel 75.

52. Hughes to Harding, July 8, 1921, *RDS*, 812.00/25094b, Reel 75.

53. Conference, PAFL Executive Committee, and Roberto Haberman, July 26, 1921, *AFL Records*, Reel 121. Clippings of these editorials are enclosed in Summerlin to Secretary of State, July 16, 1921, *RDS*, 812.00/25111, Reel 75.

54. Summerlin to Secretary of State, October 28, November 18, 1921, *RDS*, 812.00/25223, 812.00/25258, Reel 75; Morones to Gompers, November 15, 1921, *AFL Records*, Reel 105. The quote is in E. C. Davison to Gompers, December 5, 1921, *AFL Records*, Reel 105.

55. Gompers to Morones, December 22, 1921, *AFL Records*, Reel 105.

56. Lorenzo Meyer, *Mexico and the United States in the Oil Controversy, 1917–1942*, trans. Muriel Vasconcellos (Austin: University of Texas Press, 1977), 85–88; Smith, *The United States and Revolutionary Nationalism in Mexico*, 207–213. See also idem, "The Formation and Development of the International Bankers Committee on Mexico," *Journal of Economic History* 23 (December 1963): 574–586.

57. Harding to Hughes, March 21, 1922, *RDS*, 812.00/25494, Reel 77.

58. Gompers to Hughes, July 1, 1922, *RDS*, 812.00/25747, Reel 78. AFL locals also pressured the State Department to recognize Obregón, often linking those who opposed recognition to the open shop movement in the United States. See, for example, J. H. Williamson, Recording Secretary, District No. 8, International Association of Machinists, Chicago, to President Harding, June 27, 1922, and R. E. Paschall, Secretary, Sherman Central Labor Union, Sherman, Texas, to President Harder [*sic*], June 28, 1922, *RDS*, 812.00/25728, 812.00/25759, Reel 78.

59. Summerlin to Hanna, May 30, 1922, *RDS*, 812.00/25708, Reel 78.

60. Bowman to Secretary of State, June 30, 1922, *RDS*, 812.00/25751, Reel 78. Other consuls echoed the sentiments of Bowman and argued for

direct U.S. intervention. See, for example, Walter F. Boyle to Secretary of State, February 26, 1923, *RDS*, 812.00/26226, Reel 79. See also Hanna to Secretary of State, June 30, 1922, *RDS*, 812.00/26066, Reel 79.

61. Dawson's unrestrained plea for a coup to overthrow Obregón startled his superiors in the State Department. Attached to his report is a memorandum from the Office of the Director of the Consular Service to Matthew Hanna, Chief of the Division of Mexican Affairs: "Do you not think this is a pretty dangerous sort of thing for Dawson to be engaging in?" See Dawson to Secretary of State, June 1, 1922, *RDS*, 812.00/25671, Reel 77.

62. Dawson to Secretary of State, January 16, 1924, *RDS*, 812.00/26866, Reel 81.

63. Blocker to Secretary of State, January 24, 1922, *RDS*, 812.504/327, Reel 163.

64. Summerlin to Secretary of State, August 4, September 1, 1922, *RDS*, 812.00/25845, 812.00/25895, Reel 78; Snow, *The Pan-American Federation of Labor*, 114.

65. A translation of this article, which appeared on May 31, 1922, is enclosed in Dawson to Secretary of State, June 1, 1922, *RDS*, 812.00/25671, Reel 77.

66. Whittaker, "American Labor Looks South," 546–548; Buford, "A Biography of Luis N. Morones," 49; Summerlin to Secretary of State, March 15, 1923, *RDS*, 812.504/465, Reel 163.

67. Buford, "A Biography of Luis N. Morones," 49; Conference on Efforts to Resume Diplomatic Relations Between Mexico and the United States, April 25, 1923, *AFL Records*, Reel 122.

68. Samuel Gompers, "Treacherous, Tyrannical, Barbarous," *American Federationist* 30 (July 1923): 368–370; Buford, "A Biography of Luis N. Morones," 242. The Mexican government tried to exploit U.S. fears about contacts with the Soviet Union to gain diplomatic recognition in late 1922. Lázaro Basch, the Mexican consul general in Copenhagen, Denmark, visited the American Legation to report that the Mexican government commissioned him during the summer of 1922 to visit the Soviet Union to establish commercial relations. Soviet officials insisted upon immediate mutual recognition before signing a commercial agreement. Basch said that he would recommend that Obregón not recognize the Soviet Union if the American Legation in Copenhagen would advise the State Department to grant diplomatic recognition to Mexico immediately. The American Legation refused to strike such a deal. See John Dyneley Prince to Secretary of State, November 15, 1922, United States Department of State Records, *Political Relations Between Mexico and Other States, 1910–1929*, 712.6–1/2, Reel 2.

69. Conferences on Conducting a Publicity Campaign to Inform American Labor of the Situation in Mexico, April 12, 14, 19, 1923, *AFL Records*, Reel 122.

70. PAFL Executive Committee, Conference on Efforts to Resume Dip-

lomatic Relations between Mexico and the United States, April 25, 1923, *AFL Records*, Reel 122.

71. Conference on the American Advisory Commission to Mexico, May 4, 1923, *AFL Records*, Reel 122.

72. *The Great Rebellion*, 401. Villa had developed a friendship with de la Huerta, who negotiated his retirement from politics in 1920. Villa promised to end his retirement if de la Huerta ever needed his political assistance. Thus, many charged that Calles masterminded Villa's assassination to advance his presidential ambitions. Villa's widow, Luz Corral, believed that Obregón and Calles gave orders to have her husband killed in order to prevent him from honoring his promise to de la Huerta. See Ronald Atkin, *Revolution! Mexico 1910–20* (London: Panther Books Limited, 1972), 355. José Vasconcelos, Obregón's Minister of Education who later resigned, claims that Jesús Salas Barraza, Villa's assassin, visited the residence of Calles after the assassination. See Vasconcelos, *El desastre* (México: Ediciones Botas, 1938), 240.

73. See, for example, memoranda prepared by Consul Dawson in Mexico City, enclosed in Summerlin to Secretary of State, February 20, March 17, 1923, *RDS*, 812.20211/6, 812.20211/10, Reel 138. The American consul in San Luis Potosí suggested that Mexican capitalists would support the establishment of an American protectorate. Walter F. Boyle to Secretary of State, February 26, 1923, *RDS*, 812.00/26226, Reel 79.

74. John W. F. Dulles, *Yesterday in Mexico: A Chronicle of the Revolution, 1919–1936* (Austin: University of Texas Press, 1961), 163–165; Ruiz, *The Great Rebellion*, 401–402; Summerlin to Secretary of State, June 1, 23, 1923, *RDS*, 812.00/26379, Reel 80.

75. "Latin America: Laboratory of American Foreign Policy in the Nineteen-Twenties," 23.

76. Some members of the Harding administration moderated the antilabor views of State Department officials. Williams, "Latin America: Laboratory of American Foreign Policy," 3–30, discusses the role of Secretary of Commerce Herbert Hoover in shaping the Republicans' policy of pushing foreign economic expansion to stabilize Latin America. Hoover hoped to capitalize on a developing cooperative relationship with Gompers and extend labor-capital cooperation on domestic issues into the arena of foreign policy. Williams notes that Secretary of State Hughes's ideas were similar enough to allow Hoover to exercise an influence on State Department policies. Williams emphasizes that Gompers also favored greater labor-capital cooperation to solve the domestic and international problems of production that plagued the postwar world economy.

Even before the establishment of diplomatic relations with Obregón, Hoover had taken a more favorable view of the investment climate and political conditions in Mexico. See, for example, Summerlin to Secretary of State, January 12, 1923, *RDS*, 812.00/26171, Reel 79. See also Smith, *The United States and Revolutionary Nationalism in Mexico*, 202.

77. AFL Information and Publicity Service, press release, September 8, 1923, *AFL Records*, Reel 118.

78. Gompers, Address to El Paso Chamber of Commerce, October 26, 1923, *AFL Records*, Reel 118.

79. Ibid.

5. LABOR'S ROLE IN THE DE LA HUERTA REBELLION
AND ELECTION OF CALLES

1. A copy of this report, which was prepared on December 28, 1923, is enclosed in DeNette to W. J. Burns, December 28, 1923, *DJBI*, 64–0–365.

2. Ibid.

3. Dulles, *Yesterday in Mexico*, 183–198.

4. Conference on Efforts to Resume Diplomatic Relations Between Mexico and the United States, April 25, 1923, *AFL Records*, Reel 122. A copy of Brown's letter to Gompers is in Conferences Between the Executive Committee of the Pan-American Federation of Labor and Representatives of the Mexican Federation of Labor, October 25, 1923, *AFL Records*, Reel 123.

5. Conferences Between the Executive Committee of the Pan-American Federation of Labor and Representatives of the Mexican Federation of Labor, October 25, 1923, *AFL Records*, Reel 123.

6. Ibid.

7. Ibid.

8. Ibid.

9. Ibid.

10. Ibid.

11. Ibid.

12. Address delivered by President Gompers at a mass meeting in the city hall in the city of Juárez, Mexico, October 27, 1923, *AFL Records*, Reel 118. Relations between Gompers and de la Huerta had soured after an incident in the latter's office in January 1921. Upset by something de la Huerta said, Gompers walked out of his office and refused to attend a reception hosted by him. See Conference on Conditions in Mexico, April 19, 1924, *AFL Records*, Reel 123, and Gompers, *Seventy Years of Life and Labor*, II, 319.

13. Summerlin to Secretary of State, November 20, 1923, *RDS*, 8112.00/ 26525, Reel 80; Gompers, Press statement for the *New York Times*, November 8, 1923, *AFL Records*, Reel 118.

14. See, for example, Vasconcelos, *El desastre*, 240. On the details of Villa's assassination, see Dulles, *Yesterday in Mexico*, 177–180.

15. Alonso Capetillo, *La rebelión sin cabeza* (México: Imprenta Botas, 1925), 91–92. See Dulles, *Yesterday in Mexico*, 181–217, for a discussion of the political conflicts which precipitated de la Huerta's action.

16. Carr, *El movimiento obrero y la política en México*, 146–149; Ruiz, *Labor*

and the Ambivalent Revolutionaries, 100; Schmitt, *Communism in Mexico*, 10–11.

17. Morones to Gompers, December 13, 1923, in PAFL, *Proceedings, 1924*, 36.

18. AFL Information and Publicity Service, Press Statement, December 12, 1923, *AFL Records*, Reel 118. AFL leaders had not denounced Obregón's use of military force to oust Carranza in 1920.

19. Jorge Prieto Laurens to Gompers, December 27, 1923, enclosed in Gompers to Obregón, January 29, 1924, in PAFL, *Proceedings, 1924*, 44.

20. Gompers to Obregón, January 29, 1924, in PAFL, *Proceedings, 1924*, 44. See also Gompers to Hughes, January 30, 1924, RDS, 812.00/26912, Reel 81.

21. Gompers to Hughes, December 18, 1923, in PAFL, *Proceedings, 1924*, 36–37. On the cooperation between the IFTU and PAFL leaders, see PAFL, *Proceedings, 1924*, 41–43.

22. *New York Times*, January 14, 1924; E. C. Davison to Charles E. Hughes, January 26, 1924, RDS, 812.00/26900, Reel 81; Edwin Denby, Department of the Navy, to Secretary of State, January 8, 1924, RDS, 812.00/26738, Reel 81; Adolfo de la Huerta to Secretary of State, January 12, 1924, in ibid. De la Huerta invited Gompers, Santiago Iglesias, Davison, and other AFL leaders to Veracruz at his expense. See Gompers to Obregón, January 29, 1924, enclosed in Gompers to Hughes, January 30, 1924, RDS, 812.00/26912, Reel 81. Gompers later requested that the American consul in Mérida, Yucatán, take action to protect "members of the personal and official family of the late Felipe Carrillo" but was told that the State Department could not intervene, since these persons were not U.S. citizens. Gompers to Secretary of State, February 25, 1924, and William Phillips, Under Secretary of State, to Gompers, February 29, 1924, RDS, 812.00/27043, Reel 81.

23. Gompers to Obregón, January 29, 1924, enclosed in Gompers to Hughes, January 30, 1924, RDS, 812.00/26912, Reel 81. On the appeal from Villarreal, see Villarreal to Gompers, January 12, 1924, enclosed in ibid.

24. *New York Times*, January 23, 1924.

25. W. O. Jenkins to Claude Dawson, January 20, 1924, enclosed in Dawson to Secretary of State, January 23, 1924, RDS, 812.00/26933, Reel 81. See also John Wood to Secretary of State, December 21, 1923, and February 23, 1924, RDS, 812.00/26647, 812.00/27026, Reels 80, 81; Summerlin to Secretary of State, December 14, 1923, RDS, 812.00/26601, Reel 80. The American consul in San Luis Potosí complained that official mourning in that state over the death of Lenin was "a slap at the United States to advertise to the Mexican mob that while the superior diplomacy of Mexico is forcing the support of the United States for the Government in power, that their sentiments are purely anti American, that Calles controls in San Luis Potosí and no matter what steps President Obregón may take, he is still the 'Red' leader, and that the only true support the Government may look for comes from the 'Red' element, which is dominated by Calles."

Walter F. Boyle to Secretary of State, January 28, 1924, *RDS*, 812.00/26926, Reel 81.

26. Marsh to Secretary of State, December 14, 1923, *RDS*, 812.00/26686, Reel 80.

27. Marsh to Secretary of State, April 19, 1924, *RDS*, 812.00/27226, Reel 82.

28. Summerlin to Secretary of State, January 10, 18, 1924, *RDS*, 812.00/26818, 812.00/26876, Reel 81.

29. Dawson to Secretary of State, January 16, 1924, *RDS*, 812.00/26866, Reel 81.

30. A translation of this article is enclosed in Summerlin to Secretary of State, January 18, 1924, *RDS*, 812.00/26876, Reel 81.

31. Conference on Conditions in Mexico, April 19, 1924, *AFL Records*, Reel 123.

32. Conference on Mexican Affairs, April 23, 1924, *AFL Records*, Reel 123.

33. Luncheon given by the Executive Council for the President-elect of Mexico, August 8, 1924, *AFL Records*, Reel 119.

34. Quoted in *New York Times*, October 29, 1924.

35. AFL, *Proceedings*, 1924, 125.

36. Ibid., 221. See also ibid., 303.

37. Ibid., 225.

38. Ibid., 220.

39. Ibid., 124–125.

40. Ibid., 166–167; Executive Council Minutes, October 20, 1924, *AFL Records*, Reel 7; Conference with Mexican labor representatives, November 15, 1924, *AFL Records*, Reel 123.

41. David A. Shannon, *The Socialist Party of America: A History* (New York: The Macmillan Company, 1955), 169–175. On Hillquit's endorsement of the PAFL, see Morris Hillquit, Speech at the International Socialist Congress at Marseilles, August 24, 1925, *Morris Hillquit Papers* (Microfilm edition: State Historical Society of Wisconsin, 1969), Reel 6 (hereafter cited as *Hillquit Papers*, followed by reel number).

42. Shannon, *The Socialist Party*, 176–181.

43. Manuel Sorola, reports, July 2, September 27, 1924, enclosed in Hoover to Lane, July 16, 1924, and Hoover to Director, Military Intelligence Division, October 3, 1924, *DJBI*, 25–230–52, 25–230–54.

44. Confederación Regional Obrera Mexicana Comité Central to the Socialist Party of America, October 6, 1924, enclosed in Bertha Hale White to Morris Hillquit, October 21, 1924, *Hillquit Papers*, Reel 3. On Wolfe's expulsion, see Schmitt, *Communism in Mexico*, 11–12.

45. PAFL, *Proceedings*, 1924, 3.

46. Address at the opening of the Pan American Federation of Labor Convention, December 3, 1924, *AFL Records*, Reel 119.

47. Jones to Harrison, February 6, 1925, enclosed in Anderson to Secretary of State, February 10, 1925, *RDS*, 812.00/27501, Reel 83.

48. Alexander Weddell to Department of State, January 6, 1925, *RDS*, 812.00/27495, Reel 83.

49. Sheffield to Kellogg, April 6, 1925, *RDS*, 812.00/27533, Reel 83.

50. AFL, *Proceedings*, 1924, 285–287. Woll's opposition to the resolution will be discussed in greater detail in Chapter Seven.

6. ROBERT HABERMAN, THE AFL, AND MEXICAN RADICALISM, 1917–1924

1. Grupo Acción consisted of eighteen members when it was formed in 1918, and at no time during its existence did it have more than twenty. Clark, *Organized Labor in Mexico*, 63–64. On Haberman's offer to spy for the U.S. Justice Department, see Hoover, memorandum, August 2, 1921, *DJBI*, 25–230.

2. Recent works have shed greater light on Haberman's contributions to the Mexican Revolution. His activities in Yucatán have received the most attention. Among those studies which contain important information on his involvement in Yucatán's reform movement are James C. Carey, *The Mexican Revolution in Yucatán, 1915–1924* (Boulder, Colo.: Westview Press, 1984); David Franz, "Bullets and Bolshevists: Radical Reformers in the Yucatán Peninsula" (Ph.D. diss., University of New Mexico, 1973); G. M. Joseph, *Revolution from Without: Yucatán, Mexico, and the United States, 1880–1924* (Cambridge: Cambridge University Press, 1982); and Francisco J. Paoli and Enrique Montalvo, *El socialismo olvidado de Yucatán* (México: Siglo Veintiuno Editores, 1977).

Whittaker, "American Labor Looks South," covers Haberman's activities in Yucatán and his involvement in Pan-American labor affairs, but the most thorough analysis of Haberman's role in the Mexican Revolution is Christopulos, "American Radicals and the Mexican Revolution, 1900–1925," which draws on a vast array of U.S. archival sources and radical periodicals to produce a fine study of how American radicals, including Haberman, reacted to the Mexican Revolution. What I am adding to her profile of Haberman comes largely from materials released to me by the Department of Justice through the Freedom of Information Act. The Justice Department's Bureau of Investigation assembled a massive file on Haberman, who was also watched carefully by the State Department and other branches of U.S. intelligence.

3. *New York Times*, March 5, 1962; John B. Murphy, report, July 3, 1917, *DJBI*, 25–230–0; Report Submitted by Plant Protection Section, United States Shipping Board, Emergency Fleet Corporation, Sisal Fibre Department, October 16, 1918, enclosed in Norman MacLeod to A. Bruce Bielaski, October 17, 1918, *DJBI*, 25–230–1.

Haberman passed the California State Board of Pharmacy's examination and worked for a while as a pharmacist. "Memorandum in re Robert Haberman," March 12, 1924, *DJBI*, 25–230–46.

4. Murphy, report, July 3, 1917, *DJBI*, 25–230–0; Report Submitted by

Plant Protection Section, U.S. Shipping Board, Emergency Fleet Corporation, October 16, 1918, enclosed in MacLeod to Bielaski, October 17, 1918, *DJBI*, 25–230–1; Carleton Beals, *Glass Houses: Ten Years of Free Lancing* (New York: J. B. Lippincott Company, 1938), 71.

The Office of Naval Intelligence claimed that a "reliable source" implicated Haberman in an alleged Hindu plot to smuggle machine guns into India through China. Office of Naval Intelligence to Bielaski, July 6, 1917, *DJBI*, 25–230–0.

5. William Foder, report, April 19, 1917, *DJBI*, 25–230–0.

6. William M. Offley to L. A. Merryman, July 17, 1917; Acting Chief, Bureau of Citizenship, to Bielaski, November 13, 1917, *DJBI*, 25–230–0.

7. Marsh to Secretary of State, June 12, 1917, enclosed in Leland Harrison to Bielaski, June 29, 1917, *DJBI*, 25–230–0.

8. John B. Murphy, reports, June 26, July 2, July 3, 1917, *DJBI*, 25–230–0.

9. "Memorandum for Mr. Hoover," August 13, 1921, *DJBI*, 25–230–1; "Memorandum in re Robert Haberman," March 12, 1924, *DJBI*, 25–230–46; "Memorandum on Robert Haberman," March 10, 1926, General Records of the Department of State, Office of the Counselor, Record Group 59, National Archives, Washington, D.C., File no. 862.2–224 (hereafter cited as *Office of the Counselor*, followed by file no.).

10. An excellent study of the internal and external conditions that undermined Yucatán's reform movement is Joseph, *Revolution From Without.* See also Carey, *The Mexican Revolution in Yucatán*; Franz, "Bullets and Bolshevists"; Paoli and Montalvo, *El socialismo olvidado de Yucatán*; and Gilbert M. Joseph, "The Fragile Revolution: Cacique Politics and Revolutionary Process in Yucatán," *Latin American Research Review* 15 (Number 1, 1980), 39–64.

11. Clark, *Organized Labor in Mexico,* 202; Franz, "Bullets and Bolshevists," 179. On the translated excerpt from Haberman's speech to the Motul Workers' Congress, see Paoli and Montalvo, *El socialismo olvidado de Yucatán,* 62–63.

12. John Morrison to Gompers, July 23, 1917; Morrison to Frank Duffy, July 23, 1917; *AFL Records,* Reel 86.

13. On Haberman's participation in the Liberty Loan campaign and cooperation with U.S. officials to promote publicity for the Allied war effort, see Division of Mexican Affairs, "Memorandum on Robert Haberman," September 13, 1923, enclosed in Armour to Burns, September 14, 1923, *DJBI*, 25–230–33; and Marsh to Secretary of State, October 11, 1918, *RDS*, 812.00/22315, Reel 64.

14. Marsh to Secretary of State, October 11, 1918, *RDS*, 812.00/22315, Reel 64; Franz, "Bullets and Bolshevists," 194; Joseph, *Revolution From Without*, 194.

15. Marsh to Secretary of State, October 11, 1918, *RDS*, 812.00/22315, Reel 64.

16. Ibid.

17. Ibid.

18. Memorandum, August 16, 1918, *Office of the Counselor*, 862.2–224.

19. Marsh to Secretary of State, January 21, 1919, *RDS*, 812.00/22480; E. P. Grosvenor to Leland Harrison, January 9, 1919, and Roger Welles, Office of Naval Intelligence, to Department of State, January 20, 1919, *Office of the Counselor*, 862.2–224; Division of Mexican Affairs, "Memorandum on Robert Haberman," September 13, 1923, enclosed in Armour to Burns, September 14, 1923, *DJBI*, 25–230–33.

20. Christopulos, "American Radicals and the Mexican Revolution," 370–371; Franz, "Bullets and Bolshevists," 194. On Haberman's certification as a draft evader, see, for example, Department of Justice, "Memorandum for Mr. Hoover," August 13, 1921, *DJBI*, 25–230–1.

21. *Bolchevismo y democracia en México*, 331, 334–335. Franz, "Bullets and Bolshevists," 195–196, disputes that the cooperative movement failed because of possible misappropriation of funds for personal use by Haberman, Carrillo Puerto, and others. He blames the disappearance of the cooperatives on Carranza's military action against the Yucatecan Socialists in 1919. Carey, *The Mexican Revolution in Yucatán*, 130, stresses that although critics have furnished no proof that Haberman sabotaged the cooperatives, dissatisfaction with him on the part of others involved in the reform movement played a role in his departure from Yucatán. For a view that places the demise of the cooperatives in the context of a monocultural economy dependent on the export of food and provisions from the United States, see Joseph, *Revolution From Without*, 194.

22. A copy of the U.S. Postal Censorship's summary of this letter from N. B. Breckenbridge, Mérida, to First Lieutenant C. E. Athey, Camp Logan, Houston, Texas, January 7, 1919, is in Military Intelligence Division to L. Lanier Winslow, January 31, 1919, *Office of the Counselor*, 862.2–224.

23. Gus T. Jones, Special Agent in Charge, "Confidential Memorandum for the Director," May 25, 1926, enclosed in Director, Bureau of Investigation, to Jones, June 8, 1926, *DJBI*, 25–230–65.

24. Beals, *Glass Houses*, 58, 69. On Beals's activities in Mexico, see Christopulos, "American Radicals and the Mexican Revolution," 443–444, 454; John A. Britton, *Carleton Beals: A Radical Journalist in Latin America* (Albuquerque: University of New Mexico Press, 1987); and idem, "In Defense of Revolution: American Journalists in Mexico, 1920–1929," *Journalism History* 5 (Winter 1978–79): 124–136.

25. Beals, *Glass Houses*, 71.

26. A translation of Haberman's letter to Marvini, September 18, 1920, is included in Matthew C. Smith, Colonel, General Staff, Military Intelligence Division, to Chief, Bureau of Investigation, December 16, 1920, *DJBI*, 25–230–0.

27. Report, September 22, 1920, enclosed in John M. Dunn to W. L. Hurley, October 15, 1920, *DJBI*, 25–230–0.

28. Haberman to Marvini, September 18, 1920, in Smith to Chief, Bureau of Investigation, December 16, 1920, *DJBI*, 25–230–0; Beals, *Glass Houses*, 71; Christopulos, "American Radicals and the Mexican Revolution," 411–412; Carleton Beals and Robert Haberman, "Mexican Labor and the Mexican Government," *The Liberator* 3 (October 1920): 20–23.

29. Whittaker, "American Labor Looks South," 665–667; Department of State, Memorandum, March 10, 1926, enclosed in Kirk to Hoover, March 13, 1926, *DJBI*, 25–230–63; PAFL, *Proceedings*, 1921, 4–6; AFL, *Proceedings*, 1921, 83.

30. "Mexico, the Hopeful: A Survey of Her Political and Industrial Situation As She Takes Her First Steps in Reconstruction," *American Federationist* 12 (December 1920): 1088.

31. AFL, *Proceedings*, 1921, 84; W. J. Burns to W. L. Hurley, November 14, 1921, *Office of the Counselor*, 862.2–224; Christopulos, "American Radicals and the Mexican Revolution," 412–413.

32. On Gale's activities in Mexico and his deportation, court martial, and imprisonment in the United States, see Christopulos, "American Radicals and the Mexican Revolution," especially 378–387, 390–391, and 415–432. A prison stretch in Leavenworth convinced Gale to recant his radicalism.

33. Quoted in Christopulos, "American Radicals and the Mexican Revolution," 383, 422.

34. Ibid., 422–423.

35. Haberman to Marvini, September 18, 1920, in Smith to Chief, Bureau of Investigation, December 16, 1920; W. L. Hurley to Hoover, November 1, 1920; "Memorandum in re Robert Haberman," March 12, 1924; all in *DJBI*, 25–230–0, 25–230–46.

36. Arthur Bliss Lane to Alexander C. Kirk, November 4, 1925, *Office of the Counselor*, 862.2–224; Department of State, memorandum, June 20, 1924, *DJBI*, 25–230.

37. W. A. Wiseman, report, November 26, 1921, *DJBI*, 25–230–4; Burns to Hurley, November 14, 1921, *Office of the Counselor*, 862.2–224.

38. See, for example, circulars enclosed in Charles M. Doherty, American Vice-Consul in Charge, Nogales, to Secretary of State, May 30, 31, 1921, *RDS*, 812.00/25014, 812.00/25029.

39. Christopulos, "American Radicals and the Mexican Revolution," 433–434. For Jackson's analysis of political conditions and the incident in the Chamber, see his letters dated May 16, 19, 1921, enclosed in Herbert Hoover to Henry P. Fletcher, June 8, 1921, *RDS*, 812.00/25037, Reel 75.

40. Hart, *Anarchism and the Mexican Working Class*, 160; Christopulos, "American Radicals and the Mexican Revolution," 424–433.

41. Matthew C. Smith to J. Edgar Hoover, June 16, 1921, *DJBI*, 25–230–0. The quote is in Cornelius Ferris, Jr., to Secretary of State, July 6, 1921, *DJBI*, 25–230–0.

42. W. A. Wiseman, report, November 14, 1921, *DJBI*, 25–230–4. J. Ed-

gar Hoover, "Memorandum in re Robert Haberman," March 12, 1924, *DJBI*, 25–230–46, notes that some doubt existed as to whether Haberman was deported at this time.

43. Calles to Gompers, July 14, 1921, *AFL Records*, Reel 105.

44. Conference, PAFL Executive Committee and Roberto Haberman, July 26, 1921, *AFL Records*, Reel 121; Hoover, memorandum, August 2, 1921, *DJBI*, 25–230.

45. Hoover, memorandum, August 2, 1921, *DJBI*, 25–230.

46. Ibid.

47. Christopulos, "American Radicals and the Mexican Revolution," 434.

48. "Good Stuff, Steffens," *Good Morning* 3 (May 1–15, 1921): 4.

49. Agent P-134, report, September 1, 1921, *DJBI*, 25–230–0.

50. Roberto Haberman to Mother Jones, April [?], 1921, in Foner, ed., *Mother Jones Speaks*, 647.

51. Quoted in Burns to Hurley, November 14, 1921, *Office of the Counselor*, 862.2–224.

52. Conference, PAFL Executive Committee and Haberman, July 26, 1921, *AFL Records*, Reel 121.

53. Quoted in *New York Times*, November 1, 1920.

54. Conferences, PAFL Executive Committee and Haberman, July 26, August 1, 1921, *AFL Records*, Reel 121; Agent P-134, report, September 1, 1921, *DJBI*, 25–230–0. On Haberman's efforts to attract foreign capital, see Gus T. Jones, report, December 7, 1922, *DJBI*, 25–230–32.

55. Conferences, PAFL Executive Committee and Haberman, July 26, August 1, 1921, *AFL Records*, Reel 121.

56. Hoover, memorandum, August 2, 1921, *DJBI*, 25–230.

57. Assistant Attorney General to Harry Weinberger, January 20, 1922, *DJBI*, 25–230–8.

58. Wiseman, report, November 26, 1921, *DJBI*, 25–230–4; E. Kosterlitzky, report, December 10, 1921, *DJBI*, 64–0–8; Marsh to Secretary of State, January 24, 1922, enclosed in Hurley to Burns, February 4, 1922, *DJBI*, 25–230–10.

59. O. Gaylord Marsh to Secretary of State, January 24, 1922, enclosed in W. L. Hurley to W. J. Burns, February 4, 1922, *DJBI*, 25–230–10; Marsh to Secretary of State, May 11, 1922, *RDS*, 812.00/25608, Reel 77.

60. Schmitt, *Communism in Mexico*, 8–9; Carey, *The Mexican Revolution in Yucatán*, 112.

61. Christopulos, "American Radicals and the Mexican Revolution," 460–475; AFL, *Proceedings*, 1924, 305.

62. Christopulos, "American Radicals and the Mexican Revolution," 467–470.

63. *New York Times*, June 28, 1922. While in New York negotiating a bankers' agreement in June 1922, de la Huerta complained to Obregón that Haberman was impeding his work by sending messages urging labor lead-

ers to call strikes in Yucatán and Veracruz should a debt accord be reached. Dulles, *Yesterday in Mexico*, 152.

64. E. Kosterlitsky, report, November 14, 1922; Louis DeNette, report, November 15, 1922; *DJBI*, 25-230-29, 25-230-30.

65. DeNette, report, November 15, 1922, *DJBI*, 25-230-30. When streetcar workers who belonged to the CGT went on strike just a couple of months after Haberman informed the Bureau of Investigation agent about the plan to crush the left-wing union, CROM scabs backed by troops attacked a meeting of CGT strikers. Casualties resulted from the attack, which had been advocated by Morones, and more than one hundred CGT members were jailed. Buford, "A Biography of Luis N. Morones," 48–49.

66. DeNette, report, November 15, 1922, *DJBI*, 25-230-30. On Haberman's alleged ties to the IWW and Communist Party, see W. H. Cowles, Military Intelligence Division, to Burns, August 25, 1922, and DeNette, report, August 16, 1922, *DJBI*, 25-230-18, 25-230-14.

67. DeNette, report, November 15, 1922, *DJBI*, 25-230-30.

68. Ibid. For reports of Haberman's alleged contacts with Soviet representatives, see, for example, Division of Mexican Affairs, "Memorandum on Robert Haberman," September 13, 1923, enclosed in Armour to Burns, September 14, 1923, *Office of the Counselor*, 862.2-224; J. V. McConville to Burns, August 3, 1922, and Kosterlitsky, report, January 30, 1923, *DJBI*, 25-230-11, 25-230-33.

69. Gus T. Jones, General Intelligence Bulletin, Mexican Affairs, San Antonio District, May 26, 1923, enclosed in Burns to Hurley, June 11, 1923, *DJBI*, 64-0-187.

70. Bertram D. Wolfe, "Take the Road to the Left," *The Liberator* 7 (April 1924): 21–22.

71. Dawson to Secretary of State, September 5, 1923, *RDS*, 812.00/ 26455. On the incident in the National Preparatory School, see Carr, *El movimiento obrero*, 145, n. 72.

72. *The Liberator* 6 (October 1923): 7.

73. J. Ramírez, "Mr. Hughes Surprises Himself," *The Liberator* 6 (November 1923): 21.

74. Dawson to Secretary of State, September 29, 1923, *RDS*, 812.20211/ 15, Reel 138; Armour to Burns, October 30, 1923, *DJBI*, 25-230-42.

75. Dawson to Secretary of State, November 9, 1923, *RDS*, 812.00/ 26509, Reel 80.

76. A translation of the editorial in *Excelsior*, November 7, 1923, is enclosed in ibid.

77. Ibid.; Conferences between the Executive Committee of the PAFL and Representatives of the Mexican Federation of Labor, October 25, 1923, *AFL Records*, Reel 123.

78. DeNette, report, October 27, 1923; Burns to E. J. Brennan, November 14, 1923; *DJBI*, 25-230-41, 25-230-42; Address by Gompers in Juárez, Mexico, October 27, 1923, *AFL Records*, Reel 118.

79. Manuel Sorola, report, December 18, 1923, enclosed in Director to Norman Armour, January 4, 1924, *DJBI*, 64-0-314; Shanton to Burns, December 20, 1923, enclosed in Burns to Armour, December 20, 1923, *Office of the Counselor*, 862.2-224.

80. PAFL, *Proceedings*, 1924, 38.

81. *The Pan-American Federation of Labor*, 119.

82. Manuel Sorola, report, July 2, 1924, enclosed in Hoover to Lane, July 16, 1924, *DJBI*, 25-230-52.

83. Ibid. See also Sorola, report, September 27, 1924, enclosed in Acting Director, Bureau of Investigation, to Director, Military Intelligence Division, October 3, 1924, *DJBI*, 25-230-54.

84. Wolfe, "Take the Road to the Left," 22.

85. Michael J. Johannes, report, June 21, 1924, enclosed in Hoover to Lane, June 26, 1924; Gus T. Jones, report, June 26, 1924; *Office of the Counselor*, 862.2-224.

86. Luncheon given by the Executive Council for the President-elect of Mexico, August 8, 1924, *AFL Records*, Reel 119.

87. Executive Council Minutes, October 20, 1924, *AFL Records*, Reel 7.

88. AFL, *Proceedings*, 1924, 166.

89. Ibid., 126.

90. AFL, *Proceedings*, 1924, 123–124; R. Lee Guard to Haberman, November 25, 1924, *AFL Records*, Reel 108.

91. Ambassador James R. Sheffield to Secretary of State, January 26, 1926, *RDS*, 812.20211/21, Reel 138, contains a report of this incident compiled by John Page, a newspaper correspondent in Mexico City. See also Department of State, memorandum, March 10, 1926, enclosed in Kirk to Hoover, March 13, 1926, *DJBI*, 25-230-63.

92. Sheffield to Secretary of State, January 26, 1926, *RDS*, 812.20211/21, Reel 138.

93. Sorola, report, July 2, 1924, enclosed in Hoover to Lane, July 16, 1924, *DJBI*, 25-230-52.

94. AFL, *Proceedings*, 1924, 166–167.

95. On the role of Beals, Tannenbaum, and Gruening, see Britton, *Carleton Beals*; idem, "In Defense of Revolution," 124–136; and Helen Delpar, "Frank Tannenbaum: The Making of a Mexicanist, 1914–1933," *The Americas* 45 (October 1988): 153–171. On State Department concerns over the activities of American journalists in Mexico, see Consul General Dawson, memorandum, March 16, 1923, enclosed in Summerlin to Secretary of State, March 17, 1923, *RDS*, 812.20211/10, Reel 138.

96. Hoover, "Memorandum in re Robert Haberman," March 12, 1924, *DJBI*, 25-230-46.

97. For conservative complaints about Haberman and the AFL, see, for example, Adolfo Ferrer to Secretary of State, August 20, 1924, and Wilbur Bates to Secretary of State, September 11, 1925, *RDS*, 812.00/27347, 812.00/27604, Reels 82, 83.

98. Jones, "Confidential Memorandum for the Director," May 25, 1926,

attached to Director, Bureau of Investigation, to Jones, June 8, 1926, *DJBI*, 25–230–65. See also Olmsted, memorandum, September 6–11, 1925, enclosed in Clark to Secretary of State, September 24, 1925, *Office of the Counselor*, 862.2–224.

The State Department requested a Justice Department investigation of Haberman's role as an intermediary between U.S. citizens seeking a divorce in Mexico and an attorney who was involved in the granting of bogus divorce decrees in the state of Morelos. S. P. Cowley, "Memorandum for the Director," March 16, 1934, U.S. Department of Justice, Division of Investigation, File no. 62–31219–2.

This study has uncovered no evidence which indicates that IAM officials working with Haberman tried to profit corruptly or illegally from the Mexican government's arrangement to buy union-made goods in the U.S. However, the business agent for a Machinists' local in New York City accused Davison and Johnston of trying to impose a commission on such purchases and thereby prompting the Mexicans to renege on the agreement. Perlman, *The Machinists*, 71.

99. For a thumb-nail sketch of Haberman's career in Mexico, see his obituary in the *New York Times*, March 5, 1962.

100. A copy of this resolution is enclosed in Gompers to Hughes, *RDS*, 812.00/25747, Reel 78.

101. Haberman also endorsed female suffrage in Mexico. Sorola, report, September 27, 1924, enclosed in Acting Director, Bureau of Investigation, to Director, MID, *DJBI*, 25–230–54.

102. The State Department had unsubstantiated reports that Haberman was involved in drug smuggling, and it requested investigations to determine whether he had violated the White Slave Traffic Act. His use of free railway passes in Mexico and the United States prompted an inquiry to explore whether a case could be made against him for violating the Erdman Act. See Loring Olmsted, memorandum, September 6–11, 1925, enclosed in Reed Paige Clark, American Consul in Charge, to Secretary of State, September 24, 1925, *Office of the Counselor*, 862.2–224; R. T. Crandall, report, November 4, 1922, enclosed in W. J. Burns to Gus T. Jones, November 16, 1922, *DJBI*, 25–230–28; Jones to Director, November 21, 1922, *DJBI*, 25–230–31; Arthur Bliss Lane to Alexander C. Kirk, November 4, 1925, *Office of the Counselor*, 862.2–224.

103. Levenstein, *Labor Organizations*, 135.

7. THE AFL AND U.S. HEGEMONY IN LATIN AMERICA

1. *Organized Labor in Latin America*, 251–252.

2. Studies of American labor's activities in Latin America are too numerous to mention exhaustively, but the following critical works are especially illuminating: Ibid., Chapter Six; Foner, *U.S. Labor and Latin America*; Scott, *Yankee Unions, Go Home!*; Radosh, *American Labor and United States Foreign Policy*, Chapters Eleven–Thirteen; Bodenheimer, "U.S. Labor's

Conservative Role in Latin America," 26–30; Berger, "Unions and Empire," 34–48; idem, "Union Diplomacy"; Larson, "U.S. Intervention in Nicaragua," 61–82; Levenstein, *Labor Organizations*; Torrence, "American Imperialism and Latin American Labor."

On labor's current policies in Central America, see Tom Barry and Deb Preusch, *AIFLD in Central America: Agents As Organizers* (Albuquerque: Inter-Hemispheric Education Resources Center, second printing, 1987); Chris Norton, "Build and Destroy," *NACLA Report on the Americas* 19 (November/December 1985): 25–36; Daniel Cantor and Juliet Schor, *Tunnel Vision: Labor, the World Economy, and Central America* (Boston: South End Press, 1987); Al Weinrub and William Bollinger, *The AFL-CIO in Central America: A Look at the American Institute for Free Labor Development (AIFLD)* (Oakland, Cal.: Labor Network on Central America, 1987); National Labor Committee in Support of Democracy and Human Rights in El Salvador, "The Search for Peace in Central America" (New York: n.p., 1985); Hobart A. Spalding, Jr., "Unions Look South," and "AIFLD Amok," *NACLA Report on the Americas* 22 (May/June 1988): 14–19, and 20–27; David Slaney, "Solidarity and Self-Interest," *NACLA Report on the Americas* 22 (May/June 1988): 28–36.

3. John Barrett to Gompers, January 29, 1910, *AFL Records*, Reel 71; Robert Seidel, "Progressive Pan Americanism: Development and United States Policy Toward South America, 1906–1931" (Ph.D. diss., Cornell University, 1973), 26–27.

4. Seidel, "Progressive Pan Americanism," 53–54, 72–74; Mark T. Gilderhus, "Wilson, Carranza, and the Monroe Doctrine: A Question in Regional Organization," *Diplomatic History* 7 (Spring 1983): 106.

5. "Progressive Pan Americanism," 27–28.

6. Snow, *The Pan-American Federation of Labor*, 9–10; Samuel Gompers, "Labor's Participation in Government," *American Federationist* 23 (February 1916): 107–108; Gompers to William G. McAdoo, June 23, 1915, *AFL Records*, Reel 79.

7. William G. McAdoo to Gompers, June 29, 1915, *AFL Records*, Reel 79.

8. Gompers to McAdoo, July 2, 1915, *AFL Records*, Reel 79. Berger, "Union Diplomacy," 4–5, also stresses that despite Gompers's support for expanding the export sector, his top priority was to raise the purchasing power of American workers to increase demand for goods.

9. On the contacts among the White House, Labor Department, State Department, Judge Douglas, and AFL Leaders during the Pershing crisis, see especially Florence C. Thorne, memoranda, June 23, 24, 1916, *AFL Records*, Reel 80; John Murray, memorandum, June 24, 1916, *AFL Records*, Reel 80; Thorne, memorandum, June 21, 1916, *AFL Records*, Reel 119.

10. Memorandum, October 12, 1916, *AFL Records*, Reel 81; Haley, *Revolution and Intervention*, 227–247.

11. Conference with John Murray and Chester Wright on Mexico, November 16, 1916, *AFL Records*, Reel 119.

12. Gompers to McAdoo, February 5, 1917, *AFL Records*, Reel 82.

13. Smith, *The United States and Revolutionary Nationalism in Mexico,* 94–99.

14. Memoranda, February 3, 14, 16, 1917, *AFL Records,* Reel 82.

15. See, for example, Woodrow Wilson to Secretary of State, June 17, 18, 1915, *RDS,* 812.00/15285–1/2, 812.00/15286–1/2.

16. The Bureau of Investigation agent's report is enclosed in A. Bruce Bielaski to Leland Harrison, October 11, 1917, *RDS,* 812.00/21377, Reel 61. On Douglas's efforts to gain corporate support for Carranza, see also Delbert J. Haff to Robert Lansing, May 5, 1917, *RDS,* 812.00/21233, Reel 61.

17. Enclosed in Bielaski to Harrison, October 11, 1917, *RDS,* 812.00/21377, Reel 61.

18. Snow, *The Pan-American Federation of Labor,* 35–36; Smith, *The United States and Revolutionary Nationalism in Mexico,* 117–119, 126–128.

19. Henry Bruére and Thomas Lill, Memorandum for President Wilson in Reference to Mexico, August 15, 1918, *AFL Records,* Reel 97.

20. J. R. Phillips, memorandum, August 1, 1918, enclosed in E. H. Greenwood to President Wilson, August 1, 1918, *AFL Records,* Reel 97.

21. E. H. Greenwood to Gompers, July 7, 1918, *AFL Records,* Reel 96. See also Greenwood, memoranda, July 17, 18, 1918; J. R. Phillips to Greenwood, July 26, 1918; *AFL Records,* Reel 96.

22. Snow, *The Pan-American Federation of Labor,* 43–46. On Warfield's views, see Warfield to Woodrow Wilson, July 2, 1918, *Wilson Papers,* Reel 216.

23. "Liberty's Hope Is In Thy Keeping, Organized Labor," *American Federationist* 23 (July 1916): 577.

24. Foner, *U.S. Labor Movement and Latin America,* 172–173.

25. "To Pan-Americanize Labor," *American Federationist* 24 (March 1917): 208.

26. "American Labor Looks South," 593, n. 33.

27. Ygnacio Bonillas, "Labor Legislation in Mexico: Importance of International Labor Organization," *American Federationist* 25 (August 1918): 682–683.

28. On Pani's ideology, see Keith Haynes, "Order and Progress: The Revolutionary Ideology of Alberto J. Pani" (Ph.D. diss., Northern Illinois University, 1981).

29. *The Mexican Question: Mexico and American-Mexican Relations Under Calles and Obregón* (New York: Robins Press, 1927), 95.

30. Warfield to Woodrow Wilson, July 2, 1918, *Wilson Papers,* Reel 216.

31. Phillips to E. H. Greenwood, July 26, 1918, *AFL Records,* Reel 96.

32. The AFL called for a Pan American Economic Conference after the war to upgrade the living standards of Latin American workers. See John Murray to Gompers, February 21, 1919, *AFL Records,* Reel 100.

33. Snow, *The Pan-American Federation of Labor,* 52–59; Levenstein, *Labor Organizations,* 78–89.

34. AFL, *Proceedings,* 1918, 251–252.

35. AFL, *Proceedings,* 1919, 417–418.

36. Captain Louis C. Richardson, report, March 11, 1919, enclosed in Josephus Daniels, Navy Department, to Secretary of State, March 13, 1919, *RDS*, 812.00/22562, Reel 65.

37. Ibid.

38. Ibid.

39. AFL, *Proceedings*, 1920, 125–126.

40. Snow, *The Pan-American Federation of Labor*, 51–52. Greenwood defended the ILO, whose creation was called for in the Versailles Treaty, from attacks by the left and the right. Despite U.S. refusal to ratify the Treaty of Versailles and the failure of the Chamber of Commerce to respond to an invitation to attend the opening session in an unofficial capacity, Greenwood continued to promote cooperation between the AFL and the Chamber in an effort to pressure the United States into joining the ILO in the 1920s. See Ernest H. Greenwood, "Labor and the League of Nations," *American Federationist* 27 (January 1920): 51–56; Gompers, "Pan-American Labor Congress at Mexico City," *American Federationist* 28 (March 1921): 194; Daniel P. Moynihan, "The Washington Conference of the International Labor Organization," *Labor History* 3 (Fall 1962): 307–334; Extract of Executive Council minutes concerning a meeting of the International Labor Office to be held in Geneva, February 14–20, 1923, *AFL Records*, Reel 122. For Greenwood's views on how the United States should promote the postwar economic development of Latin America, see Greenwood and Hugh Reid, "Financing a Continent," *The Nation's Business* 8 (March 1920): 18–20.

41. AFL, *Proceedings*, 1920, 128–130; Resolution submitted by Gompers to the Pan American Financial Congress, January 21, 1920, *AFL Records*, Reel 120; Remarks of Gompers to the Second Pan-American Financial Conference, Committee on Guatemala, January 19, 1920, *AFL Records*, Reel 114.

On Kemmerer's activities as a financial expert in Latin America and the broader implications of "private" U.S. foreign financial advising during this period, see Emily S. and Norman L. Rosenberg, "From Colonialism to Professionalism: The Public-Private Dynamic in United States Foreign Financial Advising, 1898–1929," *Journal of American History* 74 (June 1987): 59–82; Robert N. Seidel, "American Reformers Abroad: The Kemmerer Missions in South America, 1923–31," *Journal of Economic History* 32 (June 1972): 520–545; Donald L. Kemmerer and Bruce R. Dalgaard, "Inflation, Intrigue, and Monetary Reform in Guatemala, 1919–1926," *Historian* 46 (November 1983): 21–38; Edwin W. Kemmerer, "Economic Advisory Work for Governments," *American Economic Review* 17 (March 1927): 1–12; idem, *Inflation and Revolution: Mexico's Experience of 1912–1917* (Princeton, N. J.: Princeton University Press, 1940); Paul W. Drake, *Money Doctor in the Andes: The Kemmerer Missions, 1923–1933* (Durham, N.C.: Duke University Press, 1989).

Kemmerer had assisted Henry Bruére and Thomas Lill in their work on behalf of Carranza in 1917. Merle Curti and Kendall Birr, *Prelude to Point*

Four: American Technical Missions Overseas, 1838–1938 (Madison: University of Wisconsin Press, 1954), 160–161.

42. Seidel, "Progressive Pan Americanism," 35.

43. Resolution submitted by Gompers to the Pan American Financial Congress, January 21, 1920, *AFL Records*, Reel 120.

44. L. S. Rowe to Gompers, February 21, 1920, in AFL, *Proceedings, 1920*, 129–130.

45. Conference of Samuel Gompers with Dr. L. S. Rowe, Director-General of the Pan American Union, February 1, 1923, *AFL Records*, Reel 122.

46. Snow, *The Pan-American Federation of Labor*, 69–70.

47. Ibid., 70–71; Minutes of the PAFL Executive Committee, December 5, 1923, *AFL Records*, Reel 123; PAFL, *Proceedings, 1924*, 124–125.

48. *El Universal*, June 12, 1921, enclosed in George Summerlin to Secretary of State, June 17, 1921, *RDS*, 812.00/25057, Reel 75.

49. Summary of article in *Excelsior*, March 5, 1923, enclosed in Summerlin to Secretary of State, March 9, 1923, *RDS*, 812.00/26253, Reel 79; Thomas Horn, Jr., Vice Consul at Tampico, Document File Note, February 23–24, 1924, *Records of the Department of State Relating to Political Relations Between Mexico and Other States, 1910–1929*, File number 712.52/2, Reel 2. U.S. officials were especially worried about challenges from Spain and Mexico in Central America. See Richard V. Salisbury, *Anti-Imperialism and International Competition in Central America, 1920–1929* (Wilmington, Del.: Scholarly Resources, 1989).

50. Warfield to President Wilson, July 2, 1918, *Wilson Papers*, Reel 216. Enclosed in this letter are a memorandum dated June 27, 1918, and a copy of a previous letter to the White House dated July 18, 1917.

51. Conference on Americanizing Puerto Rico and Economic Conditions in Puerto Rico and the Virgin Islands, January 31, 1923, *AFL Records*, Reel 122.

52. Address Delivered by President Gompers Before the Committee on Foreign Relations of the Civic Federation, January 17, 1923, *AFL Records*, Reel 118.

Gompers had developed a cooperative relationship with Roosevelt during the war when the latter was assistant secretary of the navy. Roosevelt believed that labor-capital collaboration could stabilize industrial relations, counter radical forces, and promote economic expansion abroad. Radosh, "Development of the Corporate Ideology of American Labor Leaders," 96–97.

53. C. A. Vargas, Memorandum Submitted for the Consideration of the Executive Committee of the Pan-American Federation of Labor, December 5, 1923, *AFL Records*, Reel 105.

54. Address delivered by Gompers before the Committee on Foreign Relations of the Civic Federation, January 17, 1923, *AFL Records*, Reel 118.

55. Ibid.

56. Ibid.

57. AFL, *Proceedings*, 1920, 473–474.

58. "The World's Choice: League of Nations or League of Financiers," *American Federationist* 31 (January 1924): 17–18.

59. AFL, *Proceedings*, 1924, 285–287.

60. Ibid., 285.

61. Ibid., 285–286.

62. Ibid., 286–287.

63. Warfield to Wilson, July 2, 1918, *Wilson Papers*, Reel 216.

64. "Drift or Mastery?," 327.

65. Warfield to Wilson, July 2, 1918, *Wilson Papers*, Reel 216. See also Radosh, *American Labor and United States Foreign Policy*, 353–354.

66. On the opposition of embassy and consular officials to the AFL's activities in Mexico, see, for example, Summerlin to Secretary of State, January 10, 18, 1924; Dawson to Secretary of State, January 16, 1924; *RDS*, 812.00/26818, 812.00/26876, 812.00/26866, Reel 81.

67. "Mexico's President-Elect in Washington," *American Federationist* 31 (December 1924): 983. On the favorable accounts of Gompers's influence in Mexico, see, for example, E. R. Jones to Fairfax Harrison, February 6, 1925, enclosed in Henry Anderson to Secretary of State, February 10, 1925; and Alexander Weddell to Department of State, January 6, 1925; *RDS*, 812.00/27501, 812.00/27495, Reel 83.

68. Gompers, *Seventy Years of Life and Labor*, II, 540–541; *New York Times*, October 29, 1924; Smith, *The United States and Revolutionary Nationalism*, 230–231; Sheffield to Kellogg, April 6, 1925, *RDS*, 812.00/27533, Reel 83. Levenstein, *Labor Organizations*, Chapter Nine, contains a good discussion of the AFL's defense of Calles and the CROM between 1925 and 1928.

69. AFL, *Proceedings*, 1924, 88.

70. Santiago Iglesias, "The Child of the A.F. of L.," *American Federationist* 32 (October 1925): 928.

71. Gompers, "A Vision of Service," *American Federationist* 31 (June 1924): 497.

72. *Seventy Years of Life and Labor*, II, 320.

73. Venezuela's dictator Juan Vicente Gómez complained to the State Department about Gompers's criticisms of labor conditions in his country and blamed the PAFL for Mexico's decision to break off diplomatic relations with Venezuela. See Venezuelan Legation, Document File Note, January 24, 1924, United States Department of State, *Political Relations Between Mexico and Other States, 1910–1929*, 712.31/18, Reel 2.

74. On the divisions within the business community and the Republican Party, see, especially, Joan Hoff Wilson, *American Business & Foreign Policy, 1920–1933* (Lexington: University Press of Kentucky, 1971).

75. Maier, "The Politics of Productivity," 629.

76. See, for example, William Appleman Williams, *The Tragedy of American Diplomacy* (Cleveland: World Publishing Company, 1959); idem, "Latin America: Laboratory of American Foreign Policy in the Nineteen-Twenties," 3–30; Maier, "The Politics of Productivity," 607–633; idem,

"The Two Postwar Eras and the Conditions for Stability in Twentieth-Century Western Europe," 327–352; McCormick, "Drift or Mastery?," 318–330; Michael J. Hogan, "Revival and Reform: America's Twentieth-Century Search for a New Economic Order Abroad," *Diplomatic History* 8 (Fall 1984): 287–310; idem, "Corporatism: A Positive Appraisal," 363–372; Carl Parrini, *Heir to Empire: United States Economic Diplomacy, 1916–1923* (Pittsburgh: University of Pittsburgh Press, 1969); Thomas Ferguson, "From Normalcy to New Deal: Industrial Structure, Party Competition, and American Public Policy in the Great Depression," *International Organization* 38 (Winter 1984): 41–94.

77. Despite the potent attacks on organized labor in the 1920s, there were important cooperative contacts between AFL leaders and Herbert Hoover on the issue of increasing productivity and efficiency. See, for example, Gompers to Hoover, May 24, 1924; Hoover to Gompers, May 28, 1924; *AFL Records*, Reel 107. See also Robert H. Zieger, "Herbert Hoover, the Wage-earner, and the 'New Economic System,' 1919–1929," *Business History Review* 51 (Summer 1977): 161–189; Radosh, "Development of the Corporate Ideology of American Labor Leaders," especially 81–96.

8. LEGACY

1. Chester Wright, "Mexico the Hopeful," 1093. Gompers criticized the rise of a fascist movement in Mexico, pointing out that the movement was completely unwarranted, due to the nonradical orientation of Mexican workers. See Summerlin to Secretary of State, December 1, 1922, *RDS*, 812.00/26136, Reel 79.

2. On the imposition of corporatist controls over the Mexican labor movement in the 1930s, see, for example, Joe C. Ashby, *Organized Labor and the Mexican Revolution under Lázaro Cárdenas* (Chapel Hill: University of North Carolina Press, 1963). For discussions of Mexican corporatism and the modern state and Latin American corporatist thought in general, see especially James D. Cockcroft, *Mexico: Class Formation, Capital Accumulation, and the State* (New York: Monthly Review Press, 1983); Nora Hamilton, *The Limits of State Autonomy: Post-Revolutionary Mexico* (Princeton, N. J.: Princeton University Press, 1982); Nora Hamilton and Timothy Harding, eds., *Modern Mexico: State, Economy, and Social Conflict* (Beverly Hills: Sage, 1985); José Luis Reyna, "Redefining the Authoritarian Regime," in José Luis Reyna and Richard S. Weinert, eds., *Authoritarianism in Mexico* (Philadelphia: Institute for the Study of Human Issues, 1977), 155–171; Susan Kaufman Purcell, *The Mexican Profit-Sharing Decision: Politics in an Authoritarian Regime* (Berkeley, Los Angeles, London: University of California Press, 1975); James W. Wilkie, Michael C. Meyer, and Edna Monzón de Wilkie, eds., *Contemporary Mexico: Papers of the Fourth International Congress of Mexican History* (Berkeley, Los Angeles, London: University of California Press, 1975); James Malloy, ed., *Authoritarianism and Corporatism in Latin America* (Pittsburgh: University of Pittsburgh Press,

1977); Howard J. Wiarda, "Toward a Framework for the Study of Political Change in the Iberic-Latin Tradition: The Corporative Model," *World Politics* 25 (January 1973): 206–235; and Frederick B. Pike and Thomas Stritch, eds., *The New Corporatism: Social-Political Structures in the Iberian World* (South Bend, Ind.: Notre Dame University Press, 1974).

On the fragile nature of corporatist controls over the Mexican labor movement, see especially Ian Roxborough, *Unions and Politics in Mexico: The Case of the Automobile Industry* (Cambridge: Cambridge University Press, 1984); Charles L. Davis and Kenneth M. Coleman, "Structural Determinants of Working-Class Politicization: The Role of Independent Unions in Mexico," *Mexican Studies/Estudios Mexicanos* 5 (Winter 1989): 89–112; Charles L. Davis, *Political Control and Working Class Mobilization: Venezuela and Mexico* (Lexington: University of Kentucky Press, 1989); Raul Trejo Delarbe, "The Mexican Labor Movement: 1917–1975," *Latin American Perspectives* 3 (Winter 1976): 133–153; and Francisco Zapata, "Labor and Politics: The Mexican Paradox," in Edward C. Epstein, ed., *Labor Autonomy and the State in Latin America* (Boston: Unwin Hyman, 1989), 155–171.

3. V. I. Lenin, *Imperialism: The Highest Stage of Capitalism* (New York: International Publishers, 1939), Chapter Eight.

4. For a discussion of the process of state-formation in Mexico in the 1920s, see Richard Tardanico, "Perspectives on Revolutionary Mexico: The Regimes of Obregón and Calles," in Richard Rubinson, ed., *Dynamics of World Development* (Beverly Hills: Sage Publications, 1981), 69–88.

5. *The United States and Revolutionary Nationalism in Mexico,* 99.

6. On the differences between the AFL and the CIO in regard to Mexico in the 1930s, see Levenstein, *Labor Organizations,* Chapter Ten; and Norman Caulfield, "Mexican Labor and the State in the Twentieth Century: Conflict and Accommodation" (Ph.D. diss., University of Houston, 1990), 238–243.

7. Hillquit, Speech at the International Socialist Congress at Marseilles, August 24, 1925, *Hillquit Papers,* Reel 6.

8. Smith, *The United States and Revolutionary Nationalism in Mexico,* 230–231.

9. The AFL-dominated Organización Regional Interamericana (ORIT), created by the AFL in 1951, defended the U.S.-backed coup that overthrew Guatemalan president Jacobo Arbenz in 1954. On the ORIT, see Torrence, "American Imperialism and Latin American Labor."

In response to Fidel Castro and the Cuban Revolution, the AFL-CIO helped to create the American Institute for Free Labor Development (AIFLD) in 1961. Business leaders, many of whom had extensive financial interests in Latin America, joined labor leaders on AIFLD's board of directors to work with American officials to prevent the spread of Cuban-style revolutions. AIFLD supported the overthrow of elected governments in Guyana (1963), Brazil (1964), the Dominican Republic (1963–65), and Chile (1973). Most recently, AIFLD has worked to advance U.S. policies in El Salvador and Nicaragua. See, for example, Barry and Preusch, *AIFLD in*

Central America; Spalding, *Organized Labor in Latin America,* Chapter Six; idem, "Unions Look South," and "AIFLD Amok"; Weinrub and Bollinger, *The AFL-CIO in Central America*; Norton, "Build and Destroy"; Cantor and Schor, *Tunnel Vision*; and Slaney, "Solidarity and Self-Interest."

10. McCormick, "Drift or Mastery?": 327–328.

11. National Labor Committee in Support of Democracy and Human Rights in El Salvador, "The Search for Peace in Central America"; Cantor and Schor, *Tunnel Vision*, 10–11.

12. Quoted in Cantor and Schor, *Tunnel Vision*, 3.

Bibliography

MANUSCRIPT COLLECTIONS AND
ARCHIVAL MATERIALS

American Federation of Labor Records: The Samuel Gompers Era. Microfilming Corporation of America: Microfilm edition, 1979.
Morris Hillquit Papers. Microfilm edition. State Historical Society of Wisconsin. Madison.
United States Department of Justice, Bureau of Investigation. File number 25–230 on Robert Haberman released through Freedom of Information Act. Washington, D.C.
United States Department of State, General Records of the Department of State, Office of the Counselor/Undersecretary and the Chief Special Agent, Central file 1918–1927. File number 862.2–224 on Robert Haberman. Record Group 59. National Archives. Washington, D.C.
———. Records Relating to Internal Affairs of Mexico, 1910–1929. Record Group 59. National Archives. Washington, D.C.
———. Records Relating to Political Relations Between Mexico and Other States, 1910–1929. Record Group 59. National Archives, Washington, D.C.
———. Records Relating to World War I and Its Termination, 1914–1929. Record Group 59. National Archives. Washington, D.C.
Woodrow Wilson Papers. Presidential Papers Microfilm. Library of Congress. Washington, D.C.

PUBLIC DOCUMENTS

American Federation of Labor. *Reports of Proceedings of the Annual Conventions.* 1898–1924. Washington, D.C.
Pan American Federation of Labor. *Reports of Proceedings of the Conventions.* 1919–1924. Washington, D.C.
United States Department of State. *Papers Relating to the Foreign Relations of the United States: The Lansing Papers, 1914–1920.* 2 vols. Washington, D.C. 1939–1940.
United States Senate. Committee on Foreign Relations. *Investigation of Mexican Affairs.* S. Doc. 285. 66th Cong., 2nd sess., 1919–1920.

NEWSPAPERS AND PERIODICALS

American Federationist
Excelsior
New York Call
New York Times

BOOKS, DISSERTATIONS, AND THESES

Alba, Victor. *Politics and the Labor Movement in Latin America.* Stanford: Stanford University Press, 1968.

Alexander, Robert. *Communism in Latin America.* New Brunswick, N.J.: Rutgers University Press, 1957.

Ambrosius, Lloyd E. *Woodrow Wilson and the American Diplomatic Tradition: The Treaty Fight in Perspective.* New York: Cambridge University Press, 1987.

Anderson, Rodney D. *Outcasts in Their Own Land: Mexican Industrial Workers, 1906–1911.* DeKalb: Northern Illinois University Press, 1976.

Appel, John C. "The Relationship of American Labor to United States Imperialism, 1895–1905." Ph.D. diss., University of Wisconsin, 1950.

Araiza, Luis. *Historia del movimiento obrero mexicano.* 4 vols. México: Editorial Cuahtemoc, 1964–1965.

Ashby, Joe C. *Organized Labor and the Mexican Revolution under Lázaro Cárdenas.* Chapel Hill: University of North Carolina Press, 1963.

Atkin, Ronald. *Revolution! Mexico, 1910–20.* London: Panther Books, 1972.

Baker, Ray Stannard. *Woodrow Wilson: Life and Letters.* 8 vols. Garden City, N.Y.: Doubleday, Doran & Company, Inc., 1927–1939.

Barry, Tom and Deb Preusch. *AIFLD in Central America: Agents as Organizers.* Albuquerque: Inter-Hemispheric Education Resource Center, 1987.

Basurto, Jorge, *El proletariado industrial en México (1850–1930).* México: Universidad Nacional Autónoma de México, 1975.

Beals, Carleton. *Glass Houses: Ten Years of Free Lancing.* New York: J. B. Lippincott Company, 1938.

Berger, Henry Weinberg. "Union Diplomacy: American Labor's Foreign Policy in Latin America, 1932–1955." Ph.D. diss., University of Wisconsin, 1966.

Bergquist, Charles. *Labor in Latin America: Comparative Essays on Chile, Argentina, Venezuela, and Colombia.* Stanford: Stanford University Press, 1986.

Blaisdell, Lowell. *Desert Revolution, Baja California, 1911.* Madison: University of Wisconsin Press, 1962.

Blakeslee, George H., ed. *Mexico and the Caribbean: Clark University Addresses.* New York: G. E. Stechert and Co., 1920.

Blasier, Cole. *The Hovering Giant: U.S. Response to Revolutionary Change in Latin America.* Pittsburgh: University of Pittsburgh Press, 1976.

Brading, D. A., ed. *Caudillo and Peasant in the Mexican Revolution*. Cambridge: Cambridge University Press, 1980.

Britton, John A. *Carleton Beals: A Radical Journalist in Latin America*. Albuquerque: University of New Mexico Press, 1987.

Buford, Camile Nick. "A Biography of Luis N. Morones, Mexican Labor and Political Leader." Ph.D. diss., Louisiana State University, 1971.

Calhoun, Frederick S. *Power and Principle: Armed Intervention in Wilsonian Foreign Policy*. Kent, Ohio: Kent State University, 1986.

Cantor, Daniel and Juliet Schor. *Tunnel Vision: Labor, the World Economy, and Central America*. Boston: South End Press, 1987.

Cardoso, Ciro F. S., Francisco G. Hermosillo, and Salvador Hernández. *La clase obrera en la historia de México: de la dictadura porfirista a los tiempos libertarios*. México: Siglo Veintiuno Editores, 1980.

Carey, James C. *The Mexican Revolution in Yucatán, 1915–1924*. Boulder, Colo.: Westview Press, 1984.

Carr, Barry. *El movimiento obrero y la política en México 1910–1929*. México: Ediciones Era, 1979 [1981].

Caulfield, Norman. "Mexican Labor and the State in the Twentieth Century: Conflict and Accommodation." Ph.D. diss., University of Houston, 1990.

Christopulos, Diana K. "American Radicals and the Mexican Revolution, 1900–1925." Ph.D. diss., State University of New York at Binghamton, 1980.

Clark, Marjorie Ruth. *Organized Labor in Mexico*. Chapel Hill: University of North Carolina Press, 1934.

Clements, Kendrick A. *Woodrow Wilson: World Statesman*. Boston: Twayne, 1987.

Coatsworth, John H. *Growth Against Development: The Economic Impact of Railroads in Porfirian Mexico*. DeKalb: Northern Illinois University Press, 1981.

Cockcroft, James D. *Intellectual Precursors of the Mexican Revolution, 1900–1913*. Austin: University of Texas Press, 1968.

———. *Mexico: Class Formation, Capital Accumulation, and the State*. New York: Monthly Review Press, 1983.

Córdova, Arnaldo. *La ideología de la Revolución Mexicana: La formación del nuevo régimen*. México: Ediciones Era, 1973.

Cumberland, Charles C. *Mexican Revolution: Genesis under Madero*. Austin: University of Texas Press, 1952 [1974].

———. *Mexican Revolution: The Constitutionalist Years*. Introduction and additional material by David C. Bailey. Austin: University of Texas Press, 1972 [1974].

Curti, Merle and Kendall Birr. *Prelude to Point Four: American Technical Missions Overseas*. Madison: University of Wisconsin Press, 1954.

Davis, Charles L. *Political Control and Working Class Mobilization: Venezuela and Mexico*. Lexington: University Press of Kentucky, 1989.

Dick, William M. *Labor and Socialism in America: The Gompers Era*. Port Washington, N.Y.: Kennikat Press, 1972.

Drake, Paul W. *Money Doctor in the Andes: The Kemmerer Missions, 1923–1933*. Durham, N.C.: Duke University Press, 1989.

Dubofsky, Melvin. *We Shall Be All: A History of the Industrial Workers of the World*. New York: Quadrangle Books, 1969.

Dulles, John W. F. *Yesterday in Mexico: A Chronicle of the Revolution, 1919–1936*. Austin: University of Texas Press, 1961.

Fabela, Isidro. *Historia diplomática de la Revolución Mexicana, 1912–1917*. 2 vols. México: Fondo de Cultura Económica, 1958–1959.

Filippelli, Ronald L. *American Labor and Postwar Italy, 1943–1953: A Study of Cold War Politics*. Stanford: Stanford University Press, 1989.

Foner, Philip S. *History of the Labor Movement in the United States*. 7 vols. New York: International Publishers, 1947–1987.

———, ed. *Mother Jones Speaks: Collected Writings and Speeches*. New York: Monad Press, 1983.

———. *U.S. Labor and Latin America: A History of Workers' Response to Intervention*, Vol. I, *1846–1919*. South Hadley, Mass.: Bergin & Garvey Publishers, Inc., 1988.

Foster, James C., ed. *American Labor in the Southwest: The First One Hundred Years*. Tucson: University of Arizona Press, 1982.

Franz, David. "Bullets and Bolshevists: Radical Reformers in the Yucatán Peninsula." Ph.D. diss., University of New Mexico, 1973.

Gardner, Lloyd C. *Safe for Democracy: The Anglo-American Response to Revolution, 1913–1923*. New York: Oxford University Press, 1984.

———. "Woodrow Wilson and the Mexican Revolution." In *Woodrow Wilson and a Revolutionary World, 1913–1921*, 3–48. Edited by Arthur S. Link. Chapel Hill: University of North Carolina Press, 1982.

Gilderhus, Mark T. *Diplomacy and Revolution: U.S.-Mexican Relations Under Wilson and Carranza*. Tucson: University of Arizona Press, 1977.

———. *Pan American Visions: Woodrow Wilson in the Western Hemisphere, 1913–1921*. Tucson: University of Arizona Press, 1986.

Gilly, Adolfo, Arnaldo Córdova, Armando Bartra, Manuel Aguilar Mora, and Enrique Semo. *Interpretaciones de la Revolución Mexicana*. Prologue by Héctor Aguilar Camín. México: Editorial Nueva Imagen, 1979.

Gómez-Quiñones, Juan. *Sembradores: Ricardo Flores Magón y el Partido Liberal Mexicano: A Eulogy and a Critique*. Los Angeles: Aztlán Publications, 1973.

Gompers, Samuel. *American Labor and the War*. New York: George H. Doran Co., 1919.

———. *Seventy Years of Life and Labor: An Autobiography*. 2 vols. New York: E. P. Dutton Company, 1925; reprint ed., New York: Augustus M. Kelley, 1967.

González Casanova, Pablo. *La clase obrera en la historia de México: en el primer gobierno constitucional (1917–1920)*. México: Siglo Veintiuno Editores, 1980.

González Navarro, Moisés. *El porfiriato: la vida social*. México: El Colegio de México, 1966.

Green, Marguerite. *The National Civic Federation and the American Labor Movement, 1900–1925*. Washington, D.C.: Catholic University of America Press, 1956.

Grieb, Kenneth J. *The United States and Huerta*. Lincoln: University of Nebraska Press, 1969.

Grubbs, Frank L., Jr. *The Struggle for Labor Loyalty: The A. F. of L. and the Pacifists, 1917–1920*. Durham, N.C.: Duke University Press, 1968.

Gruening, Ernest. *Mexico and Its Heritage*. New York: D. Appleton-Century Company, 1934.

Haley, P. Edward. *Revolution and Intervention: The Diplomacy of Taft and Wilson with Mexico, 1910–1917*. Cambridge, Mass.: MIT Press, 1970.

Hall, Linda B. *Álvaro Obregón: Power and Revolution in Mexico, 1911–1920*. College Station: Texas A & M University Press, 1981.

Hamilton, Nora. *The Limits of State Autonomy: Post-Revolutionary Mexico*. Princeton: Princeton University Press, 1982.

Hamilton, Nora and Timothy Harding, eds. *Modern Mexico: State, Economy and Social Conflict*. Beverly Hills: Sage Publications, 1985.

Hansen, Roger D. *The Politics of Mexican Development*. Baltimore: Johns Hopkins University Press, 1971.

Hansis, Randall George. "Álvaro Obregón, the Mexican Revolution, and the Politics of Consolidation, 1920–1924." Ph.D. diss., University of New Mexico, 1971.

Hart, John M. *Anarchism and the Mexican Working Class, 1860–1931*. Austin: University of Texas Press, 1978.

———. *Revolutionary Mexico: The Coming and Process of the Mexican Revolution*. Berkeley, Los Angeles, London: University of California Press, 1987.

Harvey, Rowland Hill. *Samuel Gompers: Champion of the Toiling Masses*. New York: Octagon Books, 1975.

Haynes, Keith. "Order and Progress: The Revolutionary Ideology of Alberto J. Pani." Ph.D. diss., Northern Illinois University, 1981.

Hill, Larry D. *Emissaries to a Revolution: Woodrow Wilson's Executive Agents in Mexico*. Baton Rouge: Louisiana State University, 1974.

Hoff-Wilson, Joan. *American Business and Foreign Policy, 1920–1933*. Lexington: University Press of Kentucky, 1971.

Hogan, Michael J. *The Marshall Plan: America, Britain, and the Reconstruction of Western Europe, 1947–1952*. Cambridge: Cambridge University Press, 1987.

Jordan, David Starr. *The Days of a Man: Being Memories of a Naturalist, Teacher and Minor Prophet of Democracy*. 2 vols. Yonkers-on-Hudson, N.Y.: World Book Company, 1922.

Joseph, G. M. *Revolution From Without: Yucatán, Mexico, and the United States, 1880–1924*. Cambridge: Cambridge University Press, 1982.

Karson, Marc. *American Labor Unions and Politics, 1900–1918.* Carbondale: Southern Illinois University Press, 1958.

Katz, Friedrich. *The Secret War in Mexico: Europe, the United States, and the Mexican Revolution.* Portions translated by Loren Goldner. Chicago: University of Chicago Press, 1981.

Kaufman, Stuart Bruce. *Samuel Gompers and the Origins of the American Federation of Labor, 1848–1896.* Westport, Conn.: Greenwood Press, 1973.

————, ed. *The Samuel Gompers Papers.* 3 vols. Urbana: University of Illinois Press, 1986–89.

Kaufman Purcell, Susan. *The Mexican Profit-Sharing Decision: Politics in an Authoritarian Regime.* Berkeley, Los Angeles, London: University of California Press, 1975.

Keen, Benjamin, and Mark Wasserman. *A Short History of Latin America.* 3rd ed. Boston: Houghton Mifflin Company, 1988.

Kemmerer, E. W. *Inflation and Revolution: Mexico's Experience of 1912–1917.* Princeton, N.J.: Princeton University Press, 1940.

Kipnis, Ira. *The American Socialist Movement 1897–1912.* New York: Columbia University Press, 1952.

Knight, Alan. *The Mexican Revolution.* 2 vols. Cambridge: Cambridge University Press, 1986.

————. "The Political Economy of Revolutionary Mexico, 1900–1940." In *Latin America, Economic Imperialism and the State: The Political Economy of the External Connection from Independence to the Present,* 288–317. Edited by Christopher Abel and Colin M. Lewis. London: The Athlone Press, 1985.

Kolko, Gabriel. *The Triumph of Conservatism: A Reinterpretation of American History, 1900–1916.* New York: Free Press, 1963.

LaFrance, David. *The Mexican Revolution in Puebla, 1908–1913: The Maderista Movement and the Failure of Liberal Reform.* Wilmington, Del.: Scholarly Resources, 1989.

Lane, Anne Wintermute and Louise Herrick Wall, eds. *The Letters of Franklin K. Lane, Personal and Political.* Boston: Houghton Mifflin Company, 1922.

Larson, Simeon. *Labor and Foreign Policy: Gompers, the AFL, and the First World War, 1914–1918.* Rutherford, N.J.: Fairleigh Dickinson University Press, 1975.

Laslett, John H. M. *Labor and the Left: A Study of Socialist and Radical Influences in the American Labor Movement, 1881–1924.* New York: Basic Books, 1970.

Lenin, V. I. *Imperialism: The Highest Stage of Capitalism.* New York: International Publishers, 1939.

Levenstein, Harvey A. *Labor Organizations in the United States and Mexico: A History of Their Relations.* Westport, Conn.: Greenwood Publishing Company, 1971.

Levin, N. Gordon, Jr. *Woodrow Wilson and World Politics: America's Response to War and Revolution.* London: Oxford University Press, 1968.

Link, Arthur S. *Wilson: Campaigns for Progressivism and Peace*. Princeton, N.J.: Princeton University Press, 1965.

————. *Wilson: Confusions and Crises, 1915–1916*. Princeton, N.J.: Princeton University Press, 1964.

————. *Woodrow Wilson: Revolution, War, and Peace*. Arlington Heights, Ill.: Harlan Davidson, Inc., 1979.

Link, Arthur S., ed. *Woodrow Wilson and a Revolutionary World, 1913–1921*. Chapel Hill: University of North Carolina Press, 1982.

Lombardo Toledano, Vicente. *Teoría y práctica del movimiento sindical mexicano*. México: Universidad Obrera de México, 1974.

Lorwin, Lewis L. *Labor and Internationalism*. New York: The Macmillan Company, 1929.

Lustig, R. Jeffrey. *Corporate Liberalism: The Origins of Modern American Political Theory, 1890–1920*. Berkeley, Los Angeles, London: University of California Press, 1982.

McKee, Delber Lee. "The American Federation of Labor and American Foreign Policy, 1886–1912." Ph.D. diss., Stanford University, 1952.

MacLachlan, Colin M. *Anarchism and the Mexican Revolution: The Political Trials of Ricardo Flores Magón in the United States*. Berkeley, Los Angeles, Oxford: University of California Press, 1991.

Malloy, James, ed. *Authoritarianism and Corporatism in Latin America*. Pittsburgh: University of Pittsburgh Press, 1977.

Mandel, Bernard. *Samuel Gompers: A Biography*. Yellow Springs, Ohio: Antioch Press, 1963.

Marchand, C. Roland. *The American Peace Movement and Social Reform, 1898–1918*. Princeton, N.J.: Princeton University Press, 1972.

Mena Brito, Bernardino. *Bolchevismo y democracía en México: Pugna entre dos partidos políticos en Yucatán durante de la Revolución Mexicana*. México: n.p., 1933.

Meyer, Eugenia. *Conciencia histórica norteamericana sobre la Revolución de 1910*. México: Instituto Nacional de Antropología e Historia, 1970.

Meyer, Lorenzo. *Mexico and the United States in the Oil Controversy, 1917–1942*. Translated by Muriel Vasconcellos. Austin: University of Texas Press, 1977.

Meyer, Michael C. *Huerta: A Political Portrait*. Lincoln: University of Nebraska Press, 1972.

Meyer, Michael C. and William Sherman. *The Course of Mexican History*. 4th ed. New York: Oxford University Press, 1990.

Montgomery, David. *The Fall of the House of Labor: The Workplace, the State, and American Labor Activism, 1865–1925*. Cambridge: Cambridge University Press, 1987.

————. *Workers' Control in America: Studies in the History of Work, Technology, and Labor Struggles*. Cambridge: Cambridge University Press, 1976.

Moody, J. Carroll and Alice Kessler-Harris, eds. *Perspectives on American Labor History: The Problems of Synthesis*. DeKalb: Northern Illinois University Press, 1989.

Painter, Nell Irvin. *Standing at Armageddon: The United States, 1877–1919*. New York: W. W. Norton & Company, 1987.

Paoli, Francisco J. and Enrique Montalvo. *El socialismo olvidado de Yucatán*. México: Siglo Veintiuno Editores, 1977.

Parrini, Carl. *Heir to Empire: United States Economic Diplomacy, 1916–1923*. Pittsburgh: University of Pittsburgh Press, 1969.

Perlman, Mark. *The Machinists: A New Study in American Trade Unionism*. Cambridge, Mass.: Harvard University Press, 1961.

Pike, Frederick B. and Thomas Stritch, eds. *The New Corporatism: Social-Political Structures in the Iberian World*. South Bend, Ind.: Notre Dame University Press, 1974.

Quirk, Robert E. *An Affair of Honor: Woodrow Wilson and the Occupation of Veracruz*. Lexington: University Press of Kentucky, 1962.

Raat, W. Dirk. *Revoltosos: Mexico's Rebels in the United States, 1903–1923*. College Station: Texas A & M University Press, 1981.

———. *The Mexican Revolution: An Annotated Guide to Recent Scholarship*. Boston: G. K. Hall & Co., 1982.

Raat, W. Dirk and William H. Beezley, eds. *Twentieth-Century Mexico*. Lincoln: University of Nebraska Press, 1986.

Radosh, Ronald. *American Labor and United States Foreign Policy*. New York: Random House, 1969.

———. "The Development of the Corporate Ideology of American Labor Leaders, 1914–1933." Ph.D. diss., University of Wisconsin, 1967.

Rayback, Joseph G. *A History of American Labor*. Expanded and updated edition. New York: The Free Press, 1966.

Reyna, José Luis. "Redefining the Authoritarian Regime." In *Authoritarianism in Mexico*, 155–171. Edited by José Luis Reyna and Richard S. Weinert. Philadelphia: Institute for the Study of Human Issues, 1977.

Richmond, Douglas W. *Venustiano Carranza's Nationalist Struggle, 1893–1920*. Lincoln: University of Nebraska Press, 1983.

Rodríguez, Jaime E., ed. *The Revolutionary Process in Mexico: Essays on Political and Social Change, 1880–1940*. Los Angeles: UCLA Latin American Center, 1990.

Rosenberg, Emily S. *Spreading the American Dream: American Economic and Cultural Expansion, 1890–1945*. New York: Hill and Wang, 1982.

Roxborough, Ian. *Unions and Politics in Mexico: The Case of the Automobile Industry*. Cambridge: Cambridge University Press, 1984.

Ruiz, Ramón Eduardo. *Labor and the Ambivalent Revolutionaries: Mexico, 1911–1923*. Baltimore: Johns Hopkins University Press, 1976.

———. *The Great Rebellion: Mexico, 1905–1924*. New York: W. W. Norton & Company, 1980.

———. *The People of Sonora and Yankee Capitalists*. Tucson: University of Arizona Press, 1988.

Salazar, Rosendo. *La Casa del Obrero Mundial*. México: Costa-Amic, 1962.

Salazar, Rosendo and José G. Escobedo. *Las pugnas de la gleba, 1907–1922*. México: Comisión Nacional Editorial, 1972.

Salisbury, Richard V. *Anti-Imperialism and International Competition in Central America, 1920–1929.* Wilmington, Del.: Scholarly Resources, 1989.

Schmitt, Karl M. *Communism in Mexico: A Study in Political Frustration.* Austin: University of Texas Press, 1965.

Schmitter, Philippe. "Still the Century of Corporatism." In *The New Corporatism: Social-Political Structures in the Iberian World*, 85–131. Edited by Frederick B. Pike and Thomas Stritch. South Bend, Indiana: Notre Dame University Press, 1974.

Scott, Jack. *Yankee Unions, Go Home! How the AFL Helped the U.S. Build an Empire in Latin America.* Vancouver: New Star Books, 1978.

Seidel, Robert Neal. "Progressive Pan Americanism: Development and United States Policy Toward South America, 1906–1931." Ph.D. diss., Cornell University, 1973.

Sessions, Tommie Gene. "American Reformers and the Mexican Revolution: Progressives and Woodrow Wilson's Policy in Mexico, 1913–1917." Ph.D. diss., American University, 1974.

Shannon, David A. *The Socialist Party of America: A History.* New York: The Macmillan Company, 1955.

Silva Herzog, Jesús. *Breve historia de la Revolución Mexicana: La etapa Constitucionalista y la lucha de facciones.* México: Fondo de Cultura Económica, 1980.

Smith, Robert Freeman. *The United States and Revolutionary Nationalism in Mexico, 1916–1932.* Chicago: University of Chicago Press, 1972.

Snow, Sinclair. *The Pan-American Federation of Labor.* Durham, North Carolina: Duke University Press, 1964.

Spalding, Hobart A., Jr. *Organized Labor in Latin America: Historical Case Studies of Urban Workers in Dependent Societies.* New York: Harper Torchbooks, 1977.

———. "U.S. and Latin American Labor: The Dynamics of Imperialist Control." In *Ideology & Social Change in Latin America*, 55–91. Edited by June Nash, Juan Corradi, and Hobart A. Spalding, Jr. New York: Gordon and Breach, 1977.

Stearn, Gerald Emanuel, ed. *Gompers.* Englewood Cliffs, N.J.: Prentice-Hall, Inc., 1971.

Steel, Edward M., ed. *The Correspondence of Mother Jones.* Pittsburgh: University of Pittsburgh Press, 1985.

Stimson, Grace H. *The Rise of the Labor Movement in Los Angeles.* Berkeley and Los Angeles: University of California Press, 1955.

Taft, Philip. *Defending Freedom: American Labor and Foreign Affairs.* Foreword by Robert M. Murphy. Los Angeles: Nash Publishing, 1973.

———. *The A. F. of L. in the Time of Gompers.* New York: Harper and Brothers, 1957.

Tannenbaum, Frank. *Peace By Revolution.* New York: Columbia University Press, 1933.

———. *The Mexican Agrarian Revolution.* Washington, D.C.: Brookings Institution, 1929.

Tardanico, Richard. "Perspectives on Revolutionary Mexico: The Regimes of Obregón and Calles." In *Dynamics of World Development*, 69–88. Edited by Richard Rubinson. Beverly Hills: Sage Publications, 1981.

Tomlins, Christopher L. *The State and the Unions: Labor Relations, Law, and the Organized Labor Movement in America, 1880–1960*. Cambridge: Cambridge University Press, 1985.

Torrence, Donald R. "American Imperialism and Latin American Labor 1959–1970: A Study of the Role of the Organización Regional Interamericana de los Trabajadores in the Latin American Policy of the United States." Ph.D. diss., Northern Illinois University, 1975.

Toth, Charles William. "The Pan-American Federation of Labor." Master's thesis, University of Illinois, 1947.

Tulchin, Joseph S. *The Aftermath of War: World War I and U.S. Policy Toward Latin America*. New York: New York University Press, 1971.

Turner, John Kenneth. *Barbarous Mexico*. Introduction by Sinclair Snow. Austin: University of Texas Press, 1969.

Tutino, John. *From Insurrection to Revolution in Mexico: Social Bases of Agrarian Violence*. Princeton: Princeton University Press, 1987.

Uloa, Berta. *La Revolución intervenida: Relaciones diplomáticas entre México y Estados Unidos (1910–1914)*. México: El Colegio de México, 1971.

Van Tine, Warren R. *The Making of the Labor Bureaucrat: Union Leadership in the United States, 1870–1920*. Amherst: University of Massachusetts Press, 1973.

Vasconcelos, José. *El desastre*. México: Ediciones Botas, 1938.

Walling, William English. *The Mexican Question: Mexico and American-Mexican Relations Under Calles and Obregón*. New York: Robins Press, 1927.

Weinrub, Al and William Bollinger. *The AFL-CIO in Central America: A Look at the American Institute for Free Labor Development (AIFLD)*. Oakland, Cal.: Labor Network on Central America, 1987.

Weinstein, James. *The Corporate Ideal in the Liberal State: 1900–1918*. Boston: Beacon Press, 1968.

———. *The Decline of Socialism in America, 1912–1925*. New York: Monthly Review Press, 1967.

Whittaker, William. "American Labor Looks South: The Gompers Era, 1894–1924." Ph.D. diss., Georgetown University, 1965.

Wilkie, James. *The Mexican Revolution: Federal Expenditure and Social Change Since 1910*. Berkeley and Los Angeles: University of California Press, 1967.

Wilkie, James W., Michael C. Meyer and Edna Monzón de Wilkie, eds. *Contemporary Mexico: Papers of the Fourth International Congress of Mexican History*. Berkeley, Los Angeles, London: University of California Press, 1975.

Williams, William Appleman. *The Tragedy of American Diplomacy*. Cleveland: World Publishing Company, 1959.

Wolf, Eric R. *Peasant Wars of the Twentieth Century*. New York: Harper Torchbooks, 1973.

Wolfskill, George and Douglas W. Richmond, eds. *Essays on the Mexican Revolution: Revisionist Views of the Leaders*. Introduction by Michael C. Meyer. Austin: University of Texas Press, 1979.

Womack, John, Jr. *Zapata and the Mexican Revolution*. New York: Vintage Books, 1968.

Zapata, Francisco. "Labor and Politics: The Mexican Paradox." In *Labor Autonomy and the State in Latin America*, 173–193. Edited by Edward C. Epstein. Boston: Unwin Hyman, 1989.

Zieger, Robert H. *Republicans and Labor, 1919–1929*. Lexington: University Press of Kentucky, 1969.

Zorrilla, Luis G. *Historia de las relaciones entre México y los Estados Unidos 1800–1958*. 2 vols. México: Editorial Porrúa, S. A., 1966.

ARTICLES

Anderson, Rodney D. "Mexican Workers and the Politics of Revolution, 1906–1911." *Hispanic American Historical Review* 54 (February 1974): 94–113.

Andrews, Gregg. "Robert Haberman, Socialist Ideology, and the Politics of National Reconstruction in Mexico, 1920–25." *Mexican Studies/Estudios Mexicanos* 6 (Summer 1990): 189–211.

Bailey, David C. "Revisionism and the Recent Historiography of the Mexican Revolution." *Hispanic American Historical Review* 58 (February 1978): 62–79.

Beals, Carleton and Robert Haberman. "Mexican Labor and the Mexican Government." *The Liberator* 3 (October 1920): 20–23.

Berger, Henry W. "Unions and Empire: Organized Labor and American Corporations Abroad." *Peace and Change* 3 (Spring 1976): 34–48.

Bernstein, Harry. "Marxismo en México, 1917–1925." *Historia Mexicana* 7 (April-June 1958): 497–516.

Bodenheimer, Susanne. "U.S. Labor's Conservative Role in Latin America." *The Progressive* 31 (November 1967): 26–30.

Britton, John A. "In Defense of Revolution: American Journalists in Mexico, 1920–1929." *Journalism History* 5 (Winter 1978–79): 124–136.

Carr, Barry. "Marxism and Anarchism in the Formation of the Mexican Communist Party, 1910–1919." *Hispanic American Historical Review* 63 (May 1983): 277–306.

———. "Las peculiaridades del norte mexicano, 1880–1927: Ensayo de interpretación." *Historia Mexicana* 3 (January-March 1972): 320–346.

Clements, Kendrick A. "Woodrow Wilson's Mexican Policy, 1913–15." *Diplomatic History* 4 (Spring 1980): 113–136.

Coleman, Kenneth M. and Charles L. Davis. "Preemptive Reform and the

Mexican Working Class." *Latin American Research Review* 18 (Number 1, 1983): 3–31.

Cox, Robert W. "Labor and Hegemony." *International Organization* 31 (Summer 1977): 385–424.

Davis, Charles L. and Kenneth M. Coleman. "Structural Determinants of Working-Class Politicization: The Role of Independent Unions in Mexico." *Mexican Studies/Estudios Mexicanos* 5 (Winter 1989): 89–112.

Davis, Horace B. "American Labor and Imperialism Prior to World War I." *Science and Society* 27 (Winter 1963): 70–76.

Debs, Eugene V. "The Crisis in Mexico." *International Socialist Review* 12 (July 1911): 23.

Erickson, Kenneth Paul, Patrick V. Peppe, and Hobart A. Spalding, "Dependency vs. Working-Class History: A False Contradiction." *Latin American Research Review* 15 (Number 1, 1980): 177–181.

Ferguson, Thomas. "From Normalcy to New Deal: Industrial Structure, Party Competition, and American Public Policy in the Great Depression." *International Organization* 38 (Winter 1984): 41–94.

Frey, John P. "Trade Unions and the Civil War in Mexico." *American Federationist* 31 (April 1924): 303–308.

Gaddis, John Lewis. "The Corporatist Synthesis: A Skeptical View." *Diplomatic History* 10 (Fall 1986): 357–362.

Gilderhus, Mark T. "Senator Albert B. Fall and 'The Plot Against Mexico.'" *New Mexico Historical Review* 48 (October 1973): 299–311.

———. "Wilson, Carranza, and the Monroe Doctrine: A Question in Regional Organization." *Diplomatic History* 7 (Spring 1983): 103–115.

Gompers, Samuel. "Labor's Menace in Mexico." *American Federationist* 26 (May 1919): 404.

———. "Labor's Participation in Government." *American Federationist* 23 (February 1916): 105–110.

———. "Liberty's Hope Is in Thy Keeping, Organized Labor." *American Federationist* 23 (July 1916): 575–577.

———. "Pan-American Labor Congress at Mexico City." *American Federationist* 28 (March 1921): 193–200.

———. "The Mexican Government Should Be Recognized." *American Federationist* 29 (March 1922): 197–198.

———. "The World's Choice—League of Nations or League of Financiers." *American Federationist* 31 (January 1924): 17–41.

———. "To Pan-Americanize Labor." *American Federationist* 24 (March 1917): 208.

———. "Treacherous, Tyrannical, Barbarous." *American Federationist* 30 (July 1923): 368–370.

———. "United States—Mexico—Labor—Their Relations." *American Federationist* 23 (August 1916): 633–652.

Greenwood, Ernest H. "Labor and the League of Nations." *American Federationist* 27 (January 1920): 51–55.

Greenwood, Ernest H. and Hugh Reid. "Financing a Continent." *The Nation's Business* 8 (March 1920): 18–20.

Hart, John M. "The Urban Working Class and the Mexican Revolution: The Case of the Casa del Obrero Mundial." *Hispanic American Historical Review* 58 (February 1978): 1–20.

Hawley, Ellis. "The Discovery and Study of a 'Corporate Liberalism.'" *Business History Review* 52 (Fall 1978): 309–320.

Hogan, Michael J. "Corporatism: A Positive Appraisal." *Diplomatic History* 10 (Fall 1986): 363–372.

———. "Revival and Reform: America's Twentieth-Century Search for a New Economic Order Abroad." *Diplomatic History* 9 (Fall 1984): 287–310.

Iglesias, Santiago. "The Child of the A. F. of L." *American Federationist* 32 (October 1925): 928–931.

Kane, N. Stephen. "American Businessmen and Foreign Policy: The Recognition of Mexico, 1920–1923." *Political Science Quarterly* 90 (Summer 1975): 293–313.

———. "Bankers and Diplomats: The Diplomacy of the Dollar in Mexico, 1921–1924." *Business History Review* 47 (Autumn 1973): 335–352.

Katz, Friedrich. "Labor Conditions on Haciendas in Porfirian Mexico: Some Trends and Tendencies." *Hispanic American Historical Review* 52 (February 1974): 1–47.

———. "Pancho Villa and the Attack on Columbus, New Mexico." *American Historical Review* 83 (February 1978): 334–336.

Knight, Alan. "The Working Class and the Mexican Revolution, c. 1900–1920." *Journal of Latin American Studies* 16 (May 1984): 51–79.

Larsen, A. Simeon. "U.S. Intervention in Nicaragua: The Reaction of Organized Labor, 1920–1927." *New Labor Review* 6 (Spring 1984): 61–82.

Levenstein, Harvey A. "The AFL and Mexican Immigration in the 1920s: An Experiment in Labor Diplomacy." *Hispanic American Historical Review* 48 (May 1968): 206–219.

Maier, Charles. "The Politics of Productivity." *International Organization* 31 (Autumn 1977): 607–633.

———. "The Two Postwar Eras and the Conditions for Stability in Twentieth-Century Western Europe." *American Historical Review* 86 (April 1981): 327–352.

McCormick, Thomas J. "Drift or Mastery? A Corporatist Synthesis For American Diplomatic History." *Reviews in American History* 10 (December 1982): 318–330.

Meyer, Jean. "Los obreros en la Revolución Mexicana: Los 'Batallones Rojos.'" *Historia Mexicana* 21 (July–September 1971): 1–37.

Miller, Richard Ulric. "American Railroad Unions and the National Railways of Mexico: An Exercise in Nineteenth-Century Proletarian Manifest Destiny." *Labor History* 15 (Spring 1974): 239–260.

Moynihan, Daniel P. "The Washington Conference of the International Labor Organization." *Labor History* 3 (Fall 1962): 307–334.

Murray, John. "Labor's Call Across the Border." *The Survey* 42 (April 5, 1919): 46–47.

———. "The Private Prison of Díaz." *International Socialist Review* 9 (April 1909): 737–752.

Panitch, Leo. "The Development of Corporatism in Liberal Democracies." *Comparative Political Studies* 10 (April 1977): 61–90.

———. "Trade Unions and the Capitalist State." *New Left Review* 125 (January-February 1981): 21–43.

Parlee, Lorena. "The Impact of United States Railroad Unions on Organized Labor and Government Policy in Mexico (1880–1911)." *Hispanic American Historical Review* 64 (August 1984): 443–475.

Pregger-Román, Charles G. "Dependence, Underdevelopment, and Imperialism in Latin America: A Reappraisal." *Science and Society* 47 (Winter 1983–84): 406–426.

Raat, William Dirk. "The Diplomacy of Suppression: *Los revoltosos,* Mexico, and the United States, 1906–1911." *Hispanic American Historical Review* 56 (November 1976): 529–550.

———. "US Intelligence Operations and Covert Action in Mexico, 1900–47." *Journal of Contemporary History* 22 (1987): 615–638.

Radosh, Ronald and Horace B. Davis. "American Labor and the Anti-Imperialist Movement: A Discussion." *Science and Society* 8 (Winter 1964): 91–104.

Ramírez, J. "Mr. Hughes Surprises Himself." *The Liberator* 6 (November 1923): 21–22.

Richmond, Douglas W. "Nationalism and Class Conflict in Mexico, 1910–1920." *The Americas* 43 (January 1987): 279–303.

Rosenberg, Emily S. and Norman L. Rosenberg. "From Colonialism to Professionalism: The Public-Private Dynamic in United States Foreign Financial Advising, 1898–1929." *Journal of American History* 74 (June 1987): 59–82.

Seidel, Robert N. "American Reformers Abroad: The Kemmerer Missions in South America, 1923–31." *Journal of Economic History* 32 (June 1972): 520–545.

Seltzer, Alan L. "Woodrow Wilson As 'Corporate-Liberal': Toward a Reconsideration of Left Revisionist Historiography." *Western Political Quarterly* 30 (June 1977): 183–212.

Sklar, Martin J. "Woodrow Wilson and the Political Economy of the Modern United States Liberalism." *Studies on the Left* 1 (Fall 1960): 17–48.

Slaney, David. "Solidarity and Self-Interest." *NACLA Report on the Americas* 22 (May/June 1988): 28–36.

Smith, Robert Freeman. "The Formation and Development of the International Bankers Committee on Mexico." *Journal of Economic History* 23 (December 1963): 574–586.

Sofer, Eugene. "Recent Trends in Latin American Labor Historiography." *Latin American Research Review* 15 (Number 1, 1980): 167–176.

Spalding, Hobart A., Jr. "AIFLD Amok." *NACLA Report on the Americas* 22 (May/June 1988): 20–27.

———. "Solidarity Forever? Latin American Unions and the International Labor Network." *Latin American Research Review* 24 (Number 1, 1989): 253–265.

———. "Somethings Old and Somethings New." *International Labor and Working-Class History* 36 (Fall 1989): 37–43.

———. "The Parameters of Labor in Hispanic America." *Science and Society* 36 (Summer 1972): 202–216.

———. "Unions Look South." *NACLA Report on the Americas* 22 (May/June 1988): 14–19.

Taft, Philip. "Differences in the Executive Council of the American Federation of Labor." *Labor History* 5 (Winter 1964): 40–56.

———. "The Bisbee Deportation." *Labor History* 13 (Winter 1972): 3–40.

Taibo, Paco Ignacio, II. "El breve matrimonio rojo: Comunistas y anarcosindicalistas en la CGT en 1921," *Historias* 7 (octubre-diciembre 1984): 45–71.

Tardanico, Richard. "State, Dependency, and Nationalism: Revolutionary Mexico." *Comparative Studies in Society and History* 24 (July 1982): 400–423.

Toth, Charles W. "Samuel Gompers, Communism, and the Pan American Federation of Labor." *The Americas* 23 (January 1967): 273–278.

———. "The Pan American Federation of Labor: Its Political Nature." *Western Political Quarterly* 18 (March 1965): 615–620.

Trejo Delarbe, Raul. "The Mexican Labor Movement: 1917–1975." Translated by Aníbal Yañez. *Latin American Perspectives* 3 (Winter 1976): 133–153.

Trow, Clifford W. "Woodrow Wilson and the Mexican Interventionist Movement of 1919." *Journal of American History* 58 (June 1971): 46–72.

Viotta da Costa, Emilia. "Experience versus Structures: New Tendencies in the History of Labor and the Working Class in Latin America—What Do We Gain? What Do We Lose?" *International Labor and Working-Class History* 36 (Fall 1989): 3–24.

Walker, David W. "Porfirian Labor Politics: Working Class Organizations in Mexico City and Porfirio Díaz, 1876–1902." *The Americas* 37 (January 1981): 257–289.

Walling, William E. "Financial Intervention in Mexico." *New Review* 2 (June 1914): 327–329.

Whittaker, William G. "Samuel Gompers, Anti-Imperialist." *Pacific Historical Review* 55 (November 1969): 429–445.

———. "Samuel Gompers, Labor, and the Mexican-American Crisis of 1916: The Carrizal Incident." *Labor History* 17 (Fall 1976): 551–567.

Wiarda, Howard J. "Toward a Framework for the Study of Political

Change in the Iberic-Latin Tradition: The Corporative Model." *World Politics* 25 (January 1973): 206–235.

Williams, William Appleman. "Latin America: Laboratory of American Foreign Policy in the Nineteen-Twenties." *Inter-American Economic Affairs* 11 (Autumn 1957): 3–30.

Wolfe, Bertram D. "Take the Road to the Left." *The Liberator* 7 (April 1924): 21–23.

Woll, Matthew. "Why Intervention—Also for Whom?" *American Federationist* 26 (September 1919): 830–831.

Womack, John, Jr. "The Mexican Economy during the Revolution, 1910–1920: Historiography and Analysis." *Marxist Perspectives* 4 (Winter 1978): 80–123.

Wright, Chester M. "De la Huerta's Black Escapade." *American Federationist* 31 (February 1924): 146–147.

———. "How the Propagandists Work for War with Mexico." *American Federationist* 27 (June 1920): 550–554.

———. "Mexico, the Hopeful: A Survey of Her Political and Industrial Situation As She Takes Her First Steps in Reconstruction." *American Federationist* 27 (December 1920): 1087–1094.

Zapata, Francisco. "Labor and Politics: The Mexican Paradox." In *Labor Autonomy and the State in Latin America*, 155–171. Edited by Edward C. Epstein, Boston: Unwin Hyman, 1989.

Zieger, Robert H. "Herbert Hoover, the Wage-earner, and the 'New Economic System,' 1919–1929." *Business History Review* 51 (Summer 1977): 161–189.

Index

Designer: U.C. Press Staff
Compositor: Prestige Typography
Text: 10/13 Palatino
Display: Palatino
Printer: Bookcrafters, Inc.
Binder: Bookcrafters, Inc.

DATE DUE

BRODART, INC.

Cat. No. 23-221